The Women of Watergate

The Women of Watergate

MADELEINE EDMONDSON

and ALDEN DUER COHEN

STEIN AND DAY/*Publishers*/New York

First published in 1975
Copyright © 1975 by Madeleine Edmondson and Alden Duer Cohen
All rights reserved
Designed by David Miller
Printed in the United States of America
Stein and Day/*Publishers*/Scarborough House,
Briarcliff Manor, N.Y. 10510

Library of Congress Cataloging in Publication Data

Edmondson, Madeleine.
　　The women of Watergate.

　　　1.　Watergate Affair, 1972-　　2.　Women—United
States—Biography.　I.　Cohen, Alden Duer, joint
author.　II.　Title.
E860.C63　　　973.924　　　74-30126
ISBN 0-8128-1775-3

For M.F. and C.F., with many thanks

M. E.

For those who stood by with special grace

A. D. C.

ACKNOWLEDGMENTS

We want to thank the women of Watergate who granted us interviews, as well as their friends and classmates, colleagues and collaborators, neighbors and relatives who offered additional insights and background. We are also grateful to those members of the press, some of them distinguished reporters indeed, who so generously shared their information and files with us.

It was these people who gave their time, sometimes under difficult circumstances, to provide us with material that had not been published previously. Without the cooperation of all these primary sources, we could not have told the full story of the women of Watergate.

M.E. and A.D.C.

Contents

Prologue

Those actions collectively and conveniently christened Watergate, actions that eventually coalesced to overwhelm the Nixon Administration, were almost exclusively committed by men. Most were respectable citizens in dark suits—short-haired, efficient, resolutely bland. A nationwide audience soon learned their names, and even to recognize and differentiate among them, though that was more difficult, for these were faceless men, not noted for color, wit, intellect, excess, or eccentricity, interesting only because of their unprecedented situation.

And yet these interchangeable men were not the only people whose lives were being wrenched and transformed by Watergate. Women, too, were caught up in it. Initially, the women of Watergate were not central to the drama. They were the supporting cast. Watergate had its roots in the corruption bred by power, and women have not often had enough power to be in any danger of corruption.

There were secretaries, to be sure, and they knew a good deal about one thing and another, but they were paid for their discreet inability to discern an emergent pattern. There were wives, too, but they were peripheral—glittering tokens in the political game. They could be seen holding the Bible at a husband's swearing-in, or gazing up raptly as he recited a familiar speech. They and their bright, healthy children were on display, living passports validating the humanity of their menfolk.

Certainly some of these women were close to men in power, often exceedingly close, but they were never included in the secret councils of the inner circle. The everyday transactions revealed in the transcripts are those of a thoroughly masculine business life, where women are scarcely thought of unless their public appearance might be of potential use.

9

But with the discovery of what was then called the Watergate caper, the situation changed, and women began to emerge. It was then that the long, bitter conflict began—a conflict between the outsiders, probers both official and unofficial, who were determined to uncover at least a partial and approximate truth, and the insiders, who fought, for varying motives, to preserve their secrets and their anonymity. There were women on both sides of this lethal tug-of-war.

Some, of course, were eager to see the truth come out, perhaps undertaking to help uncover it themselves. Martha Mitchell, the volatile, outspoken wife of the Attorney General, was certainly one of these. So was Pat Ellsberg, who felt herself one of the principal victims of Nixonian persecution. There was Jill Volner, the talented young lawyer on the Watergate special prosecutor's staff. And when events moved inexorably toward impeachment, the two most eloquent members of the House Judiciary Committee proved to be Elizabeth Holtzman and Barbara Jordan. Less visibly, another woman, Katharine Graham of the *Washington Post*, was responsible for the first and perhaps most valuable of all investigations into the Watergate affair. John Mitchell called her Katie when a brash reporter woke him near midnight with a question. "Katie Graham's going to get her tit caught in a big fat wringer," he threatened, "if that's published." The story, and many more damning, ran. Today, in memory of that remark, Katharine Graham wears two appropriate gold miniatures around her neck on a chain.

Other women played their part in the unfolding drama as adjuncts to their men. The TV cameras lingered on the bland, blond, egglike face of Maureen Dean, whose ever-changing wardrobe fascinated the photographers and whose marital history inspired the gossip columnists. Rose Mary Woods, wifeliest of loyal office wives, provided comic relief. Could she have caused that famous eighteen-and-a-half-minute gap by holding her foot flexuously and thoughtlessly on the pedal of her tape recorder while reaching for the phone? And was she or wasn't she out of favor with her boss in consequence of her irresponsible garrulity?

There, too, were those radiant, steadfast wives, paradigms of femininity, still appearing in cameo roles, still costumed in good Republican cloth coats. But now their importance was not being exaggerated by the camera as in the past; no longer were they merely standing by, lending moral support, looking pretty, ready to be photographed smiling or kissing. For now that everyone was being buffeted by the wild currents of accusation and discovery, their well-ordered lives were just as much at hazard as anyone else's—and not because of things they had done, words they had spoken, decisions they had made. They would stand or fall with their men: they had not played the game, but their stakes were the same.

So different are these women—and their viewpoints—from each other that it is hard at first to think of them as a group at all. They seem to have little in common beyond the fact that all of them were involved in a great historic cataclysm and that their story—perhaps partly because they are women—has remained obscure and incomplete.

Yet there is one thing they do have in common that makes them more than simply subjects of natural curiosity: all of them, because Watergate was for so long a central part of their lives, have been forced to come to terms with it. They have had to try to understand it, judge it, and decide what, for them, it meant.

The rest of us could flick the dial, fold the newspaper, cultivate our garden. We could leave it to history to make uncluttered sense out of each day's new proliferation of detail. But decisions about meaning cannot be postponed indefinitely. Consciously or unconsciously, as time passes we are making them. Eventually each of us will arrive at a judgment of our own about the significance of Watergate.

These women have already made their judgments, for whatever they are worth, and however idiosyncratic or self-serving they may seem. So they are a little ahead of us on a road we all must travel

Katharine Graham

The press has no damn business doing
good or doing evil.

Again and again throughout the Watergate era the story surfaced
that Katharine Graham held a special grudge against Richard Nixon
and was out to destroy him. Somehow, the whisper went, he had
slighted her, and she, like the bad fairy at the christening, was going
to avenge the insult by putting her curse on him. One person who
gave currency to this rumor—and, considering his position, a measure
of credibility—was the chairman of the Republican National Committee, Senator Robert Dole. He publicly charged that Kay Graham
had told someone at a dinner party that she intended to "get Nixon."
She was, of course, in an excellent position to do this, since she
headed a communications empire that included *Newsweek* as well as
the capital's most powerful newspaper, the *Washington Post*.

Katharine Graham's distress when reports of this reached her can
only be imagined. She thinks of it even today with visible pain,
characterizing it as "just outrageous and preposterous." As she told
the authors of this book, "I never said anything like it. I said the
opposite. I mean, I emphasized again and again . . ." Her outrage
faded into disbelief, then to amusement as she explained that
months later she was about to disembark from a plane when a
courteous gentleman appeared in the aisle to introduce himself as
Senator Dole. He proffered an aide to help with her bags, a lift to her
destination. Amazed by all this cordiality, she decided to broach the
delicate topic. "If you don't mind my saying so," she began, "I never
said that about getting Nixon, and I don't think it." "Oh, of course
not," he quickly soothed her. "*You* know how they put those things
in your hand at the last minute."

This whispering campaign, though perhaps the most pointedly
personal, was no isolated attack on Katharine Graham and the *Washington Post*. The *Post*'s Watergate coverage had aroused the ire of

12

Nixon loyalists both within and without the Administration —and indeed, as the tapes would later show, of Nixon himself. Immediately after the overwhelming victory of 1972 there was a concerted effort to punish the *Post*. Officials in various agencies began to "forget" to invite *Post* reporters to meetings and press conferences. A grandmotherly sixty-eight-year-old social reporter was banned from White House functions. A *Washington Star-News* reporter told a friend at the *Post* that Charles Colson had called him in and confided that the Administration had every intention of burying the *Post* in the next four years. "Come in with your breadbasket and we'll fill it," Colson promised. This was followed by Nixon's granting of a rare exclusive interview to a *Star-News* writer. More ominously, there were challenges to the license renewals of two *Post*-owned television stations. Nixon associates were involved in both.

The fact is that the *Post* had indeed made a decision to devote considerable energy, manpower, and money to its thorough ongoing coverage of Watergate developments—even when, as sometimes happened, there seemed to be none—an attitude in marked contrast to that of much of the media. One analyst of Watergate journalism figured out in early 1973 that of the 433 reporters based in Washington bureaus with staffs of ten or more, fewer than fifteen were assigned full time to Watergate. He speculated that it was entirely possible that more man-hours of investigative journalism had been invested in the rumor that John Kennedy had a secret marriage in his past than had been devoted to the Watergate affair.

Katharine Graham is not surprised that the *Post* stayed with the story; what surprises her is that others devoted less attention to it (though she admits to a certain jealousy of the few that did and occasionally beat out her paper). Far from being out to get anyone, she says, the *Post* stayed on the story as a simple matter of journalistic responsibility. "We obviously thought," she continues, substituting "you" for "I" as she often does, "that the reporting was reliable enough or you obviously wouldn't have risked the whole paper, which essentially you were doing by running those stories. If you thought there was more there, there was no way you were going to take reporters off the story." As for the swirl of rumors, she dismisses them with finality. "What they were trying to do was attack the paper's credibility, to try to persuade people that we weren't telling the truth, that we had these motives that they said we had. I never did anything but say all we are doing is a piece of investigative reporting and we have no other motive at all."

Indeed it is impossible to imagine Katharine Graham committing any such clumsy indiscretion as the one alleged in the much-circulated anecdote. The publisher of the *Washington Post* and the chairman of the board of the Washington Post Company is a tall, slender woman, groomed and dressed with expensively casual simplicity. Her brown eyes are direct, her smile friendly, her laugh infectious. Yet at the same time there are unmistakable hints here of well-controlled power. Spare, supple, alert, testing each word for accuracy, probing for the genuine, Kay Graham proceeds always as if on intellectual thin ice. Any weaknesses she may have will be born of caution, not of careless pride.

When she first took over the leadership of the *Post* after the death of her husband, she was quite a different woman. Painfully shy, and accustomed to a sheltered life, she was only a figurehead then, but even that was difficult. Four months after her accession she was asked to make a one-minute speech to assembled *Post* employees at their Christmas party. Supplied with a few jokes by old family friend Art Buchwald, she practiced them over and over before the mirror, working to perfect every inflection, her voice quavering with nervousness as her children encouraged her.

Perhaps it is not surprising that Katharine Graham grew up less than aggressively self-confident, child as she was of two such crushingly formidable parents as Eugene and Agnes Meyer. Eugene had made millions on Wall Street and then devoted years to government service; but his fame today rests largely on the fact that in 1933 he spent $825,000 to acquire the *Washington Post,* at that time an unimpressive scandal sheet with a circulation of 40,000, and began the process that was to turn it into one of the world's great newspapers.

Agnes was far more spectacular, and her influence on her children hardly the ideal envisaged by the developmental psychologist. A dynamo of wit, charm, beauty, intelligence, and social commitment (among other things), she has been likened to a galleon in full sail, all guns firing. She once accused her husband of having no ego, to which he replied, "That's all right, my dear. You have enough for both of us."

In her youth Agnes, always mistress of her own destiny, attracted the friendship of the great Rodin, then as famous for his romantic conquests as for his art. When he unsubtly attempted to convert their relationship from that of pupil and teacher into something more intimate, Agnes rose to the occasion by falling to her knees. In fluent (though perhaps less perfect than she believed) French, she pleaded: "Dear friend, you cannot imagine what you mean to me. You are the greatest artist, the greatest teacher I have ever known. Dear, dear friend, there are many men in the world. There is only one Rodin. I don't wish to lose him." Awed, crushed, or possibly ennobled by this speech, Rodin remained her friend.

As mother of five children, Agnes continued under full sail, managing nurses, menus, servants, travel, art, profuse writings and translations, a complex and teeming social life complete with constant houseguests, and games ranging from baseball to dominoes. Eugene once said he felt like a boarder in his own house, as well he might. The children grew up in an atmosphere of constant action and interaction. The house was filled with the interesting and the famous, with ideas and argument, and, above all, with competition. Both parents were unassailably successful. Never shrinking from competition in their own lives—even within their own relationship—they expected no less of their children.

Warmth and mothering were in short supply. Agnes, presented for the first time with her infant daughter Florence, eyed the baby with distaste. "Take her away," she commanded. Later she became what she herself would call "a conscientious but scarcely a loving mother." A description of life at the Meyer "farm" in summer shows just how formidably conscientious she could be. She never left her children to drift or idle; their time was organized constructively for them. Agnes seldom appeared at the breakfast table, but the children breakfasted with their father, whose rule was that they appear on time after making their own beds. At breakfast they reported to him on their activities of the previous day, or conducted one of their intense family debates. After Meyer left for the office, the children were taught their lessons, mainly arithmetic and French, by a Swiss governess her former pupil recalls as "nutty as a fruitcake." Afternoons they were tutored by a mademoiselle imported for the purpose of making French the family's second language. (This never quite worked out: Katharine Graham today describes her French as that of a fluent nine-year-old.)

To get the children "out of the groove of conventional living," Agnes led them on pack trips, evidently conceived as ventures into the wilderness but including enough expensive amenities to remove them conclusively from the category of roughing it. A child had to be nine years old before being permitted to participate in these excursions. Alternate summers, there were European tours, which allowed further cultural elevation. Agnes was particularly careful that the

children should be correctly introduced to great art: to cut down on
the number of bewildering visual impressions, they were instructed
in art galleries never to look until she gave the signal.

These children who were being so carefully nurtured, so
judiciously strengthened, so dosed with appropriate educational
stimulation, were being groomed for stardom. And they were expected to earn it. All the Meyer children had trust funds, established
by their father when they were babies, but they were not to begin
drawing income until they were twenty-one and could not touch the
principal until they were thirty. They were supposed to behave as if
there were no money, and in practice there was little. Though their
surroundings were lavish in the extreme, the children were not well
dressed; they were not supposed to care about that. They were
taught to abhor the very thought of waste; turning out unused lights
was a central article of faith. They all had allowances that were
supposed to cover incidentals; in college they had more, but not
ostentatiously more.

In addition to all this, they were expected to be brilliant,
charming, witty, and slightly eccentric. Kay, growing up, believed
that she alone of the Meyer children was failing to achieve these
goals. She was, of all of them, the quietest, perhaps even rather stolid.
She did not join the great wide-ranging intellectual battles, the
showing off, the singing, that characterized the Meyer table. Until
she was in college she withdrew into herself and let the storm rage
about her. While her siblings engaged with Agnes in terrible combat,
Kay kept her eyes down. Katharine Graham today admits that for
years she thought of herself as "a Mongolian." She has referred to her
younger self as a peasant in almost every interview she has given.

Of course, peasants are strong and durable, and it was Kay who
would end up the only Meyer child of large accomplishment and
influence. Yet no one could measure up to Agnes' vast expectations.
Once, years later, when she was talking with Kay's husband and Kay
approached, Agnes waved her daughter grandly off with "Go away,
dear. We're having an intellectual discussion." And when Kay was
honored, along with three other women, for her achievements in
journalism, Agnes was heard to remark, "They all made it on their
own—all but Kay, that is." The highest compliment Katharine
Graham ever received from her mother was apropos of a speech she
had given long before. "You reminded me," Agnes said looking
back on it, "of myself."

With a mother so hard to please, Kay quite naturally inclined
toward a father who was not so ready to point out his children's

shortcomings. Though she says now that she did not realize she was his favorite, she was noticeably closer to him than were her brother and sisters. Most strikingly, she was the only one of his children to share his interest in journalism. Early on, there was the school paper; later, at Vassar, a real job. Summers, while the others traveled, she stayed in Washington with her father, performing "all kinds of lowly jobs" at the *Post*.

After two years at Vassar, she transferred to the University of Chicago, graduating in 1938. With the help of one of her professors, Paul (later Senator) Douglas, she got a job on a Chicago paper, but she fell in love with San Francisco while on a trip there with her father and she accepted his help in getting a job as a $21-a-week reporter on the *San Francisco News*. Not knowing the city, and assigned to cover an unfamiliar subject (labor), she was soon ready to quit, but her father came out and persuaded her to persevere. Then, at the end of a year, he brought her back to the *Post*.

Not long after that, however, she met Philip Graham, and her first journalistic career was ended, in spirit if not in fact. Graham came into Kay Meyer's life like a cyclone. The third time they saw each other they decided to marry. Agnes was in Nassau at the time with another of her daughters, but Kay's father, she explains, "sort of wormed it out of me" that she was interested in this unknown young man. He asked if she was really serious; she said she thought she was; Graham was bidden to dinner. Almost immediately, father and fiancé were deep in political dispute, with Kay worrying that the two would never get on; in truth Meyer was delighted with a young man daring enough to argue with him, and he gave the prospective match his blessing.

The evening of Agnes' return from Nassau, Meyer planned to inform her of Kay's engagement, but she had a great deal of information to impart about her trip and hardly paused even to draw breath. When her husband at last managed to interrupt this torrent of detail he said, "Well . . . Mother . . . we're having champagne tonight." "Good," she replied, and went on talking. "Don't you want to know *why* we're having champagne?" asked Meyer at the next opportunity. This time his wife looked at him and noticed that he seemed inordinately pleased about something. Bethinking herself of his long-time rivalry with Cissy Patterson, owner of the *Post*'s bitter rival, the *Washington Times-Herald*, she made a triumphant guess: "Cissy's gone out of business!"

Never very enthusiastic about any achievement of Kay's, Agnes' only comment when she did eventually meet her prospective son-in-law was that he had "a fine jawline." But in later years she would come to share the majority view, which was that if you couldn't get Phil Graham, perhaps you could settle for God Almighty. Phil Graham was, by all accounts, one of the most brilliant, charming, talented, and endearing persons that most who met him had ever known. And somehow Kay Meyer, the quiet one, the Mongolian, had achieved the delightfully improbable success of being chosen by him. She was still in awe of natural aristocrats of the charming-witty-eccentric variety, and if her parents and siblings had made her feel outclassed, surely Phil Graham could produce the same effect, and more convincingly. But Kay Meyer had no objection to that. She had no wish to compete in the center of the arena; her only ambition was to absent herself from the self-aggrandizing intellectual Donny-brook she had grown up in. What she wanted was to be Phil Graham's wife, the mother of his children, to keep house, to learn to cook. She did continue to work at the *Post* after her marriage, but not because she chose to: it was done at her husband's insistence. He told her she would regret it if she quit her job. He pointed out that he would not be there, that she would have nothing to do; that with the money she earned she could pay a maid. So she continued working until she had two children to justify retirement.

She claims that she never did learn how to cook, but her life at that time was, from all descriptions, admirably drab. She took her children to the Safeway. She made a good home—in fact two, both more comfortable than attractive. She was the kind of mother—devoted, warm, supportive, and, above all, *present*—that mothers in those days were supposed to be. She was not brilliant, beautiful, eccentric, or witty. Someone who knew her then sums up: "She had nothing—no opinions, no style, nothing." But it no longer mattered. Katharine Graham, in quiet rebellion against her mother, had withdrawn from all competition. Pictures of her in those days show a pleasant, smiling, rather matronly person. She has grown younger since.

The Grahams had four children. Daughter Lally, incongruously intellectual for one of such consummate chic, has edited a book of essays about Thomas Jefferson and is collaborating on another about the 1870s in America. Bill is a trial lawyer on the staff of Edward Bennett Williams; Steve works with the legendary Henri Langlois at the Cinémathèque Française in Paris. But Don, the eldest son, is the heir. When the Washington Post Company bought out the *Washington Times-Herald* in 1954, Don was eight years old. His grandfather, Eugene Meyer, explained to a friend, "The real significance of this event is that it makes the paper safe for Donnie."

Donald Graham himself is quite aware of the responsibilities that go with this enormous job that seems to be his birthright. After college he joined the Washington, D.C., police force for eighteen months, a move his mother describes as "a darn good and original idea." As she says, "He decided it would make him aware of people's lives in a way he'd never be as a reporter, even a police reporter." Clearly, it was done as a part of his apprenticeship to the *Post*.

Evidently there has been some questioning of the decision that Don and only Don can take over the empire. Katharine Graham is a trifle defensive as she explains that she "used to" assume that only one person could run something and Don—who started on the Harvard *Crimson* and is now sports editor of the *Post*—was "the one who had been in journalism consistently." Picking her way carefully, she says she has changed her thinking to some extent recently, so that if any of her other children wanted a career at the *Post* it would not be closed to them. These days, since the *Post* has gone public, "there is probably room for one or two, if they are totally professional and prove themselves somewhere else. I just don't think you can make your child the movie reviewer because you like him. That louses up people's advancement. I feel very strongly that they have their own dough, that there's no need for them to do this unless they're obsessed. And able. And serious. If they are, then I think that families in newspapers can be constructive. On the other hand, if they can't pull their weight it's a bad show. It kills the newspaper."

Kay Graham herself, of course, is where she is largely for family reasons. When she first met Phil Graham, he was a promising lawyer, law clerk to a Supreme Court Justice. He had never had journalistic interests; he planned that after service in World War II he would return to Florida, practice law there, and eventually enter politics. But to the aging Eugene Meyer, Graham was clearly just what he had begun to feel a need for—a successor. In those days one did not hand over a huge and complex enterprise like the *Washington Post* to a woman, even a favorite daughter. Meyer did have a son, and rigid ideas about family obligation, so he asked that son if he wanted the job. Fortunately or unfortunately, Bill (Eugene III) Meyer, now a psychiatrist, was already studying medicine. He asked for three days to think the matter over and decided against it, whether because of a deep-seated commitment to his chosen profession or discomfort at the prospect of working with his father, no one will ever know. Meyer, released to follow his own wish in the matter, went to see Phil Graham at the Army Air Force Intelligence School in Harrisburg.

"I'm sixty-seven," he said. "I've got to know if you are interested in coming to the paper." He made it plain that the *Post* was no gold mine, but he hoped his son-in-law would see it as he did, as an opportunity to build a great newspaper.

Phil Graham took even longer to think it over than the last prospect had. His situation, of course, was far more difficult. He was being offered the makings of a classic problem: the opportunity to base his life on the generosity of his wife's father. Kay gave no advice. Her conviction, expressed later, was that "men have to do what they want to do. It's hopeless if wives begin saying, 'Do this for me.'" Eventually, Phil Graham decided to accept. Some suggest that Washington friends convinced him that ownership of a newspaper was no hindrance to political influence, if that was what he wanted.

In 1946, the war over, Graham came to the *Post* as assistant publisher. Two years later Meyer transferred the voting stock of the Washington Post Company to Phil and Kay. They used a $75,000 gift from Meyer (in the interest of fairness he had given the same sum to each of his children) as down payment and continued to pay over Phil's salary against their debt while living on Kay's income.

Phil Graham's leadership was good for the *Post*, and he continued to add to its holdings, acquiring the *Washington Times-Herald* and, eventually, *Newsweek*. And his choice of a journalistic career did not preclude political influence; he was largely responsible for the formation of the Kennedy-Johnson ticket in 1960.

Yet though Phil Graham's career was meteoric in the sense that it was brilliant and rapid, it was meteoric also in its blazing self-destructiveness. In 1957 he had begun to suffer from acute depression. The psychiatrists he was persuaded to see suggested that he give up his responsibilities at the *Post* and try to rest and relax. Taking their advice, he and Kay retired for months to their Virginia farm, Glen Welby. The prescription seemed to work. Phil was able to return to the *Post*, without his father-in-law—who had always worried about his health, calling him "too skinny and too high-powered"—having to be given more than the sketchiest of explanations.

Katharine Graham did her best to conceal her husband's problems, and this practice was to stand her in good stead later, as his life fell increasingly into disarray. Though he was still impressively effective at work, his leisure was erratic. He drank heavily. He was hyperactive, manic, dissipated. He traveled with a reporter from *Newsweek*'s Paris bureau who was introduced as his fiancée. And he was bitter. Insisting that without Eugene Meyer's help he would have made it on his own, he told his friends, "If I had gone back to

Florida to practice law, I might be in the Senate now." He was said to be leaving Kay. Then he was said to be reconciled with her.

It is certainly possible to read the story several ways, and there is still disagreement as to just how severe Phil Graham's problems were, and whether they were psychiatric or perhaps all too predictably practical. When Kay ascribed his decision to leave her to his illness, there were those who considered that explanation simply the self-saving rationalization of an abandoned wife. Others, equally Graham's admirers, felt trapped in a maze of Kafkaesque impenetrability as they tried to explain the change they saw in him to people who refused to listen. And there were those, too, who saw Phil Graham as a deeply troubled man in an untenable position, torn between two possible solutions, neither entirely acceptable.

In any case, his problems, whatever they were, reached a point where he could no longer try to deal with them alone, and he entered a psychiatric hospital. But he still retained his old charm, and ultimately it was his undoing. Fatally plausible, he managed to persuade the doctors to let him have a day at home. After six weeks in the hospital he came to Glen Welby, where he shot himself.

Katharine Graham was shy and retiring. She was inexperienced. But she was not weak. On the eve of her husband's funeral she was able to speak to a hastily summoned board meeting. "I want you all to know," she said, "that I know what you've been through this past year." Then she took over the empire.

She was doubtful, at first, of her own ability to manage so complicated a job—"as one sensibly would be," one observer of this transitional phase points out. But she never considered selling the *Post.* "Vultures and hawks" were circling around her head, she later told a reporter, but she had lived through the difficult years of the newspaper's growth, and "selling what I had seen my father and my husband create with such agony and devotion was unthinkable."

And, timid as she might appear, Katharine Graham had long been developing a tenacious strength of will. Throughout her childhood she had clung unswervingly to her own peasant independence, and those last years of Philip Graham's life had demanded, if they did not create, a resolute self-sufficiency. As her father had once said of her, Kay was like a Chinese doll: no matter how many times she might be knocked down, she always came up straight. The story of Kay's bout with tuberculosis is characteristic. She had been informed by her doctor that tests showed she was in the early stages of TB. Phil, at the time, was in New York, concluding the negotiations that would lead to the purchase of *Newsweek*, and he wanted her to join him there. As always, when he wanted her with him (and, as she notes, "he usually did"), she went, breaking the truth about her health to him only later, when she had to enter the hospital. Looking back on it, she remembers it was hard to tell him, he being already "very sick" himself.

After the shattering disaster of her husband's death, she must have been relieved and grateful for the opportunity to concentrate all her energies on a demanding job and the distraction it offered after those recent painful years. With the guidance of Frederick Beebe, then chairman of the board of the Washington Post Company and *Newsweek*, she slowly transformed herself into a first-class businesswoman. At first, because business was no part of her background, her style was traditionally feminine. She worked through men, and their devotion to her was a unifying force among them. After five years on the job, it was still possible to describe her, as one reporter did, as "the loyal lady of the house" who "accepts her responsibilities much more often than she asserts her authority."

That could hardly be said today, though she still describes her job as largely a matter of appointing people she has great confidence in and then backing them up. Not only is she generally credited with "a sense of who's good and who isn't that's eerily accurate," as one colleague describes it, but she is willing to expend the constant vigilance that is the price of confidence. Katharine Graham devotes enormous energy and concentration, as well as the knowledge she has acquired during her years of on-the-job training, to keeping abreast of every aspect of her empire. Her job as it is now constituted is a very real, and a very difficult, one: she is head, in fact as well as name, of one of the five hundred largest U.S. companies. All divisions report to her as principal financial officer. Most noticeably, it is she as publisher who takes ultimate responsibility for the character of the newspaper she runs. And many people feel (though the comparison is perhaps as unnecessary as it is inevitable) that the *Post* under Katharine Graham is a better newspaper than it was under her husband.

As she expanded her influence at the *Post*, she began to blossom socially as well, and in 1966 everybody heard of Katharine Graham as guest of honor at what Truman Capote, the host, modestly referred to as his "little masked ball for Kay Graham and all my friends," but which staid *Business Week* described as "the season's most spectacular social event." Evidently a new Katharine Graham was in the making. No longer the daughter, wife, and mother whose aim was to please others or withdraw to avoid displeasing them, this was an independent and powerful woman who was beginning to enjoy both her power and her independence. Some people credit Truman Capote with assembling this new image. "He did more than launch her," one old friend says flatly. "He put her together. He created her as a public personality. He gave her a lot of confidence at a time when she didn't have any." But it seems far likelier that Capote contributed little more than the perceptiveness to observe, before anyone else, a healing process that was already taking place.

Nowadays, Katharine Graham is a social power in her own right, with all the accouterments of wealth and celebrity. In addition to Glen Welby, her 350-acre cattle farm in Virginia, she maintains a New York apartment conveniently close to *Newsweek*, and has recently established herself on some 250 acres of Martha's Vineyard. She has invitations (most of them declined) for every night of the week, and assembles what are generally conceded to be some of Washington's most dazzling guest lists for dinner parties in the Georgetown house to whose decor Renoir, Picasso, Marin, and Brancusi contribute.

Sought after as she is, however, there are few rumors of romance in Katharine Graham's life. (A Washington newswoman, confirming this, adds regretfully, "Everyone would approve if she had an affair.") Most people who know her doubt that she will ever marry again, suggesting that it would be hard for anyone to measure up to Philip Graham, and Truman Capote has said, "Why should she? She has everything in the world." Yet a female friend of long standing suggests, "I think every woman would like it to happen, don't you?" Katharine Graham herself deprecates the idea without entirely rejecting it. Though "extremely pro-family," and thus favoring marriage in principle, she admits she is not sure she could ever "become part of a team again." Besides, she points out, she is already so committed to her job, and always so busy rushing off somewhere to do something, that "nobody would really want to marry me."

As a single person with a well-publicized metamorphosis from housewife to career woman in her background, and unchallengeable status in the present as one of the world's most powerful women (though that description, she protests, makes her sound like a weight lifter), it was only natural that Katharine Graham should attract the attention of the women's movement. In recent years she has become a favorite example of the kind of fulfillment that may be expected to follow close upon liberation. One less fulfilled feminist acidly notes that the most obvious lesson to be derived from Kay Graham's life is that inheriting a newspaper empire can have a very liberating effect. Yet unquestionably Katharine Graham has come a long way toward liberation, if only because she has had to travel a longer distance than many.

As she says herself, she started out with the viewpoint of a male chauvinist pig. "I was brought up in that world," she says, "and I considered myself a second-class citizen. I had their view of women." An old friend concurs, saying, "She used to think women were not good for much and that an intelligent woman who could perform on the job as well as a man could was just an accident, a freak of nature." She was always defensive, too, about her own abilities. If all this seems surprising, in view of the fact that her liberated mother never considered taking second place to any man, Katharine Graham today can only laugh and explain, "Well, you see, I think she considered me a second-class citizen too—so that I never would have identified with her."

She recognizes that if, over the years, she was uneasily conscious of the questions, she has been slow in finding the answers. As late as 1969 she could tell a reporter that which jobs should be held by women was "a matter of appropriateness," volunteering that "I think a man would be better at this job I'm in than a woman." Even an uprising by the women at *Newsweek*—part of her own domain— caused no real change in her attitude. Insisting that they were being relegated to inferior jobs, demanding equal representation in the ranks of *Newsweek*'s writers, they had filed a suit against the magazine. Katharine Graham, informed by telephone as she vacationed in Barbados, could not take it seriously. "Whose side," she asked, laughing, "am I supposed to be on?" The *Newsweek* women eventually reached agreement with management and their suit was withdrawn, but not because of any sisterly intervention by Katharine Graham.

Throughout those years, however, as the subject was repeatedly raised and she admitted the justice of much of the change she saw taking place, something must have had an effect, because all at once she realized that something had happened—"not in my head but suddenly in my psyche." The issue—and Kay Graham is first to admit that "obviously this is a slightly ludicrous way of suddenly discovering you've changed"—was the separation of men and women after dinner that has long been customary in Washington society. "I was so used to it," she explains, "that I did it in my own house even after I was alone. Because, after all, these great wonderful men wanted to talk to each other. So I'd send them all into the library to talk to each other. It really is very funny." One day she realized that she was "sitting there responsible for this rather big, complicated company, with an incredible number of things going on and decisions being made in which obviously a lot was involved and a lot of responsibility"—and she knew that she could no longer tolerate it. "I just wasn't up for being shoved out of the room anymore."

From then on, if there is division after dinner she simply leaves, and the custom itself seems well on its way to oblivion. "It caused a certain amount of stink sometimes," she says with equanimity. "It still does." And then she adds, with evident pleasure, "It has cheered up all the women."

This feeling of solidarity points up her increasing comfort with feminist attitudes. Not only has she begun to accuse reporters of asking her "sexist questions," but she can even joke about it. Accepting an award recently, she told her audience that she understood it had been won in the past by twenty men, and she was delighted to be the first *person* to receive it. So perhaps there is some inspiration in her inner progress toward self-esteem, if not in her outward success. After years of confusion and doubt, Katharine Graham has discovered who she is.

It was this hard-won equilibrium that was tested by the dramatic irruption of Watergate, which catapulted Katharine Graham almost overnight to heroine status. At the height of the struggle, when CRP had issued subpoenas to five of those most closely identified with the *Post*'s Watergate coverage, Kay Graham's apotheosis was exultantly summed up by executive editor Ben Bradlee: "Of course we're going to fight this one all the way up, and if the judge wants to send anyone to jail, he's going to have to send Mrs. Graham. And, my God, the lady says she'll go! Then the judge can have that on his conscience. Can't you see the picture of her limousine pulling up to the Women's Detention Center and out gets our gal, going to jail to uphold the First Amendment? That's a picture that would run in every newspaper in the world. There might be a revolution."

Events proved that particular revolution unnecessary, but Katharine Graham's picture must surely have run in most of the world's newspapers. Her own paper has won two Pulitzers for its Watergate investigation, and she herself has collected a string of awards and adorned a sheaf of magazine covers. She is in constant demand as a speaker, and her name threatens to become a household word.

Naturally, she has been insistently questioned about Watergate, which she has described as "the most serious problem the country ever faced," and she has been willing, though certainly not eager, to discuss it. As she sees it, what characterized Watergate was "not the traditional brand of influence peddling and graft, although there's some of that, but rather a pervasive and indiscriminate use of power and authority, a passion for secrecy and deception, and an astounding lack of regard for the normal constraints of democratic politics, or republican politics, if you prefer."

As she talks about it, what emerges is a clear sense that she prefers to approach Watergate not as a philosophical question—or even a political one—but simply as a news story. It was, to be sure, a news story of unprecedented scope and magnitude, but it was uncovered and fully reported by the press, and now it is at an end. The press, having fulfilled its obligation, must proceed to new and different stories, new concerns, new responsibilities.

The point made by indirection is that the Watergate cover-up was a very specific set of misdeeds committed by a certain set of persons at a particular time, for reasons implicit in their own characters. "The idea that this sort of thing goes on in every Administration," Katharine Graham concludes, "is just ludicrous." Viewed as a discrete anomaly rather than as material for moral or political speculation, Watergate becomes a more manageable story. "What you're talking about here," Katharine Graham says, "is money in totally unprecedented proportions—and it wasn't just dirty tricks. It was the perversion of the whole democratic process, as we sensed at the time and we now *know.*" Her explanation of the need for all that money and the ways in which it was spent is that "President Nixon wanted an overwhelming mandate" and that nobody was willing to risk diminishing it by so much as a fraction of a point. The mandate once achieved was intended, she suggests, to rule out any question by anyone of any conceivable action taken by the victorious Administration: "They'd be able to say, 'We have a mandate to do anything we want to do and we're going to do it.' "

Far from looking back on Watergate to search it for implications about American life and morality, Kay Graham is determinedly looking ahead. If there are lessons to be learned from Watergate, she feels it forms no part of the media's responsibility to point out what those lessons might be. Her concept of the press's role is one of computerlike neutrality; it has been said of her that she believes in straight news coverage the way other people believe in God. The *Post*, she feels, has done its part in covering Watergate. If any reflection is to take place, any search for significance, it must be done not by the media but by the individual. "It's not our responsibility," she told the authors of this book, "to reform the world now because of Watergate. I really feel very strongly that the press has no damn business doing good or doing evil. We're here to bring information. We're not, God damn it, do-gooders."

Above all, she refuses to see the downfall of the Nixon Administration as a triumph for herself or the *Post*. She admits only grudgingly to a mild satisfaction at the outcome in purely journalistic terms. "We obviously wanted our reporting validated because our credibility was totally on the line," she says. "So that, to that extent, we got some satisfaction, I suppose. When you've taken that much heat for that important a story, to have it all come out in the wash, so to speak, was important for the paper and for us."

But at the same time Katharine Graham certainly realizes that one man's hero is another's villain, and that what is seen one day as a public service of inestimable value could be viewed the next as destructive overreaction. If she appeared to accept the plaudits of her admirers for having brought down a group of dangerous malefactors, it would make her vulnerable once again to the old charge of having been the person who vindictively set out to destroy a President. She is far too shrewd to be tempted to take a bite from that particular apple.

In fact, she has only once publicly claimed a reward for her contribution to the unraveling of Watergate. Warned that she was going to be late to a Halston fashion showing, she permitted herself that luxury. "Since Watergate," she said, "I can get away with being a little late."

Dorothy Hunt

They ordered him to do this and it's wrong
for them to prosecute him.

The first woman touched by the lapping scandal of Watergate was
Dorothy Hunt. Her husband Howard was master of the inept little
band of burglars caught at the Watergate complex the night of June
17, 1972. (So incompetent were they, in fact, that they carried Hunt's
White House telephone number with them, its discovery linking
him inextricably with the break-in.) Dorothy is dead now and can
never testify as to exactly how much she knew of Watergate, but she
was certainly aware of her husband's involvement from the beginning. Eventually, with more or less sympathy and willingness, she
joined him.

As Hunt awaited trial, Dorothy's resentment on his behalf was
building. She was a friendless woman, but to her acquaintances she
whispered her bafflement and discontent. She told one that
"Howard is being made a scapegoat." Another informed *Washington Post* reporters later that during this time "Dorothy was furious
and kept saying, 'They ordered him to do this and it is wrong for
them to prosecute him.' " Then, a few weeks before the trial was to
begin, Dorothy died in a plane crash with a mysterious $10,000 in her
pocketbook, the only known Watergate-related fatality.

E. Howard Hunt joined the CIA shortly after the agency
was formed, right after World War II, and was sent to Paris. It was
there that he met Dorothy, the secretary of the local CIA station
who astonished the French by claiming to be a full-blooded American Indian. (Hunt himself later explained that she was actually
one-eighth Indian and that when they married she brought into their
home "many Sioux artifacts handed down from her mother's
family.")

Hunt's record is impressive, on paper even glamorous. In person,
however, he seems considerably less substantial, a small man all pose

and posture, boast and flimflam. "He couldn't get over the fact that he'd been a CIA agent," says a longtime associate. "You couldn't have a conversation with him for ten minutes without him bringing it up in some way." And when he and Gordon Liddy were on the return flight from Los Angeles, they were so overcome by their own derring-do in breaking into the office of Daniel Ellsberg's psychiatrist that they were unable to resist describing their exploit, only slightly veiled, to two stewardesses who were later able to identify them. Not, perhaps, the most gifted of spies.

But then, Hunt had always been a curious figure: onetime Guggenheim Fellow, archconservative, wine connoisseur, author of some forty-five novels of crime and intrigue—a romanticist, spinning out dreams of clandestine warfare and sexual conquest, who at home was Father the writer and petty tyrant.

There Dorothy presided, an enigma too in her own way. Described as warm and gay by those who knew her, emotional and outgoing, she made few claims on life. Hers had been the drab, self-effacing existence of the spy's wife, constantly on the move—to Mexico, Tokyo, Montevideo, Madrid—unable to put down roots, always without friends. Though she was an educated woman with a job as translator, the area she carved out for herself was small, its perimeters defined by what she conceived to be her duty to husband and children. Beyond that she did not venture. Years earlier, in India before her marriage to Hunt, she had had her fortune told by a wise man. She used to tell her children that she had been promised she would marry again, have ten children, and live to be seventy-five.

Perhaps it was safety that she sought with Howard, a refuge from loneliness and a failed first marriage. She was willing to ignore his extramarital experiments; they seem to have amounted to very little, in any case. According to Cuban friends, Hunt spent one night in a Miami motel with a young lady who later complained that "All he did was to keep me up all night talking about his novels." At best, Howard Hunt was a flimsy reed on which to lean. He was so busy establishing his own colorful legend that he had little time to offer emotional shelter to his wife. In fact, he used her to shield him from the conflicting demands of life, and she provided him with as near to a climate-controlled, sterile environment as possible. She became the bridge to his own children, and the channel of communication through which his messages, largely critical, were sent.

It was the children who provided sustenance; St. John, Lisa, Kevan, and David were her real friends. And while Howard wrote—between four and eight hours a day, according to his eldest son, all day on weekends—Dorothy would sit down with them and their friends, eager for talk and understanding. They stayed up late, often till two or three in the morning, discussing politics, drugs, sex, subjects where she was likely to sympathize with views Howard sharply condemned. She even proposed to buy a double bed for her son to share with his girl friend in his room, a plan quashed by Hunt after her death.

Yet she tried always to mediate between her husband and the children, making his views palatable, ensuring quiet, brooking no interference with his nightly monologue at the dinner table. She even managed to persuade her daughter Lisa to cast her first vote for Nixon, to show her father that she loved him. Dorothy, conversant with her husband's secret life, kept it from the children, telling them only that it was CIA. When one of them found his red wig and false I.D. cards (and silently assumed they meant an affair), she explained, "It's something he needs for his work. I can't tell you any more." And when Howard turned to her in the wake of the June 17 fiasco, she was there. Dorothy, alone among Watergate wives, became an active partner in the cover-up, acting as courier to transmit huge sums in cash from the White House to other defendants.

When her plane crashed and burned, Howard Hunt wept for her, moaning, "Poor Dorothy, poor Dorothy. I dragged everyone into this." He has memorialized her in the dedication of a recent novel, which reads simply: "To my beloved wife, Dorothy. Twenty-three years, three months and one day." But to her two older children, estranged now from their father, her memory is a legacy of grief, disappointment, and confusion.

Knowing something about their mother's life as a courier, they try somehow to justify it. They explain hazily, disjointedly, that she did it for the Cubans ... to help their families ... for her own children's sake. They cannot see how she could have refused their father's request. After all, they point out, she was his wife. And there was no one else.

Beyond that, they share the family conviction that it is the government's duty to see that spies are taken care of. There are rules to the espionage game, and they should be followed. That is the code. (A code, too, for wives? The children are perhaps more conventional than they imagine.)

And yet, now that their mother is dead and their family scattered, they are bitter. If only Watergate had never happened. If only their mother had refused to cooperate. If only their father had not talked her into it. If it had not been that plane. They do not know where to place the blame. They see their mother's death as a terrible penalty for what was, in their view, a mistake, a miscalculation. "It seemed like she paid for every mistake he ever made," says her son. "Her first mistake was getting married. She paid for that one her whole life."

Martha Mitchell

I'll be damned if I'll let my husband
take the rap for Mr. President.

Looking back to the beginnings of Watergate, to the days when it all looked a great deal simpler than it does today, one thing seems certain: Martha Mitchell was first to sound the alarm. In the folklore of Watergate, Martha is Cassandra. She knew the truth; she tried to tell it; and nobody was listening. But what was the truth that Martha had to tell?

The break-in at the Watergate took place on June 17. On June 22, Martha Mitchell, in California to attend a series of GOP fund-raising events, telephoned reporter Helen Thomas of UPI. In response to a question about "the alleged break-in and attempted bugging of Democratic national headquarters," Martha informed Thomas that she had given her husband an "ultimatum to get out of politics" or she would leave him. She was "sick and tired," she said, of "the whole operation." The conversation ended abruptly when, as Thomas explained, "it appeared someone took away the phone from her hand." Martha in the background could still be heard protesting, "You just get away!"

Three days later Martha was in Westchester calling Helen Thomas again. By now she was being "held prisoner" because she would not stand for "the dirty things that go on." Events in California had, it appeared, been dramatic in the extreme. Martha had been overpowered by at least five security guards. Her telephone had been ripped from the wall. She was black and blue, her hand severely cut. She had been thrown down on her bed and held there as a tranquilizer shot was administered.

People who today speculate as to the possibly sinister reasons why the country ignored Martha Mitchell's early warnings point out that the *New York Times* ran the first Thomas story on page 12, the

32

second on page 25. If only, they suggest, the world had listened, Watergate might have been unraveled far sooner than it was; the whole truth might have been uncovered then and there.

Subscribers to this view seem ready to forget that Martha never specified what those "dirty things" she spoke of might be. To most people it seemed quite likely at the time that she had in mind such foul deeds as ripping telephones from walls and forcibly tranquilizing unwilling women. Much of the press and public already suspected that Martha sometimes indulged in a drink or two beyond the social, and these lurid complaints suggested to many that a woman with an alcohol problem had been appropriately dealt with.

Martha was not questioned by any official investigative body at that time. But if inquiries had been made, what would she have told them? When she was later allowed, after prolonged insistence, to testify in the Democrats' civil suit against CRP, she had little hard information to offer. The one fact she did have in her possession—that James McCord, one of the Watergate burglars arrested at the scene, was CRP's head of security—was already known to the press. It was this identification that had prompted John Mitchell to issue a statement attempting to dissociate McCord from CRP. Martha, who knew and liked McCord, could have branded her husband's statement a lie. The fact remains, she did not choose to do so.

Indeed it was Martha herself who prevented her hints and allegations from being followed up. Within a week the signals she had sent out had been firmly recalled. All accusations forgotten, all rough handling forgiven, apparently all passion spent, she was once more a loyal Republican and devoted wife. She made no complaint to any authority; nor did anything she knew seem to have discredited John Mitchell in her eyes. And by the time Martha and John left Washington three months later she was presenting her inside knowledge of Watergate as simply the material of gossip.

Martha had long planned to write a book. Well before Watergate she had told a reporter that she intended to begin setting down her experiences "just as soon as we leave Washington." Describing herself proudly as "a sponge," she announced, "I have been soaking up material and it's fabulous." The "dirty things that go on" seemed to have become a juicy addition to this compilation. When the Mitchells moved to New York in September, reporters questioned Martha once more about Watergate. With a mischievous twinkle in her eye, she told them that those who wanted to know would just have to wait and read about it in the book she intended to write. She was going to tell everything in her book, she said, and she hoped it was going to make lots of money. In fact, she predicted confidently, it would outsell *Gone with the Wind.*

Since then, all kinds of hints have been thrown out about what Martha could have known, and why her original cryptic pronouncements were not more carefully investigated. Was there a plot, a conspiracy to discredit Martha Mitchell? Was there a public-relations campaign to make people believe her a kook and/or a lush and thus devalue any testimony she might offer about Watergate? Was her husband ordered by Nixon to maltreat and eventually divorce her, because the President wanted her silenced? Did Nixon then proceed to destroy John Mitchell, try as Martha might to save him? And did nameless enemies try to drive Martha mad so she could be locked away and forgotten—or even, as her friends have suggested, be driven to suicide?

For the answers to these Gothic questions, and many, many more, the curious will have to wait for the book Martha still promises. That book, in truth, has more substantial reality than almost any other fact of Martha's present life.

It was early in the morning of September 11, 1973, more than a year after the Watergate break-in, when John Mitchell walked out of the fourteen-room Fifth Avenue apartment he used to refer to facetiously as the Taj Mahal. Martha had said, "It has my kind of charm," when she first discovered it, but that charm no longer exerted any effect on Mitchell. By this time all he wanted to save from their sixteen-year marriage was his papers and a few clothes. Martha, he told a friend who informed the press, was "a sick woman."

Today Martha Mitchell tries for a laugh, a weak one at least, as she conjures up a picture of her husband "sneaking out of here with a few clothes and his radio under one arm"—and, she suspects, her file of telephone numbers—"trying not to wake me up." But it was not funny at the time; nor did heaving a stack of John Mitchell's clothes out into the foyer provide much relief. The following morning, when she awoke to find that the cook had walked out, too, Martha reached for the telephone. For the second time since John's departure, she called Winzola McLendon, Washington newswoman and perennial contributor to women's magazines. "I'm alone and frightened," she said, "and I don't know what to do." Winzola canceled everything and flew to New York to spend the next few weeks with Martha.

Winnie McLendon had been promised that when Martha got around to writing that long-talked-of book, they would work on it together. In one of her frantic calls, Martha had at last agreed,

"Okay, let's write the book." Publishers are discreet, but offers for the hardback advance alone are generally reported as $250,000, and a figure of $500,000 has been mentioned. Martha's lawyers have advised her to hold off, however, until a separation agreement can be reached with Mitchell. Thus, though Winzola describes the book as all but finished, no contract has been signed.

Martha has said that she long ago put all her memories on tapes and simply turned them over to Winnie to work from. "I don't know what's happened to the stuff," she told one interviewer. "Lawyer trouble, I think. I have a lapse of memory when it comes to unpleasant things." According to a reporter who has been permitted to watch the Winnie-Martha team at work, however, it has not been that simple. This observer explains their writing technique as depending not on the simple transcription of tapes but on countless interviews. These tête-à-têtes are hard to arrange and harder still to sustain. In the first place, Martha refuses to work at Winzola's Washington apartment, insisting instead on meeting in a variety of obscure hotels. After setting up the appointment over the telephone in code—and there is the added difficulty of knowing what name Martha is using that day—the moody and elusive Martha does not always feel like working. Even when she does, her mind veers frequently into other channels. She never has responded well to questioning; she must be allowed to monologue at her own discursive pace. Then she may have an impulse to make a phone call, a lengthy one. Or she may abruptly cut the session short.

Obviously, the going has not been easy. Still, the game is worth the candle. Winnie's name will appear on the book jacket in lettering no less than three quarters the size of Martha's own; if all goes well, she stands to earn several hundred thousand dollars. The book itself should provide enough definitive answers to satiate the world's curiosity about Martha Mitchell. It is said to consist largely of Watergate and political espionage stories, but it will also attempt to trace the curve of Martha's life as she now remembers it. It will chart her political career back to the time when, she contends, she converted John Mitchell from a "liberal Democrat" who once deeply offended guests by lambasting a Richard Nixon he had yet to meet; it will detail that exhilarating and exhausting period when her public appearances and speeches helped a President win overwhelming reelection. It will also discuss the leather-bound book that "included the whole procedures of everything that has happened," she says, "from a to zeta." Martha is convinced it was the Gemstone file—the record of CRP's bugging of the Democrats' Watergate headquarters—though Republican insiders suggest that it sounds remarkably like the theoretically secret procedural book CRP issued to every Republican candidate. Last, but by no means least intriguing, Martha and Winnie will analyze the Mitchell marriage, offering an explanation of its decline from its early romantic beginnings to those sad later days when Martha began to believe that her husband wanted her committed to a mental institution.

Martha Mitchell has been a national figure almost since her arrival in Washington. From the beginning, she was the darling of the press; among all those drab, button-down Nixonians she provided a gaudy splash of color. Her iconoclastic if conservative views, uninhibited style, and honeyed Southern charm brought her so much publicity that by the time she had been on the Washington scene for two years, a Gallup poll showed that 74 per cent of the American people knew who she was, at least well enough to give her a positive or negative rating. If only 43 per cent of those ratings were favorable, it still added up to an astonishing degree of celebrity.

People who had known her way down home in Pine Bluff, Arkansas, were nonplussed. "We certainly never would have predicted she'd ever have an opinion on a national issue worth listening to," said one of her old teachers. Pine Bluff remembered, though, that Martha's high school yearbook had included a verse beneath her picture that still seemed appropriate thirty years later:

> I love its gentle warble,
> I love its gentle flow,
> I love to wind my tongue up,
> And I love to let it go.

Martha Beall (pronounced Bell) was an only child and apparently felt neglected, though her mother would later annoy her by following her around "like a puppy dog" until her death in 1967. Her father, a cotton broker, died early, but at least provided a very prosperous milieu. The Martha-Winzola book will tell of the car she owned at fourteen, the tour of Europe while in college. Martha, who grew up pretty, has said that she "liked boys at an awful early age." Hardly an intellectual, she was thought to have a good but very much under-employed mind. As one old acquaintance summed it up, "She was a pretty, happy, empty-headed little girl."

Like many another unintellectual Southern belle, Martha chose Stephens College, known in those days as a "charm school." Later, stirred by uncharacteristic ambition, she transferred to the University of Arkansas, where she enrolled in a premed program. Ambition proved fleeting and she gave that up ("With my Southern accent I decided I couldn't master roreign languages," she explained), but it was there that she got to know William (later Senator) Fulbright, with whom, her book will disclose, she used to play tennis. At her next school, the University of Miami, from which she graduated, she became acquainted with Bebe Rebozo, then known as the biggest man around town because he drove the biggest car. These were athletic days for Martha, whose book will describe her as a good tennis player and excellent swimmer. Finally, after flirting with the notion of becoming an actress (her mother, herself an elocution teacher, squelched that), she settled for teaching seventh grade in Mobile. "I despised it," Martha says cheerfully, and she barely lasted out the year. Returning to Pine Bluff, she found work at the arsenal there as receptionist to the commanding general, who eventually provided an escape route: when he was transferred to Washington in 1945, he took her along.

The next decade was a detour in Martha's life. In 1946 she married a handbag manufacturer, Clyde Jennings of Lynchburg, Virginia, and they settled in New York. After ten years and one son, Clyde Jay, they were divorced. Martha's book may reveal what it was, aside from the fact that Jennings was constantly on the road as a salesman, that caused the collapse of the marriage. Jennings himself never will. He is, as his son says, "what I would call, in every sense of the word, a Virginia gentleman." Reflecting that inflexibly courteous tradition, he makes no comment on his ex-wife; the most he has ever told a reporter is that he has had little contact and "no rapport at all" with her since the divorce in 1956, four months before she married Mitchell.

Martha met John Mitchell through common friends during the early fifties (although dates tend to blur in conversations that turn on just when that was). He was a successful lawyer specializing in municipal bonds, divorced from his first wife. The minute Martha laid eyes on him she knew he was "an extremely outstanding person." She was most impressed with his suavity and intellect—and, perhaps, his equable temperament. As she later said, "He's very easy to please. Nothing bothers him."

Their first married home was on Gramercy Park, a high-rent square in the midst of New York City where gracious nineteenth-century buildings surround a well-manicured garden. But that was followed by a series of moves that led from one affluent New York suburb to another ending in Rye where the Mitchells led a quiet, if immensely comfortable, life. Martha's game was bridge, and one prominent neighbor and friend of John's says, "I never heard of anyone there who really knew her." During this time Martha's son from her previous marriage, Jay, lived with her, though for the most part he was away at military school. And in 1961, after four years of marriage, forty-three-year-old Martha bore Mitchell a daughter, named after her mother and called Marty.

People who knew the Mitchells when Marty was very young describe them as doting on her in a fashion almost grandparental. The child was sent to Catholic schools because Martha approved the discipline, and Marty seemed a proper product of her schooling. Martha once proudly announced that her daughter, on hearing of a Beatle drug arrest, had broken her beloved collection of their records. Marty traveled with her parents, and was devoted to her mother. That relationship, once so close, seems ended now. Mitchell, Martha contends, has turned her daughter against her. She has seen her only three times since she went off to boarding school just before her parents' separation in 1973. On one of those occasions, Martha recalls, Marty told her: "My father told me a child only needs one parent. You don't have a car and a chauffeur, and you can't take care of me. My father says you're running around with a wild set of people and you'd better watch your step." To another reporter Martha quoted Marty as saying, "It's all your fault that Daddy is in trouble. You're the one who talked."

"I spoiled her," Martha concedes, "but he has brainwashed her against me." She remembers happier times. One day just before John Mitchell left, he sent his secretary out with Marty to get her long auburn hair cut off. "He never told me," Martha says sadly. "I used to get up a half hour early in Washington to fix it for her. It hung all the way down her back and had never been cut. It was beautiful."

One morning late in the fall of 1974, Martha drove to Marty's convent school in Connecticut to try to bring her daughter home. At her request she was accompanied by a CBS-TV reporter. "I wanted someone to go up with me to see that I try my best to do what I'm supposed to do as a mother," she explained. Three nuns and the business manager met them at the door, prepared to block the way. Marty's father pays all school fees and, according to Martha, has instructed Sacred Heart to forbid Martha access to her daughter. But maybe she was convincing that day, or desperate, or full of charm. As Martha viewed the situation, "Nothing's legally defined. I'm still her mother."

Emerging from the building after a short time, she admitted to the reporter, who had not been allowed to accompany her, that the school authorities had let her speak with Marty and that she had lost control and struck her daughter when the child refused to leave with her. Once back at her Fifth Avenue apartment, Martha refused to confirm the story. "It was a little scuffle, let's put it that way," was all she would say.

Jay Jennings, Martha's son, sympathizes deeply with Marty. He sees the saddest part of Watergate as its impact on the children touched by it. "If you had to say this whole thing has been unfair to someone," he says, "you'd have to say it's been most unfair to the younger children of parents involved in this thing." He worries about Watergate's effect on Marty. Without naming his half sister, he talks about the "young people who did nothing but exist, the ones who have had all this come down on their heads. It's crushed so much of their world, made them old before their time."

Jay Jennings, at twenty-eight a consultant to the Senate Veterans Affairs Committee, is a very small, very polite young man; blinking owlishly behind thick glasses, he attracts attention by his very inconspicuousness. Though out of the Army since 1971 and married, he bears the stamp of eleven years of military life—in his carriage, in the care with which he shapes his sentences, in the precision of his logic—and he welcomes that. "The military tends to leave an indelible mark on you," he explains. "You try to organize your life along military lines, on basically well-organized concepts. The concepts they ingrain within an individual are basically ones of organization, everything from teaching methods to their methods of organizing your own personal welfare."

He explains that he originally chose military school because, growing up without brothers or sisters, with a father frequently absent, and never settled in one place for long, he felt a need to establish roots. "The idea of having a group of friends that I could grow with appealed to me," he recalls. Yet his insistent emphasis on organization suggests that he chose military life not for companionship alone but for its security, its order, its lack of ambiguity. Jay Jennings refuses to react hastily or intemperately to anything; he seems utterly rational. Long ago, at the time of his parents' divorce, he resolutely refused to make a choice between them, or any judgment on the rights and wrongs of their situation. "What's the point of making a judgment?" he says mildly today. Throughout his adolescence, he took care to alternate his vacations between mother and father, so there would be no favoritism. Since his mother's separation from John Mitchell, he considers that he has four parents (his father remarried in 1970). All, he insists, are held in "equal esteem."

Jay has not seen his half sister for some time, and, though he has written to her repeatedly, he has received no reply. But clearly he wishes she could learn from his example. Marty, he points out, is very young, and facing the problem for the first time. He himself learned from his mother's earlier divorce that "they were both right and they were both wrong." Marty, he recognizes with a sigh, will have to learn that for herself. He does not mention any childhood sufferings of his own, before he arrived at his detached and logical view, but when he speaks of Marty's situation, it is possible to guess at them and imagine a small boy determined to steer his lonely, independent course regardless of the emotional gales buffeting him. "As you know," he says, "the younger a child is, the more godly their parents are, and when their image is held up and destroyed, it's a very, very hard thing."

As for what has happened between John Mitchell and his mother, Jay does not take sides, explaining, "I chose to, as best I could, remain intimate with both." Any problems that exist between the two, he says, can be resolved only between them, and "I would be a fool to make any personal judgment about it." He simply recognizes that "it's regrettable and unfortunate, but my parents grew apart," and adds, "I don't even attempt to understand why my stepfather has treated my mother in the way he has since he's left." He does suggest diffidently that "these are developments which have occurred since the inception of Watergate" and that "what has happened since that particular incident has changed them both." Before, they were "very happy, very contented," but "since that time so many things seem to have changed."

Jay's regard for John Mitchell is not one of them. Though he has not seen him recently, Jay still feels close to his stepfather, who, he says sympathetically, "has more problems than any one man should ever have to bear." He describes him as "a very warm man" who "rarely shows it." The warmth is visible, he explains, "in the form of a certain kind of look, a certain kind of smile, a pat on the back." Jay does willingly concede Mitchell's complexity, however. "I'm not sure," he muses, "that anybody in this world, including himself, can honestly and forthrightly say they fully and totally understand John Mitchell—not his own children, my mother, or myself." Still, he concludes, Mitchell "is without a doubt in my mind a very great man. I have the utmost respect for him."

Clearly, Jay remembers the Mitchell marriage with nostalgia. "When I think of my mother and my stepfather," he says, "when I look back to the time we spent together, I can't remember any dissension, any major flaw." But he recognizes the facts of today and insists on facing them squarely. "The Mitchell family," he concludes, "is no longer extant. What used to be is no longer. And the members of the family are just going to have to live with that."

The Mitchells' move to Washington after Nixon's narrow victory over Hubert Humphrey in 1968 seems to have marked the turning point in their marriage, though Martha had no premonition of disaster when John Mitchell first installed her and Marty in their $140,000 duplex in Watergate East. As the new Attorney General, John was making $60,000 a year, no princely sum compared with his former income, reputedly between $200,000 and $300,000 a year as Nixon's law partner, and Martha made no effort to conceal her opinion that the move from Rye represented something of a sacrifice. But Washington offered many compensations.

The nation's capital provided the perfect stage for Martha Mitchell. She adored dressing up, though in a day of maxis, minis, and midis she kept her hemline just above the knee and had, lining one closet's walls, more than a hundred (one fashion columnist insisted it was three hundred) pairs of spike-heeled slingbacks, a shoe so outmoded that it had to be made up specially for her at Saks Fifth Avenue. Unquestionably, Martha reveled in Washington social life. *Time* reported that on a "typical" day in 1970 she gave a coffee party for a friend in the morning, attended a reception for Mamie Eisenhower in the afternoon, and dined (she and John were guests of honor) at the Uruguayan embassy at night. "It's almost required of you to attend those foreigners' functions," she sighed. "If you miss one, they get upset—even if there are five cocktail parties in one night."

She did good works, too. She earned points with Washington activists by helping with District drug programs. Keeping an eye peeled for smoky chimneys, she campaigned against pollution. She assisted the Salvation Army. A favorite project was her antismut campaign. Son Jay suggests that if his mother has been shortchanged by the media on any aspect of her personal life, it was this interest in public service that was overlooked. He offers the example of "a young lady in Africa writing that it had been her lifelong dream to come to the United States," and Martha Mitchell somehow managing to extract permission from immigration authorities. "I don't think the press was aware of her very humanitarian instincts," Jay says. "Or, if they were, didn't choose to bring that out."

The Administration, however, soon recognized Martha's public-relations potential and what a valuable asset they had in her. She was probably the most sought-after Republican in America, after the President and possibly Spiro Agnew. She became the first Cabinet wife to be assigned a press secretary, and she campaigned tirelessly in behalf of Richard Nixon. Never much for formal speechmaking, she excelled at off-the-cuff remarks and socializing. Her guest appearances on television were hugely successful. She had carved out a constituency of her own among that silent majority Nixon hoped to appeal to in '72. She even believed it was her duty to reply personally to the floods of mail they directed to her, a custom she kept up until recently.

As Martha explains it today—totting up how hard she worked for the Nixon Administration, how much she gave—her family life was by this time beginning to disintegrate, its vitality leached away by the President and politics. Domestic tranquillity could not survive the demands of John's twelve- and fifteen-hour work days; even the Mitchells' leisure hours were eroded by constant phone calls from the President and his minions. These claims on their time and patience, she says, included the soothing of disgruntled Cabinet members and agency heads. Even Rose Mary Woods, the President's secretary, came to their Watergate apartment to cry over the treatment she was getting from Bob Haldeman. Martha, contradicting all other accounts of the Woods-Haldeman power struggle, believes John Mitchell talked Rose out of quitting.

Jay Jennings sympathizes with this view of his mother's difficulties. "People in public life," he says, "have to fight for any private life they have." Though he himself was only rarely present, he sees it from the children's angle. "I think it comes very hard to a young boy or a young lady when their parents first come to Washington and become public figures," he says. "A lot of the time, the parents' lives are literally given over to the public. I know, in our case, to a great extent family life began to deteriorate as soon as we came to Washington. There was so little time."

Martha had become a public figure largely because of her readiness to express her political views. Her first national headlines came in November 1969, when, letting go after an antiwar march on the Capitol, she told a television interviewer that her husband had said "many times" that he would like to take "some of the liberals in this country" and "change them for Russian Communists." Since the husband in question was the Attorney General of the United States, this was bound to cause something of a stir, and Mitchell followed up Martha's interpretation of his views with a detailed "clarification." But there were plenty of others to applaud both sentiment and spokeswoman.

Martha, thus encouraged, persevered. Her telephone voice was heard in the land. She was likely to call in the small hours of the morning, offering cogent advice and pithy comment to appreciative if drowsy newsmen. None made more headlines than her 2 A.M. blast to the *Arkansas Gazette* suggesting that they "crucify" Senator Fulbright, Martha's old tennis companion, for having voted against a Mitchell candidate for the Supreme Court.

Looking back on that period now, Martha says that the Administration was using her. "They would tell me to do something," she protests, "and then criticize me for doing it." She telephoned the *Gazette,* she says, only because John Mitchell asked her to call friends in Arkansas and induce them to put pressure on Fulbright —and then she was "criticized and held up to ridicule." She complains that "to this day, neither John nor anyone from the Administration has come forward to say 'We told her to do it.'" Explaining her continued cooperation in these difficult circumstances, she adds, "Publicly, I was criticized, but privately the President sent me a hand-written letter in which he encouraged me to continue speaking out."

The public record shows no trace of any such criticism. The man who was so often kept waiting while Martha primped for an evening out and then greeted her with an appreciative "Hi, gorgeous" was never disapproving. He did tell reporters that when he read about Martha's nocturnal calls he "laughed and laughed and laughed," and he did refer to her as his "unguided missile." But such things are not precisely ridicule, and he was likely to add that the President himself was amused. It was Mitchell, too, who circulated the story that Nixon had encouraged the "spunky" Martha to "give 'em hell."

Indeed she took that advice and enlarged on it. Besides Fulbright (who had not only ignored her directive on the Supreme Court vote but was, in her view, solely to blame for the prolongation of the Vietnam war), the hell prescription was meted out to labor and civil rights leaders, fashion designers, New York's Mayor John V. Lindsay (after he changed parties), Margaret Mead ("she advocates taking drugs and early marriages"), and the entire academic world.

In some of this she followed or enlarged upon Administration thinking. But it is difficult to believe that John Mitchell or anyone else advised her to tell the press that she had refused to speak to her husband for two whole weeks when two men were named to the Supreme Court instead of a woman. Nor, most likely, did he recommend her to reply, when asked for comment on a young woman who had denounced the Vietnam war at a White House party, "I think she should be torn limb from limb." And it was surely an independent Martha who publicly criticized Mitchell's decision to quit the Justice Department in favor of CRP as "a very bad move" that "just breaks my heart," and on Air Force One one day blithely told reporters, "Vietnam stinks."

Meanwhile, despite her growing success in public and all across America's airwaves, those closer to the real Martha were cooling toward her. She had, to be sure, always had her detractors. Even in her palmiest days she had outraged not only liberals but many fellow conservatives. As one Administration wife put it, "I'm embarrassed out of my socks that she's in my party." And there had been no dearth of speculation about Martha's drinking habits when her late-night phoning became a national joke. Her son Jay insists that his mother is strictly a social drinker and that her phone calls are her way of letting off emotional pressure. He himself has never seen Martha—or, for that matter, John Mitchell—showing any ill effects of liquor. (Since Jay himself vastly prefers milk shakes to alcoholic beverages, he can be considered at least a thoroughly sober witness.) On the other hand, Jeb Magruder's interpretation was that the Mitchells spent long evenings at home alone, both of them drinking heavily. John was known to keep a gallon jug of Dewar's mounted in a wooden frame near his desk for easy pouring, but he was notably a man who could hold his liquor. Martha, Jeb Magruder says, could not. Eventually, Magruder suggests, Mitchell would go off to bed, and "that was when she'd get on the phone, a lonely, frustrated woman who would pour out her soul to her secretary or a wire-service reporter or virtually anyone who would listen to her."

Martha's relationship with the Administration was disintegrating, too. Though they were quite willing to continue making use of the colorful and popular public figure she had become, the private Martha was no longer welcome. As Magruder tells it, Martha had an intense desire to be close to Nixon, whom she greatly admired. In some mysterious way, he says, she always knew when a presidential trip was scheduled and, eager to hitch a ride on Air Force One, she would telephone Jeb. It was by then part of Magruder's job to keep her off the plane. Dwight Chapin, who as Nixon's appointments secretary approved the passenger list, finally blew up at him. "We've dealt with that woman since 1968," he said, "and we're sick of her. The President doesn't want her anywhere near him. I'm not going to talk to her. She's your problem, you handle her."

There was a still more disturbing side. Martha was said to be not merely difficult and embarrassing, but emotionally unstable. Magruder sketches a dismal picture of the Mitchell ménage. They were rarely invited out, he says, because "Martha's reputation for erratic behavior had become such that many hostesses were unwilling to run the risk of inviting her to dinner." They avoided restaurants and theaters "because Martha was obsessed with the idea that someone would try to assassinate them." Magruder admits that the Mitchells had received numerous threats, but points out that they had FBI protection; he is certain that Martha's fears, which included the idea that people were following her, went "beyond the rational."

Jeb Magruder was not alone in considering Martha's emotional problems severe. One newsman who knew the Mitchells well during their Washington years says flatly that no one who had contact with Martha could have failed to notice that she was "an emotionally disturbed person."

By June of 1972 Martha was feeling overworked and undervalued. As she says now, CRP had Agnew, Bob Dole, and Martha Mitchell out on the road making speeches "while the rest of them were home doing dirty tricks." Above all, she resented the fact that Pat Nixon was not pulling her share of the load. In Martha's disdainful view, Pat "never did anything she was supposed to, other than greet people in the White House." It took some persuasion, then, to enlist Martha's cooperation in a round of political fundraising events in California, but she eventually went along.

On Saturday morning, June 17, at 7:15, the phone rang in the Mitchells' hotel bedroom, and Martha picked it up. It was, she says, Bob Haldeman calling Mitchell. Though Mitchell took the call in another room, Martha is sure in retrospect that it was the first announcement of the Watergate break-in. She believes that her ability to pinpoint the moment Mitchell first heard the news is significant and constitutes one of the many reasons why Mitchell and his former associates are "scared to death" of her.

Continuing her account of that California period, she reports that on the following day—still knowing nothing about the break-in—she had a serious talk with Mitchell about their future, in which she asked him to quit as head of CRP. He listened but turned down her request, promising her, "Honey, hang on for two and a half more months and I will take you back to New York." Then he persuaded her to stay out in California for a few days of rest, relaxation, and swimming, while he and his aides returned to Washington. It was only after Mitchell's departure that she learned about the break-in and the arrest of McCord. Jumping out of bed "like a sheet of lightning," she rushed to the telephone. Before she was able to reach Mitchell, she spoke to Jeb Magruder, who reports that she accused him of throwing McCord to the wolves.

Somehow quieted by whatever conversation she eventually had

with her husband, Martha did not rush back to Washington. She stayed where she was, but, as she describes her thoughts now, she continued to brood over Mitchell's refusal to get out of politics. "I had asked Mitchell on Sunday to resign," she says, "and I wasn't staying in this mess. I had seen what had gone on previously to some extent, had not agreed with them, had found fault with what they were doing, and had become very suspicious." From this explanation of her thinking, it appears that Martha's decision to leave her husband was purely political, its impersonal character underlined by the fact that Helen Thomas, not John Mitchell, was first to hear of it.

Martha's book will have to explain her removal from California to Westchester, accounting for the time between the unceremonious interruption of her call to Helen Thomas on one coast and its resumption on the other. Blanks in the long, hazy story she then outlined will also need to be filled in. That story has gone through many revisions and refinements since Helen Thomas first heard it. The press has intermittently updated it as Martha supplied new details. The number of manhandlers dwindled as the cast of name players was enlarged. Only in recent months has Martha told reporters of the mysterious appearance of the President's personal lawyer, Herbert Kalmbach, summoned by persons unknown, to take her to a local hospital for suturing cuts sustained when she smashed her hand through a glass door as she attempted escape; of her own terrors as, bruised and bloody, she was held captive; of her cold certainty, when Kalmbach tried to register her at the hospital as Dorothy Kalmbach, that he was consigning her to permanent oblivion. She maintains that it was only the providential appearance of a doctor who greeted her by name that saved her from that dread fate.

New ingredients are still being added to this spicy mélange of memories. As the story will be told in the book, the most lasting damage that was done in California was to Martha's relationship with daughter Marty, who, she says, was "allowed to see the condition I was in, without food, plying me with liquor. They were brainwashing Marty, allowing her to come in and see while they threw me down on a bed and they displaced my pants"—to administer the sedative Martha has sometimes referred to as "an eight-hour shot." She has lately added one more danger she was able to escape. She says that for a time (whether in California or in Westchester she does not specify) she was held at gunpoint.

With Martha holed up in Westchester after her second call to Thomas, Washington was abuzz with gossip about her. Some of the President's men implied that Martha had had a breakdown ("I wouldn't even want to ask John about it myself," said the discreet Ken Clawson, Deputy Director of Information at the White House). The more kindly characterized the entire episode as a marital spat, while there were others ready to ascribe it to menopause or alcohol.

Martha now accuses her husband of joining the rumormongers. "Mitchell," she said, "even went out and said I'm in Silver Hill [a private psychiatric hospital specializing in treatment of alcoholism]." But his quoted remarks at the time, uxorious almost to the point of fantasy, hardly bear out that accusation. Calling his wife "the greatest political phenomenon that has ever hit this country," he assured Helen Thomas that he wanted Martha to speak her mind at any time. "She's great," he said. "That little sweetheart. I love her so much. She gets a little upset about politics, but she loves me and I love her and that's what counts." He went on to assure Thomas that because "Martha has never been happy with me in politics," the Mitchells had a compact to "get the hell out of this gambit" immediately after the November election.

His actions, too, were certainly calculated to please a mutinous wife. Not only did he promptly join Martha in her Westchester retreat, but it was not long before the Mitchells were back in Washington together. The following day was enlivened for Washington gossips by the announcement of Mitchell's resignation. "I have found," said his letter to the President, "that I can no longer [carry out the job] and still meet the one obligation which must come first: the happiness and welfare of my wife and daughter. They have patiently put up with my long absences for some four years and the moment has come when I must devote more time to them."

In reply Nixon said he understood and appreciated the "compelling reasons" for Mitchell's decision, adding gallantly, "I am most appreciative of the sacrifice Martha and you have both made in the service of the country."

Martha now believes that Mitchell left his job solely because of Watergate and that she and the world were deluded by the explanation that it was done for her sake. But though there are others who share that view, Jeb Magruder is not one of them. There was speculation even then, Magruder says, that Nixon had fired Mitchell because of Watergate and that Martha provided a convenient cover, but he always doubted it. "At the time Mitchell resigned," he points out, "the Watergate affair seemed to be under control."

But for whatever reason the Mitchells were leaving, they departed for New York at the end of that summer in great good spirits. Waving a gay farewell to the capital, Martha exulted, "I'm free, free as a bird." Still nettled by those rumors of mental-health, marital, or drinking problems, she slapped at the Republicans and the city where they set the tone. "To get along in Washington," she said, "you have to put on a false face and never let anyone know what you really think or feel. I just couldn't do that. I can't be a phony. I have to be me." She also took this opportunity to identify the cad who had yanked the phone from the wall of her California villa the previous June: Steve King, her bodyguard, since promoted to security director of CRP. Apparently, however, she no longer held her husband responsible for King's behavior, the "dirty things that go on," or the later imprisonment, with or without gun.

Neither, apparently, did she blame the President. The Mitchells interrupted their new life in New York long enough to appear in Washington during inaugural week to help celebrate Nixon's landslide victory. Flashbulbs popped as an exultantly smiling Martha swept into parties, hair piled high, swathed in floor-length white mink. As the *New York Times* noted after witnessing Henry Kissinger greeting her at one of these receptions, "Everyone wanted to hug and kiss Mrs. Mitchell."

It was not until March that Martha was again heard to comment publicly on Watergate, and by now she had a different view of it. At the telephone again, she told the *New York Times* that someone was trying to make her husband "the goat" of the Watergate affair. This call may have been prompted by a *Newsweek* story that had quoted "a White House insider" as saying that Mitchell might be available for sacrifice. "I fear for my husband," Martha went on. "I'm really scared. I have definite reason. I can't tell you why. But they're not going to pin anything on him. I won't let them, and I don't give a damn who gets hurt."

In May the former Attorney General was indicted on charges of conspiring to obstruct a federal investigation. The wires burned again. Ignoring her daughter's pleas to stop, Martha spelled it out· "If my husband knew anything about the Watergate break-in, Mr. Nixon also knew about it. I think he should say goodbye, to give credibility to the Republican Party and to the United States. I think he let the country down. Mr. President should resign."

And as Mitchell prepared to appear before the Ervin committee, Martha moved to undercut his prepared testimony. "I'll be damned," she said, "if I'll let my husband take the rap for Mr. President." Unhesitatingly she proclaimed, "The President always knew."

A fiercely protective wife, fighting tooth and nail for her beloved husband? Her admirers certainly saw it that way. She was lauded in some quarters for her courage, panache, and what California Senator

John Tunney called her "ferocious love for her husband." John Mitchell put the finishing touch to this picture of embattled unity by joining Martha on one of her telephone calls, agreeing with her that "somebody has tried to make me the fall guy," but "it isn't going to work."

Yet at the same time a strange subterranean struggle was being waged between the Mitchells, their battleground the press, as they charged and countercharged not crime nor disaffection but psychological damage. In May, *Time* had reported that Martha Mitchell had "put herself under doctors' care and voluntarily entered a medical institution ... for treatment of a nervous breakdown." Martha hotly denied that when she returned to New York after five days of unexplained absence, and Mitchell would say only that Martha was "a very distraught young lady," but his friends eagerly whispered to reporters that a psychiatrist, complete with wife, was staying at the Mitchell apartment to watch over Martha, who sometimes would and sometimes would not cooperate.

Martha's friends riposted that this was not a therapeutic but a social visit. Accusations escalated. Mitchell, it was said, had twice attempted to have his wife hospitalized, but could not bring himself to go through court proceedings to have her committed.

Martha announced that she might walk out on her husband, then denied it. A pall had, according to her, been cast over her marriage by Watergate and the impending Vesco trial, and her description of Mitchell's mental state was a bleak one. "I don't talk to him anymore," she said. "I can't get through. He never moves, he won't see our friends, he's broken down." She said he was drinking heavily, taking tranquilizers. She told of having to drag him to bed many a night, helped by Marty and their faithful housekeeper.

Mitchell intimates suggested, with impressive psychological sophistication, that Martha was simply projecting her own symptoms onto John. "She transfers her problems to him," they told reporters. "She's in a state of acute depression and can't take it, so she tells everyone that John is depressed. The truth is that he's in pretty good shape for a guy who has as much trouble as he has."

Mitchell's final decision to walk out has been roundly condemned by Martha's supporters. If she was indeed in such parlous mental condition, how could her husband justify abandoning her? Some friends have criticism that cuts far deeper. They are convinced that Mitchell induced both servants to quit, thus leaving Martha entirely alone in an apartment purposely well stocked with liquor and stripped of food.

The Mitchells have not spoken since the night before "he walked out and left me with $975," but during the early months of separation Martha could write checks on an account to which John made deposits. Her efforts to make more personal contact failed, Martha explains, because Mitchell was living in a hotel under an assumed name, moving from floor to floor to elude her pursuit.

Since then, some of her claims on him have been legally enforced. Martha's separation suit demanded $3,000 a week for maintenance and $35,000 in counsel fees. Mitchell said he would be hard pressed to pay the temporary alimony of $1,000 a week granted by a New York judge, but Martha was quick to reject his argument. She told a reporter that she and John were worth several million dollars before they went to Washington and that John was still receiving about $300,000 a year from his old law firm. "I also understand," she added pointedly, "he has a Swiss bank account."

In a practical sense, then, Martha has done well. She is still in the fourteen-room apartment with its nineteen-foot ceilings, carved mantels, and velvet bergères. There is a vast entrance hall floored in black and white marble squares, a music room in blue, a maid once more installed in the renovated kitchen. A single woman should be able to scrape along on a thousand a week, and her book will surely sell. After successful guest shots on a number of television talk shows, Martha is deluged with offers. She travels widely, lacking neither luncheon invitations nor floral tributes. As Winnie McLendon told a reporter who recently requested an interview, "Martha doesn't need you. She doesn't need anybody."

Yet as she putters about the huge apartment where life-size portraits of herself and John gaze down on a dining room she says has never been used, Martha Mitchell is clearly not a happy woman. Complaining of a chronic digestive ailment, and thinner now (down to a size ten from "a large twelve or even a fourteen"), she talks longingly of times past. "They used to say we had a perfect marriage," she told an interviewer. "We did. Every day he used to tell me I was the most wonderful woman in the world." But Watergate changed all that. "I don't feel I'm a deserted woman," she insists. "This is not a normal marital breakup. It's much more intricate. Because a man doesn't change in twenty-four hours from thinking his wife is the most wonderful person in the world."

Plainly her feelings, too, have changed. Asked about chances of a reconciliation with John Mitchell, she told a reporter, "Hell, no. I'd like to throw a bottle of ink at him, right on his bald head." But then, she temporized, "In a way I feel sorry for him. He's made such a jackass out of himself and ruined everyone around him. He had everything in the world going for him, but he blew it."

At other times, she is less tolerant. She is threatened by an unnamed "they," who seem, as she talks, to have some connection with Mitchell. She told one reporter that "they're trying to blackmail me, but I'm not going to let them do it." Speaking of her husband, she says ominously, "He can't stand it that I came out clean. They're trying to drive me up the wall."

Whoever it is that threatens her, Martha is on her guard. She knows her garbage has been tampered with, and she has learned to foil the intruders by tearing up her letters and putting part of each in the garbage one day, another part the next, and the rest maybe a week thereafter.

Son Jay is not considered a member of the enemy group. She still sees him, and they even spent last Thanksgiving together. They discuss her problems. "She talks to me," he says. "She tells me about some of these things." He refuses to specify the problems they discuss, considering that privileged information, but he admits that "they prey heavily on her mind," adding, "I would say that I don't think my mother's problems in any way are finishing. I would say, if anything, they're increasing." He sympathizes but maintains his perspective. "I've frankly given her the best advice I can," he says, "but I don't seek to undertake a more active role because I honestly feel that, as much as I'd like to do something, there's a real sense of frustration to have to sit back and know that there isn't anything to do about the problems that exist between her and my stepfather. I'd love to help out, I'd love to resolve these things, but I can't." Balancing any favorable statement about his mother with one about John Mitchell, still resisting the pull of Martha's emotional field of force, Jay Jennings maintains a cool emphasis on even-handed justice that intemperate Martha must find galling.

Even more so must be his refusal to view Watergate from her standpoint. They do discuss the question and disagree, in his word, "vehemently." To start with, he has simply never accepted her account of the facts. He suggests that she and John Mitchell offer different versions of what happened, and he will not choose between parents in this area either. "I have no idea of the extent of my mother's knowledge. I don't know what she's overheard or what she's seen," he says, "but my mother always tells it as she sees it, and I would never question her veracity. I would only question the way she sees it." At the same time, he is able to listen to John Mitchell's Watergate testimony with equal respect. "It's never been in my mind," he says, "that both of them weren't telling the truth as they saw it. My stepfather's telling it from his point of view, my mother from hers."

Even when Jay and his mother agree on the facts, however, there is deep division as to how to judge them. Martha, of course, sees Watergate as a drama of deep-dyed crime and lurid intrigue; Jay Jennings has still not decided for himself whether anything that happened in the entire course of the Watergate affair was wrong.

Speaking of his "maverick view," his "unique position," he carefully sets forth his reasons for believing the Watergate conspiracy trial premature. "I think there are too many glaring constitutional issues involved that should be resolved before the question of anyone's guilt or innocence can be determined," he explains. "We can't judge until we know what the powers of the presidency really are." After all, he reflects, "there were riots in our communities, great unrest on our campuses," and there has as yet been no definitive ruling from any court on how far a President may go to meet internal challenges. "I don't know for sure," he says, "that we've found out what internal challenges Richard Nixon had to deal with." He seems to assume that the original order for the Watergate break-in must have come from the President; he wants to know, he says, "what the President's interests—perhaps legitimate interests—were in breaking into Watergate. Until then, we can't condemn anyone."

And, legitimate or not, there is the question of what to do when a President gives an order. That, Jay suggests, raises the question of loyalty; he himself, product of Army indoctrination that he is, respects a command from his commander in chief. Even beyond that looms the President's huge responsibility for national security. In cases involving the security of the nation, he maintains, a higher law is invoked. If the President were to ask Jay Jennings to break the law for national security reasons—even to commit murder—"I wouldn't question him. I probably would do it."

Martha Mitchell is not the woman to tolerate such temperate reflections as these. As Jay dryly notes, "My mother is rather instantaneous in her judgments." Seeing herself as a heroine opposing the forces of evil, it must be maddening to find her son so intransigently rational, coolly reserving judgment, insisting on constitutional clarifications. Martha is more comfortable in an atmosphere of enthusiastic approbation and supportive concern, among people willing to accept her evaluation of Watergate and her own role in it.

She finds this accepting attitude among the women of the Washington press corps, and it is to them that she most freely confides her feelings. "They have literally saved me from an asylum," she says, "and from I don't know what. And I can take it one step further. If I hadn't made that telephone call to Helen in California, the people that were behind all this, that were holding me a prisoner, would not have taken into consideration that the press knew that if anything happened to Martha Mitchell, Helen would have been there looking for me. It literally saved my life."

The newswomen claim no credit for saving Martha's life, but they do return her affection. Of course they have always been her public friends—how else would she be encouraged to call them some news-making midnight?—but they are her private friends as well, though one concedes that "Martha's long suit is neither friendship nor motherhood." Part of it may be the charm of the woman once described as a cross between Archie Bunker and Scarlett O'Hara; it is intermittent, but it is still there. In the main, however, their loyalty seems to spring from a sort of compassionate sisterhood. They, like many other women throughout the country, view Martha as a woman who, trying her best to please, has been used and then callously discarded by men. Her humiliation and pain, and her determination to rise above it all, seem to have struck a responsive chord. And if the protectiveness of the media women seems almost maternal, perhaps they recognize that if it were not for them, Martha Mitchell would hardly exist in the sense that she does.

Martha herself seems still unsure about what has happened to her life, but there is one central certainty: it was Watergate, she knows, that marked the turning point, and the significance of everything can be understood only in relation to that first warning of hers from California. Again and again, to anyone who will listen, backtracking, contradicting herself, weaving in new elements, sensing new implications, sometimes triumphantly righteous, often tearful, she insists on telling and retelling the story of that half-real time, as if hoping to discover in it some final justification of herself as a heroine, a victim, or simply as a person.

Jay, looking on, does not try to interfere. "Wishing for another person's happiness," he says, "is leaving it pretty much up to that person, but that's what I'd wish for." Is it likely that Martha's future will be happier? "I honestly don't know," he admits. "It's like looking in a cloudy crystal ball."

Deborah Sloan

This is an honest house.

Deborah Sloan lives quietly in Troy, Michigan, with her husband, Hugh, and their two children. She may be more attractive, brighter, and happier than most, but to people who meet her for the first time she must seem—as indeed she is in many ways—a very average young woman. No one would connect her at first sight with the scandals of Watergate, and that is the way she wants it.

But there is a connection. Debbie Sloan's husband, once treasurer of the finance committee of the Committee to Re-elect the President, is the only person in the Nixon Administration known to have quit his job to avoid participating in the Watergate cover-up —and Debbie herself has been regarded ever since as the woman responsible for that decision.

The Sloans have been pursued by the press, begged for interviews; several publishers have importuned them to recount their story in a book. But they have refused all offers. They have begun a new life and prefer to avoid publicity. It seems almost unfair to disinter that already distant time, and Debbie Sloan submits to it reluctantly, only because if the story must be told once more, she prefers it to be told accurately. It has been distorted in the past, and she is willing to sacrifice a portion of her privacy in order to set the record straight. The first myth she would like to see exploded is the one that cast her as the Joan of Arc of Watergate.

At the time of Hugh Sloan's resignation, an informant at CRP told the *Washington Post*'s Carl Bernstein: "Sloan is the sacrificial lamb. His wife was going to leave him if he didn't stand up and do what was right." From that point on, Debbie was identified as a heroine, a role she finds totally uncongenial. In the first place, she is amused that anyone could ever believe her capable of threatening to leave her husband. Not only was—and is—the Sloans' marriage a thoroughly happy one, but at the time Hugh decided to resign, Debbie was in an advanced stage of pregnancy.

More seriously, the implication that Hugh takes his orders from her as his moral superior seems an insult to her husband. It takes all credit for his decision away from him in order to lay it at her feet, and that suggests a thoroughly inaccurate picture of them and their relationship.

Debbie Sloan has discussed the origin of the story with her husband, and they think they understand now what kind of misunderstanding must have launched it. Just before Hugh made his decision to resign from CRP, a secretary who shared his suspicions that something was very much amiss told him she hoped he would not allow himself to be intimidated but would stand up for what he believed in, to which he lightheartedly replied, "If I didn't, my wife would leave me." This was reported seriously as Debbie's threat, and her unwelcome legend sprang instantly to life.

As treasurer of CRP, Hugh Sloan was in charge of all campaign contributions. During the last-minute rush to beat the new disclosure law which went into effect on April 7, 1972, he became custodian of an additional $1.7 million in cash, most of it in $100 bills. For some time he had been disbursing this money, with his superiors' approval, in ways that might have seemed questionable even to people considerably more hardened to the pragmatic methods of politics than gently reared Hugh Sloan. Among these transactions had been $350,-000 in a briefcase to White House aide Gordon Strachan; $250,000 to the President's personal lawyer, Herbert Kalmbach; $20,000 to Jeb Magruder—and, most suspicious of all, the $199,000 he had doled out piecemeal to Gordon Liddy, beginning in January 1972.

The break-in at the Watergate took place on June 17, 1972. Two days later Sloan was being asked by Jeb Magruder and Frederic LaRue to tell investigators that he had given Liddy a far lower amount. Sloan protested, "I've no intention to perjure myself." Magruder replied, "You may have to."

When Sloan appealed to the White House for guidance, aides turned a deaf ear to his problems. "I don't want to know any details," John Ehrlichman told him, adding that financial details would be covered by Executive privilege, "at least until after the election." Dwight Chapin, seeing that Sloan was, as he himself later described it, "overwrought," suggested that he "take a vacation." There was also some discussion of how important it was to protect the President.

The Sloans did indeed take a vacation, though not because Chapin had suggested it. They went to Bermuda on a long-planned last fling as a childless couple. From the first, both Debbie and Hugh had been suspicious of CRP involvement in the Watergate break-in; when it turned out that the money that financed it was a campaign contribution—and, according to Magruder, Hugh knew that within three days—they were virtually certain. Even so, they cannot have been deeply disturbed or frightened. Debbie recalls that while in Bermuda they heard of Martha Mitchell's threats to leave her husband because of "the dirty things that go on," and her claim that she was a political prisoner. Martha's husband was the head of CRP and thus she might have been assumed to know something of what the Sloans already suspected, yet they managed to find her outburst amusing, a reaction difficult to reconcile with Hugh's description of his own mental state as "overwrought."

But when they returned to Washington it was to questioning by the FBI. Hugh was alarmed. Even though he had known nothing about the break-in, he wondered if he might not somehow be held responsible. It was at least conceivable that since he had disbursed the money that paid the Waterbuggers, he might be criminally liable for their activities.

Sloan called his father, a vice-president of a large paper company, asking him to come to Washington. But by the time his father arrived, Hugh had already made up his mind that he could not in conscience continue at CRP. Citing "personal reasons," he resigned on July 14, approximately two weeks after G. Gordon Liddy was fired from the committee for refusing to answer questions put to him by the FBI, and two weeks after the resignation of John Mitchell. The best explanation CRP insiders could offer the press was that "He was getting an ulcer and his wife is pregnant."

Hugh's decision came as no surprise to Debbie. They had discussed the situation together throughout, and her thinking paralleled his. There were certain things that other people could perhaps justify to themselves on grounds that they were a traditional component of politics, but the Sloans had different values and wanted to maintain them. Accordingly, Hugh could no longer be a part of CRP. On the other hand, he had no intention of taking any action against those who did not feel as he did. His decision was simply to resign, not to report his suspicions to anyone. After all, he had no real proof, only suspicion, and he was not the kind of person who could be comfortable with the idea of getting his friends in trouble. Above all, he wanted to take no action that might in any way jeopardize the reelection of Richard Nixon, the President in whom both Sloans fervently believed.

The thought of leaving her White House job simply because something was wrong at CRP did not occur to Debbie, who continued to work until she was eight months pregnant. It never entered her mind that the White House could be involved in any wrongdoing. Even later, when the White House was clearly implicated, the much-used explanation that overzealous aides had exceeded their authority seemed entirely convincing to the Sloans. Both had worked in the White House, where people often joked that the President's name was frequently taken in vain. Both knew that when someone said, "Get that done immediately; the President expects it on his desk tomorrow morning," it likely meant no more than "Try harder."

But Hugh Sloan was not permitted to resign discreetly. Reporters and investigators converged on him. Debbie remembers those days as a confused jumble of people and events. She was in a very emotional state throughout that period, a fact she ascribes partly to her pregnancy and partly to her concern about her husband. Reporters came to their house; their names were in the newspaper. Hugh, despite her admiring conviction that he was the only honest man in the entire situation, was under suspicion. Looking back on it, Debbie Sloan can hardly recognize her present self in the woman who could—as she did—proclaim to a reporter: "This is an honest house!"

By that fall Hugh Sloan had become an important source for the *Washington Post*'s continuing Watergate probe. Though his lawyers told him that anything he said might be used against him in any civil suit that might arise from his role as CRP treasurer, and though the prosecutors had exacted a pledge that he would make no public statement before the Watergate trial, Sloan continued to be not only suspicious but concerned. He wanted to see a thorough investigation that would reveal the true state of affairs. Yet at the same time he was devoted to Richard Nixon and hoped to see him reelected. Afraid of damaging the campaign, he was not eager to tell what he knew or suspected. Only slowly and hesitantly, and with extreme caution, did he yield up part of what he knew.

Sloan was actually the source of the *Post*'s one major setback in its pursuit of the Watergate story. He had finally acknowledged to Woodward and Bernstein that H. R. Haldeman was one of the five men who controlled CRP's secret fund. The reporters understood him to mean he had named Haldeman before the grand jury, and identified the information as grand jury testimony in print. Since Sloan had not in fact been questioned about Haldeman, his lawyer threw the *Post* into temporary despair by denying the story, and the White House made the most of it.

In June of 1973, Hugh Sloan detailed for the Ervin committee his decision to resign his CRP post rather than join in the cover-up. "Your testimony," chairman Sam Ervin assured him, "has renewed my faith in the old expression 'An honest man is the noblest work of God.'" Debbie, sitting just behind her husband, beamed. It was in that same month, however, that Hugh told a reporter, "I'm disillusioned, of course, but my wife is more bitter than I am."

Then Hugh Sloan left Washington to take a job in private industry. It was then that he gave the only interview in which he talked at length about the impact the Watergate scandal had had on him. That interview paints a picture of Sloan as wasted, sad, and completely disillusioned in consequence of his experiences. He is quoted as saying, "I learned one thing in politics. If you go into it for a career—I mean as a matter of life's work and economics—then sooner or later you have to compromise. You either compromise or get out. It just, sooner or later, takes the edge off your values."

Debbie Sloan insists today that this interview presented an exaggerated report of her husband's feelings even at that time, and certainly does not represent his thinking today. Hugh, she says, was sorry, of course, that his career in politics had to end. He was deeply disappointed—as indeed they both were—in some of the people he had worked with. These were people he had known, trusted, and respected; naturally, their questionable judgments and decisions were disillusioning. But that disillusionment, she is sure, never extended to politics in general or to Republican politics in particular.

Debbie Sloan is able now to emphasize the positive side of Watergate, pointing out that it proved the system stronger than any individual. Watergate, she suggests, has forced the country to consider new ways of financing campaigns. Better people will be attracted into politics. There will be more small contributions, more personal involvement. She believes Watergate has brought about a raising of standards throughout government, a change of moral climate.

Yet it would be easy to understand if there had been at least temporary disillusionment—and even bitterness—at the circumstances that brought the Sloans' Washington life to a close. It had all begun so hopefully. Debbie and Hugh were outstanding examples of youthful enthusiasm and idealism in the Nixon White House, Hugh rather slightly built, boyishly appealing, evidently patrician; Debbie tall, slender, olive-skinned, with long dark hair and a winning smile. They met in the White House mess, introduced by Lucy Winchester, Mrs. Nixon's social secretary. Hugh was at that time a member of the President's appointments and scheduling staff. Debbie was Lucy Winchester's assistant. Both were dedicated admirers of the President. When the news of their engagement reached Pat Nixon, who was in Key Biscayne, she promptly telephoned her congratulations to the bride-to-be, saying that the announcement "just brightened my day."

Debbie Murray had left Rocky River, Ohio, an upper-middle-class suburb of Cleveland, where she went through the public schools, for Connecticut College, from which she graduated with honors, having been elected to Phi Beta Kappa. From there she went to Washington and a job in the Library of Congress's Far East Division, where she did research and wrote articles for a year. But throughout this time she felt she was failing to take full advantage of Washington. She had been a government major in college and had taken an interest in student government; now she wanted to see government in action, and perhaps participate in the process.

Her parents were Republicans, and she tended to be more conservative than liberal, so it was natural for her to apply for a job at the Republican National Committee, where she was hired by the Nixon-Agnew campaign as an overqualified receptionist. In that capacity it often fell to her to answer questions about where Nixon stood on this issue or that, so she began a careful study of all his programs and proposals. She had always favored Nixon's goals; now, as she continued her study of his political philosophy, she found herself increasingly dedicated to the man.

She had expected her political involvement to end with the election, but instead she was offered a job at the White House. There, as a member of Pat Nixon's staff, she saw a good deal of Mrs. Nixon, Tricia, and Julie. She prepared briefing papers for them, and sometimes ran their errands; minor shopping trips, for example, which they could not undertake themselves without attracting a crowd. She grew to admire them all. Debbie had always looked up to people in government; to her they seemed larger than life, distant, and almost inhuman. As she drew closer to those once unreal people, and the aura of history that shrouded them began to fade, she was surprised to find them human. Yet it is clear that she was still sufficiently awed to find their every small human gesture enormously magnified by her estimate of their importance.

Again and again she remarks on the warmth of Mrs. Nixon and the girls, their thoughtfulness. She lists their beneficences. Mrs. Nixon always invited her staff to the family quarters at Christmas for tea, Christmas cookies, and chat. She often forwarded the candy sent her as a gift with such messages as "You're a great staff and this will cheer you up." Debbie herself received little notes from Mrs. Nixon when she was married, and when her baby was born. When she left the White House, Mrs. Nixon asked her up to the family quarters for coffee. They talked about the forthcoming baby, and about Mrs. Nixon's own two daughters.

Debbie appreciated, too, the fact that the Nixons often offered to pose for pictures with staff members. Some of those pictures are still a proud part of their lives. Debbie especially treasures one showing herself and her first baby, Melissa, with Julie Nixon Eisenhower. It was taken at Julie's suggestion one spring day when Debbie had returned to visit Lucy Winchester and show off the baby. Julie autographed it as a souvenir for Melissa.

Because she knows Mrs. Nixon's real warmth and generosity, it angers Debbie to hear people refer to her as Plastic Pat. She thinks of her today with great admiration and sympathy. The sympathy, at least, extends to Richard Nixon. Debbie Sloan still believes in the great contributions of the man who, as she says, realigned the world. She is deeply sorry that his goals and his presidency had to end because of something so small—and yet, she reflects soberly, so terrible in the way it involved people and the things it made them do.

She has no doubt of the rightness of Ford's pardon. Nixon had already paid the highest price that could be exacted by having to resign in disgrace; prosecuting him and inflicting more pain on him and his family than they had already suffered could have served no useful purpose. And that Nixon has suffered deeply she has no doubt whatever, remembering as she does the quality of his dedication, the kind of man he was. She wonders if he can survive this last humiliation by many years.

Ironically, in hindsight she cannot resist thinking that perhaps all these terrible things need never have happened, if only the truth about the Watergate break-in had been allowed to come out at the time. She adumbrates a saving scenario. If only Mitchell or someone had gone to the President immediately after the break-in and told him what had happened, the President could have owned up to it publicly and said it could not be condoned. Then they could have fired the entire campaign organization and gotten a new staff. That done, the whole episode would have been over and done with, and soon forgotten. No one would have held it against the President; he would have been reelected easily. But somehow that was not what happened . . . and that, she feels, is the tragedy.

Debbie Sloan condemns no one. She tries instead to sympathize. She does not even criticize those who, knowing as much as Hugh Sloan did, did not make his decision. She points out that it was easier for her and Hugh; they had been saving her salary, so at least resignation was not a financial hardship. The truth is that the Sloans were never crusaders or proselytizers. They simply drew a moral line past which they would not step. Debbie Sloan thinks of each person's decisions as a matter of personal standards. She has her own, and they are gentle but stubborn. Two wrongs do not make a right. The ends do not justify the means. In the end, for her everything comes down to self-respect. Moral judgment is always an individual matter, because each person must, after all, live with himself.

Before any judgment can be made, though, there must be some awareness that a problem exists, and Debbie does find it hard to believe that other wives did not know or suspect their husbands' involvement. It is surprising, she suggests, that Watergate could be in the newspapers every day and that wives still would not ask their husbands for some kind of explanation. She can only conclude, with an edge of irony, that the interchange and communication so much a part of her own marriage are unusual; some people must communicate more frequently than others.

But it is when she talks about the other Watergate wives that Debbie Sloan's fundamental assumptions reveal themselves. However much she may refuse to criticize or condemn others, self-respect is not all that is involved in moral decisions. There is also the respect of other people, and that can be forfeited. Talking hypothetically about the feelings of a wife whose husband was involved in wrongdoing, she suggests that the wife could not know in advance what her reaction would be. Afterward, she might find that the love she felt for her husband was so intertwined with respect that she could no longer love him. Or perhaps the two feelings would prove to be not so inseparable; in that case, it might be possible to think of what had happened as a mistake to be learned from, and go on, perhaps with an even stronger relationship.

She evidently thinks that respect once lost is gone forever. That is why, when people talk about accepting those responsible for Watergate, forgetting or overlooking what they did, she is surprised. It has not seriously occurred to her that the possibility of rehabilitation exists. She points out that those who admire John Dean and are ready to praise him for telling the truth about Watergate are forgetting the essential thing about him: he was a central participant in the cover-up for a long time, and it was only when he realized that he was about to be made the scapegoat that he acted in order to save himself. She can sympathize with his sufferings throughout the cover-up, torn as he must have been by the necessity to lie; she imagines that must have been a terrible way to live. But the fact she returns to is that he was guilty and will pay the price of that all his life. Quite simply, he has forfeited her respect, and she assumes that people in general feel as she does. If she is right, Watergate will not soon be forgotten, nor the crimes of Watergate be taken lightly.

Frances Liddy

*I look up to him as someone who is
doing something for his country.*

Frances Liddy is at work on her autobiography. Since her husband,
G. Gordon Liddy, not only led the break-in at the Watergate complex but participated in many another "White House horror," her
book should cast some light on the personality and motivations of
the man who is—with the possible exception of Richard Nixon—
Watergate's most enigmatic figure. One thing can be said with certainty, however: it will not tell much about Watergate.

Gordon Liddy, who is now serving a six- to twenty-year sentence,
the longest meted out to any Watergate participant, has from the
very beginning maintained a proud silence about everything connected with Watergate. He has never breathed one word about what
happened on the night of June 17, 1972, even to his wife. The word
Watergate has never been mentioned in the Liddy household except
"occasionally, in jest." And as Frances Liddy herself admits, "I don't
understand the whole Watergate mess any more than other people
do. I still haven't separated the good guys from the bad guys."

On the other hand, she has no difficulty in understanding her
husband's motivation for remaining silent. "He is simply following
his own code," she explains. In fact, she frankly concedes, she and
their five children would have considered him a coward if he had
acted otherwise.

Not everyone shares Frances' elevated view of her obdurate husband. Most of those who have associated with him are likelier to
sympathize with the frustration and annoyance of Henry Petersen,
the Assistant Attorney General, as he discussed Liddy with Richard
Nixon. Liddy, Petersen told the President, had showed the prosecutor his arms, covered with cigarette burns, explaining that he had
endured this self-inflicted torture to prove to himself that he could
take anything. Petersen had no doubt in his mind that "you've got to

63

be a crazy man to sit there and burn yourself to see if you can withstand the pain."

Wherever he was, Liddy's garish imagination illuminated his daily activities. He was likely to offer a demonstration of how to kill someone with a pencil, or hold his hand over a candle to prove his nerve. He spoke with pride of his exploits and possessions, including a gun that could shoot underwater. Once Jeb Magruder grumbled that it would be nice to be rid of columnist Jack Anderson, a frequent embarrassment to the Administration, and Liddy strode off to carry out what he conceived to be a mission to kill. Stopped in the nick of time and assured that it was all a misunderstanding, he responded with annoyance, scolding Magruder, "Well, you'd better watch that. When you give me an order like that, I carry it out."

Another interesting sidelight on Liddy was his infatuation with Germany. Not only did he mention its spirit and accomplishments with admiring frequency, but in his house he kept shelves of books on the subject, including *Mein Kampf*—a number of them with swastikas on the jackets—prominently displayed where visitors could hardly avoid noticing them.

Perhaps one value of Frances Liddy's book will be to explain what kind of woman is attracted to a man like this. One might expect to find her lacking in some inner core of strength of her own, but Frances' life offers no indication of weakness or dependency. Quite to the contrary, she is evidently a strong and self-reliant person, possessing qualities of stoicism and self-sufficiency rather like her husband's.

Frances Liddy has had a life that demanded such qualities. Her father died when she was eighteen, and she worked in a bank to put herself through school, earning a degree in economics. Then she became an economist for a public utility and later taught computer training for IBM, supporting not only herself but her mother until she, too, died.

Frances Liddy's book will doubtless provide details of what, in view of Gordon's personality, must have been a daringly imaginative and original courtship, but their early married life seems to have been notable mainly for its lack of glamour. Gordon was in the FBI and his salary was low. Within five years the Liddys had five children and a host of financial problems—problems mitigated from 1962 to 1966 by his decision to leave the FBI and practice law in New York with his father.

But Gordon Liddy was restless. His wife explains that he wanted to go into politics because he was "concerned by what was happening in America at that time." He became assistant district attorney in Dutchess County, New York. Frances, agreeing with her husband that he had a great contribution to make to political life, wanted him to have his chance, so she began teaching school to augment his meager pay. She had been taking classes summers, nights, and weekends, and by that time had a master's degree in urban education.

When Gordon was offered a job in Washington as a special assistant to the Secretary of the Treasury, the Liddys were so deep in debt—in consequence of Gordon's unsuccessful try for a Republican congressional nomination in 1968—that Frances and the children could not afford to join him for the first year. Once reunited in Washington, however, the family worked hard, paid off their debts, bought a house, and settled down. As Gordon advanced from the Treasury to the White House, and thence to CRP, the future seemed assured.

Then came the Watergate break-in. Eleven days later, Gordon was fired from his job for refusing to answer questions from the FBI. Frances says she cried when she first realized what had happened to them. "I am not going to pretend that I meekly accepted my fate and the sequence of events that brought it about," she explains. In fact, she says that throughout the summer following the break-in she was "very upset." With Gordon back in Poughkeepsie practicing law with an old friend, Frances dealt with her emotional conflict by renewing an old interest in art, taking a course in painting "as therapy."

For some time thereafter, the Liddys' relationship seems to have been in a somewhat ambiguous and suspended state. Frances says her husband did nothing to explain or justify his actions or to persuade her to stand by him, leaving it entirely up to her to come to her own conclusions. On the other hand, he evidently found her choice of therapies encouraging and even gave her a portable easel. In addition, he considered their wedding anniversary an occasion of considerable significance. Since he was in Poughkeepsie on November 9, Frances suggested celebrating later; but Gordon—sensing, she thinks, that it might be their last anniversary together for a long time—drove the six hours to Washington to spend that day with her. The final proof that Liddy intended to make no demands whatever on his wife's loyalty was his offer of a divorce. Just before going to jail on January 30, 1973, he told her, "You have reason to divorce me if you wish. I will not contest it." He even left it up to her whether or not she would write to him in prison. "He would have understood," Frances explains, "if I had made a complete break then and there."

Frances Liddy had already had her moments of doubt about the marriage, especially since their move to Washington, and she insists that she considered her husband's offer carefully. But whatever those earlier problems may have been, and whatever reservations she may have had about Gordon's role in the Watergate affair, she eventually reached a decision. She realized, she says, that she loved him too much not to stand behind him. From that time on, Frances has been unreservedly committed to her relationship with Gordon Liddy.

From prison Gordon wrote what his wife describes as "really beautiful love letters," one each day. He wrote to the children, too, and on the outside of each envelope he printed WIN. Ostensibly, this referred to their swimming competitions (all five are champion swimmers) but to the Liddy family the word has much deeper implications. Gordon Liddy sees all of life as a competition. He himself is always in training, ready to meet any test. When Watergate came, it was an opportunity for him to prove himself—as he has to his wife's satisfaction, at least—a hero.

As Liddy maintains his obstinate silence, Frances explains: "I think he's serving his country just as many of the military men have. And I think of him and the kind of life we're living very similar to the POWs and the MIA wives, who have had it so much harder than I've had it. And I look up to him as someone who is doing something for his country, because I believe that's what he thinks he is doing and I agree with him—behaving the way he should."

Temporarily out of prison on appeal, Gordon submitted to a television interview, reputedly for a fee of $15,000, and though he of course refused to discuss any factual aspect of Watergate he was ready to outline his theories of power. Frances smiled and nodded as her husband explained that power exists to be used. "If Watergate is as it's alleged to be," he hedged, carefully giving nothing away, "it was an intelligence-gathering operation of one group of persons who were seeking power or to retain power against another group of persons who were seeking to acquire power. That's all it was." In fact, such things as Watergate were so basic, so commonplace, that "It's like brushing your teeth."

In the same interview Liddy projected a clear vision of the kind of man he would like to be and believes he is. He admires John Mitchell because he is a "whole man" who is "sufficient unto himself." Dismissing Nixon as "insufficiently ruthless," Liddy reserved his highest praise for Judge John Sirica, whom he described as tough-minded and persevering—and, above all, a man who thinks, as Gordon Liddy so proudly does, that the end justifies the means. Very like Liddy himself, Sirica "does what is necessary."

Perseverance and dedication to doing what is necessary certainly characterize Frances Liddy, too. She continues self-reliantly to teach school, bring up her children, and work on her book. And in her own way she might be described as tough-minded. On her jeep she has a bumper sticker reading WELCOME HOME, POWS. She says she intends to keep it there until she and the children can welcome home their own POW.

Gail Magruder

I don't feel he ever did lie on this to me.

In the entire scenario of Watergate, there are few scenes more vivid than that of Jeb Stuart Magruder sitting before his fireplace late one night in June 1972 as he burned the Gemstone file. Jeb, then deputy director of CRP, glanced through the fruits of the largely unproductive bugging operation at Democratic National Committee headquarters. As the house around him slept, he tossed more transcripts on the fire.

Suddenly Jeb's wife Gail appeared at the head of the stairs, awakened by noise below or the unseasonable whiff of smoke. "What in the world are you doing?" she asked. "You're going to burn the house down." Once reassured, however, that it was "just some papers I have to get rid of," Gail came and sat by the fire, keeping her husband company until the task was done. There were, by Jeb's account, no questions asked, no connections made between the blaze and the Magruders' precipitous departure from California the day before—nor would there be at any time during the next ten months before he decided to tell her the truth of his involvement in the Watergate affair.

But then, Gail Magruder was not the woman to bring up awkward, difficult subjects or ask embarrassing questions. She had grown up in a world of certainties, a fourth-generation Californian, daughter of a successful lawyer. She attended Marlborough, a private girls' school in Los Angeles, then went East, as her mother and older sister had, to Dana Hall, a boarding school outside Boston. At Vassar, she found the students cold and distant, and so transferred back to friendly California to finish up at Berkeley.

Jeb Magruder was in San Francisco that same year, a sales trainee at the Crown Zellerbach paper company. The two had once met when he was at Williams, she at Vassar, and he decided to look her up. Before long, they were seeing a good deal of each other. "Gail,"

Jeb has since explained, "had all the external qualities that I—like most young men of my generation—had always sought in the girls I dated. She was pretty and popular and from a well-to-do family." The importance of these particular attributes to Jeb would not surprise his boyhood friends. Back at Staten Island's P.S. 13, he used to tell classmates that he hoped to marry well. "He wasn't a serious-minded or deep guy, hardly an intellectual," one old school friend says. "He was lighthearted, very much a social type, concerned with meeting the right people and making good contacts."

The Magruder family prided themselves on their colonial Maryland background, but Jeb was born on Staten Island, where his father owned a modestly successful print shop. There he grew into an attractive and gregarious young man, a first-rate tennis player, successful at school, and ambitious. After an Army stint, Williams College, and the summer sales jobs that helped pay his way there, Jeb headed West, confident in his own abilities, eager for success.

Gail Nicholas was unquestionably the right girl for him. Well educated (a political science major) without being intellectual, attractive yet uncompetitive, she even shared Jeb's Reaganesque political position. And beyond those "external qualities" Jeb found so appealing, she possessed what he later described as "a maturity and an honesty and a depth of character that exceeded any I had known in other young women I had dated." In short, she was "an exceptional person," and they fell in love.

Gail was not ready to marry. She was then planning a long European trip, a reward for having finished school. But suddenly a crisis was precipitated: Jeb was being transferred to Kansas City. Convinced that he and Gail would inevitably drift apart if their relationship were subjected to the strain of prolonged separation, Jeb drove up to the Sierras, where Gail was visiting friends, to persuade her to his point of view. She yielded, and the two were married in Los Angeles in October 1959.

Their early life together was the traditional composite of mishaps, discoveries, and delights characteristic of young marriage. Their first apartment, selected by Jeb, was a disaster, small, gloomy, and dark, with hideous furniture and a lumpy three-quarter-size bed. Their neighbors were all, it appeared, old and ill, and the young Magruders were depressed by the constant aura of mortality. But soon, with Gail already pregnant, they moved to more pleasant surroundings. They met other young couples through church or through Jeb's work. They went to football games. Jeb played golf. Sometimes, as he traveled through his Midwest territory, selling the paper bags, toilet paper, and gum-label tape his company produced, Gail accompanied him on the road. It was in Kansas City, too, that Jeb began to take an active part in politics, doing precinct work in Nixon's 1960 campaign. He found selling a political candidate even more satisfying than selling a product.

By this time, however, Jeb had decided that a master's degree in business administration was essential to his further advancement, and the Magruders moved to Chicago for that purpose. Gail's life there proved less carefree than in Kansas City. With a six-month-old baby—and, before long, a second on the way—she discovered that the Chicago apartment, a third-floor walk-up, was less than ideal. Its insulation was no match for the winds whipping in from Lake Michigan; the washing machine was in the basement; and Gail was always juggling baby and bundles up and down three flights of stairs. As a shortcut she dropped the bags of wet diapers to be washed off her back porch, then hurried down to retrieve them in the alley.

By the time their second son was born in 1963, the Magruders had bought their own home. But both boys were prone to minor ailments—earaches, allergies, the kind of thing that keeps a concerned young mother close to home—and there was one serious scare that winter. Two-year-old Whitney suddenly became cross-eyed, and when his parents took him to a doctor, they were stunned to learn that without surgery there was the possibility of blindness. The operation was performed, a complete success, but it was, says Jeb, "a profoundly depressing time" for Gail.

If 1963 was depressing, 1964 was even more so. By then, a daughter, Tracy, had been born, which meant that Gail had three children under the age of four. Jeb had yet another new job, and he was more and more involved in politics, so much so, in fact, that, as he discreetly explains, his political work was causing "serious problems for our marriage" and he "resolved not to let it happen again." It was probably not an ideological disagreement that caused these problems, but simply the fact that while Gail raised her three children almost single-handedly, Jeb was increasingly absent.

The problems were solved, however, at least temporarily, when the Magruders moved back to California; solved, ironically, by the very thing that had helped to cause them—politics. In 1966 Jeb asked his company for a leave of absence in order to help run a local political campaign. Angered by management's refusal, he walked away from a $35,000-a-year job and, as events proved, Illinois. He was hired by a department store chain and assigned to its headquarters in Los Angeles.

For Gail it was a highly satisfactory move. She and Jeb took their first real vacation alone in six years of marriage—the long-deferred trip to Europe—and when they returned, it was to the kind of life she had always assumed she would someday lead. It was a sunny interlude, with a spectacular house in Santa Monica Canyon, walled in glass, not far from the Pacific Ocean; the warmth of family approval as a daughter who had married well; old friends; and at last the mobility allowed by household help. The arrival of a new baby in March 1967 caused barely a ripple in the serenity of her life.

Though Jeb was once again deep in politics, working as Southern California coordinator for Richard Nixon, family life was less skimpy than before. California evenings are long, and the Magruders often went down to the beach at sunset, or joined Gail's sister Ruth, her husband, and their eight children. One California neighbor remembers their Sunday bike rides as "mother and father duckling and all the little ducklings," adding, "The whole thing was a picture, everything perfect."

Gail had managed to fit some hospital volunteer work into even Chicago's crowded schedule; now she had more time for community activities and the local PTA. Her main interest, however, was in her own home. She considered herself primarily a mother, as indeed she still does, and she insisted that any meetings scheduled for afterschool hours must be held at her house, because, as she frequently explained, her children needed her there.

Much as some of the other mothers who worked with her were nettled by the implications of this, they conceded that Gail's concern extended to the needs of children in general. A favorite suggestion of hers was that a sort of buddy system be instituted in the local school, intended to extend her high standards of mothering to others. She had noticed that some of the children wore the same shirts and socks on consecutive days; she was aware that many mothers were not at home to await their children's arrival from school. To remedy this situation, she proposed to divide the parents into two groups, those who were bringing up their children correctly and those who were not, each good mother helping and instructing a neglectful one.

Though one woman who knew her in California and has not seen her since defends her as having "extremely good instincts as a mother and as a member of society," others were somewhat taken aback by another pet proposal of Gail's. Convinced that local people (many of whom were Jews) had adopted a pro-Israel stance without devoting sufficient attention to possible opposing arguments, she suggested that a forum be held to examine and explore the Arab point of view.

Into this pleasant life politics once again intruded. In the wake of the 1968 Nixon victory, Bob Haldeman was reorganizing his staff, and the name of Jeb Magruder, by then president of two small cosmetic companies, came to his attention. The two men met in the presidential compound at San Clemente, and Jeb returned to tell Gail that no decision had been reached. It was clear, however, that psychically he was already in Washington. Gail did not share his euphoria. The very idea of moving once again ("new schools and new friends and new stores") struck her as infinitely depressing. "Do we have any choice?" she asked. When Jeb said no, that if the job were offered he would have to take it, she made but one request: Would he talk to her at least once again before accepting anything definite? But when two weeks later Haldeman offered Jeb a job on his staff, with the title of Special Assistant to the President, it was accepted without a moment's hesitation. As always, Gail came to terms with her husband's decision.

Arrived in Washington, the Magruders, like most Nixonian families, circumspectly avoided that hotbed of liberalism they identified in Georgetown. Instead they found a house in suburban Sumner, Maryland, just across the District line. Gail initially justified their choice by explaining that Sumner had outstanding public schools, though the Magruder children in the end did not attend them. Gamely she went about the business of settling again in a new place, ready once more to try her best as wife and mother.

The Magruders are an attractive family. Jeb is athletically built and good-looking, with blue eyes, wavy brown hair, and the youthful appearance of a man who leads a healthy life. Gail is a slender woman with delicate features; her light-brown hair and hazel eyes seem to emanate a gentle glow. Their children are appealing. The Nixon Administration was known for its picture-book families; even among them, the Magruder clan stood out.

From the start, Jeb was marked as a man to watch, a political comer with the right connections in the White House. A few months after the Magruders arrived in Washington in the fall of 1969, Jeb became deputy to Herb Klein at the Office of Communications. One year later, he moved over to the newly formed Committee for the Re-election of the President, setting up its structure and acting as director until John Mitchell—or the A.G., as Jeb liked to call him—could leave Justice and publicly take charge. "Jeb had *power*," says one Washington woman, awed by a long-ago visit to one of his offices, a high-ceilinged corner room once occupied by Cordell Hull when he was Secretary of State. As in all Jeb's offices, there were framed photographs of Gail and the four children.

Washington is notoriously a bad place for wives; they are likely to be present on ceremonial occasions, overlooked when something more important is in the works. Their place is in the background. It is perhaps an indication of Gail's standing on Jeb's personal list of priorities that when Nixon spoke to the Magruders after a White House church service, Jeb was surprised and pleased that the President remembered her name. "It was a nice personal touch from a man with many other things on his mind," he said.

He did believe, however, that the attractive White House wives were a potential source of good publicity for the Administration and at one point suggested setting up a public-relations operation specifically to publicize them. He planned to start with Gail, but the project was somehow sidetracked.

Gail's activities were limited, too, by the fact that Nixon's Washington was not a very gregarious place. As she herself said later, there was very little socializing back and forth among the Administration families. She sounded wistful when she explained that "much as I would have loved to have known some of these people, they were all hardworking men and family men, so the little free time they had they spent at home with their families." In California, she had been accustomed to friends, a busy social life, playing tennis with other couples. In Washington, though she was said to be "a fabulous cook" who sometimes gave "beautiful dinner parties," she was lonely. She missed Southern California, with its bounty and sunshine. Later, in an interview, she compared her California life and what she had exchanged it for in Washington. "We had a home with a fantastic lemon tree," she said longingly, "an avocado tree, fresh tomatoes, a lovely garden. In Washington, you get lots of rain, dark weather, other things."

If she resented her exile, the neighbors did not notice it. Gail stood at her door each morning, waving Whitney, Justin, and daughter Tracy off to school. Then Jeb departed, frequently by bicycle (it was a six-mile trip each way and he did it several times a week to stay in shape for the rigors of the political fray). At first Gail's days were filled with Stuart, who was only two years old when they first arrived in Washington, but as time passed she became increasingly active in social service, especially through the Junior League. When the '72 campaign went into high gear, she signed on at the Committee for the Re-election of the President, to work one day each week as a volunteer.

Because she was there, she could observe her husband's work days. If she did not know precisely what he was doing, at least she saw its effect on him, and ascribed it to the "incredible pressure" he was under. Looking back on that time now, she insists that she began to notice a change in Jeb during the period when—as she now knows but did not then suspect—the break-in and bugging operations were being planned. "He became tenser, and more irritable," she explains, "and he was obviously not at home with himself." At the time, she attributed this change to the increasing pressure of the campaign, which, as she describes it, never let up. There were phone calls, not only until nine or ten at night, but all night long. "We had phone calls at two, and three, and five in the morning," she recalls, "usually about minor, meaningless things."

A few other people report noticing a change in Jeb at the time of the break-in. Following the arrest of the original Watergate burglars, Jeb lost weight, they say, and seemed depressed. Yet they agree that by late summer, when Watergate seemed to be having no impact on the Nixon campaign, Jeb had become his normal self again; more ebullient, in fact, for with each passing day victory came closer. At the campaign's end Jeb was put in charge of planning the inauguration, and the shadows of Watergate were dispelled.

Few doubted Jeb's emphatic denials that he knew anything whatever about the break-in. His explanation was that Gordon Liddy had planned the whole thing, and he reiterated that before investigators, grand juries, and a judge. So confident was he, in fact, that any threat to him from Watergate had been dissipated that he considered running for California Secretary of State. Such a decision would have exposed him to searching questions from the media, but Magruder seemed impervious to doubt, sunnily confident that all would be well. Looking ahead to the possible campaign, he speculated that he could be very effective on television—and that his photogenic family would be an asset.

Then came James McCord, with his letter to Judge Sirica. Announcing that "higher-ups" had been involved in the planning of the break-in, McCord told Sirica that perjury and political pressure had been part of the trial. Those words spelled the downfall of Jeb Magruder, for he, along with John Mitchell and John Dean, had known from the beginning what Gordon Liddy's intelligence-gathering scheme was all about, and he had been in charge of its unimpressive results.

The next two weeks were Jeb Magruder's time of decision. It has been described by some of the people who were in touch with him then as a frantic attempt to survive, a time of anxious patching together of stories, of desperate evasions and appeals, of panic and near-breakdown. The explanation emanating from the John Dean camp was different, ascribing a more enlightened self-interest to Magruder. According to this version, Dean's lawyer told Magruder's attorneys what Dean was planning to reveal to the prosecutors; knowing he would soon be deeply implicated, Magruder, they suggest, was forced to make the best deal he could. Jeb himself has described this period as one of solitary soul-searching. Distracted, nervous, and irritable, he began to drink too much, taking tranquilizers to help him sleep. At last, he says, "I couldn't take any more, in mind, in body, or in spirit."

In any case, the outcome was that Jeb made his decision and his lawyer negotiated an agreement with the federal prosecutors for a one-count felony indictment. It was only then that Gail was told. "I think she had guessed at the truth for months," Jeb explains, "but chose not to accept it." Now, driving home from a dinner party, he detailed the story for her. At first she failed to understand her husband's precarious situation; it took him some time to make it clear to her that serious crimes were at issue, that people—maybe including himself—were going to be sent to prison. As Magruder says with typical understatement, "This was not an easy time for Gail." They agreed that they must try to make the best of things, and minimize the harm to their children. Gail did not add to her husband's distress by reproaching him; as he says, "throughout the difficult months that followed, Gail was unfailingly understanding and considerate."

The Magruders made a poignant picture together at the televised Watergate hearings, he the epitome of boyish contrition, she of womanly constancy. Hard-bitten newsmen were touched; they described the tragedy of Jeb Magruder's downfall, the brilliant career that lay in ruins, the grim uncertainty of his family's future. Even Senator Ervin extended some encouragement to the downcast Jeb. "In spite of your very unfortunate state at the present time," he drawled with more patriarchal kindliness than clarity, "you have got about the greatest asset that any man can have. You have a wife who stands behind you in the shadows where the sun shines."

Jeb, who at the time of his decision to talk to the prosecutors had moaned to a friend, "My whole life is over. I'm ruined," soon perked up. Now he explained to reporters that there had been more than a little pragmatism in his choice of a guilty plea. Fighting prosecution and appealing a conviction could have cost him two years and $200,000, he explained, "so you go the other way. You cooperate, and get the decision over with, and then you move on."

He had made peace with himself, he said, on grounds that he

described as "corny, but we've all sinned, right?" and pointed out that "there's more rejoicing over the one lost sheep that is found, et cetera. I think I'll be able to survive and be better for it. I think I've been as down as I've ever been down, but I've never been the kind that stays down."

Jeb Magruder was resilient. Despite the fact that he had had to resign a $38,000-a-year job at the Commerce Department at the time he began to talk to the federal prosecutors, he kept on working. He established a one-man marketing consulting company, intending to use it as a springboard to an eventual management job in a major corporation. He also booked himself onto the lecture circuit, where he was to receive $1,500 to $3,000 per speech. When Judge Sirica vetoed that plan, Jeb came up with the idea of a book. The publisher reportedly paid a $100,000 advance for *An American Life: One Man's Road to Watergate.*

By the time Jeb had finished his book he had arrived at an assessment of his Watergate experience and what he had learned from it. Ambition, he said, was the force that had impelled him. Trying to rise, through whatever means, he had been blinded to real values. All his problems had been caused by the same ambition that, as he and his wife agreed, had driven him—along with the rest of the men at the top of the Nixon Administration—to a point of "all but inexcusable neglect of their wives and children." Gail had even told him once, he said, that he should be thankful for Watergate, because she could not have continued much longer in a marriage with the man he had become—"obsessed with my work, too tired and distracted to share in the give and take of real family life."

When Gail began to speak for herself in interviews, she continued this theme. Watergate, she said, had been a wonderful, wonderful thing, and she was "glad it's happened." True, it had been painful—it had hurt the country, her husband, herself, and their children—and yet, she said, "I think you can learn the most through adversity. And we've learned so much, we really have. I can't regret it." (It sounded almost as if Watergate had been arranged entirely for the Magruders' benefit, just when they needed its constructive lessons most, to ensure the future happiness of the family.) Since Watergate had cured Jeb of his ambition, they had begun a new life, and Gail described it lyrically. The most wonderful part of it, she said, was that "we have had so much more time together than we have had, really, since we've been married . . . we never had the leisure to sit and talk on a hillside. And we have that leisure now. He has a job, but it isn't one that really consumes him. And it's just been a thrilling thing."

In Gail's view, it was dedication to hard work—with its concomitant neglect of other aspects of life—that caused Watergate in the first place. Her explanation is that because Nixon was a shy man, never at ease with other people, he withdrew into work. He wanted those around him to share his preoccupation, and the atmosphere thus created made Watergate "inevitable." Her description of Nixon sounds remarkably like what on other occasions she said of her husband, though in Nixon's case shyness was the problem, in Jeb's ambition. Nixon, she said, "is not a man who enjoys small social gatherings, or things of that nature." Always working, he never took time "to sit back and enjoy a lovely day."

As for the actual decision to carry out the break-in at the Watergate—the decision in which her husband was involved—she manages to reduce it to utter unimportance. It was simply "one decision made on a day when a number of decisions of far greater importance were being made." As she spoke of it on television, she seemed to make an effort to remind herself that other people might consider the break-in significant, but through all her talk of how "perhaps" jail for the planners of Watergate was "something that has to be" it was quite clear that her real belief was that all those planners were good men who had made a minor and very understandable error of judgment and now were being punished out of all proportion to their deserts.

As Jeb awaited sentencing and worked on his book, he was living the new and different life both he and Gail recommended so highly. He had learned, he said, to give fewer orders and to pay more attention to what Gail and the children had to say. Like a person recovering from a serious illness, he found enjoyment in simple things, cooking, puttering around the house, spending time with the children.

During this time Gail told an interviewer that she was trying to work out what she would do if Jeb had to "go away" for a while. "I am not a career-type woman," she explained. "I don't like to leave my home and I don't like to leave the rearing of my children to a nanny or someone like that. Ideally, I would like to find some sort of job I could do during the day when the children are gone, then be there when they come home."

To another interviewer who asked her how she would manage without her husband, she replied that she would be lonely—"miserable inside" is how it was put on another occasion—but that Jeb Magruder's humor and wisdom would help her see it through.

Jeb finally went to jail on June 4, 1974, sentenced to a ten-month-to-four-year term. The men at Allenwood, the minimum-security prison in Pennsylvania to which he was assigned—lawbreakers of a more conventional sort—showed their disdain for those convicted of Watergate crimes. But Clifford Irving, then a prisoner there, and secure by virtue of his membership in a great criminal tradition, befriended Jeb along with fellow Watergater Howard Hunt. Irving explained that he had found physical exercise the key to survival in prison, and he advised his protégés to play lots of tennis.

Gail did not take a job. Instead she stayed at home in Washington or at a country house the Magruders had rented near the Pennsylvania border, and took the children to see their father often. Then Jeb was moved to the D.C. jail so that he could conveniently testify at the Watergate conspiracy trial. Conditions there were so bad that Gail could not bring herself to let the children visit. She has since launched a crusade for prison reform, but at the time she had little to do but consider her difficult situation.

Despite all her prior protestations of happiness and reconciliation, those who saw her throughout this time agree that Gail Magruder is bitter. It is in her tone of voice and in her words themselves. She admits that she has a great deal to say, and suggests that she will eventually speak out. Meanwhile, it seems clear enough that she feels she and her family have suffered greatly from what she still sees as a rather insignificant offense. Perhaps, too, she contrasts her situation with that of other Watergate defendants. There is a strong hint of that in her insistence on distinguishing between those who were found guilty and those who, like Jeb, chose to plead guilty. She implies that there is some superiority in Jeb's decision, though in legal fact there is no distinction whatever. And it is clear that she deeply resents the Nixon pardon; she has even expressed doubts that Richard Nixon ever suffered from phlebitis.

Of course, there is ample cause for bitterness. Gail Magruder's world has proved to be full of cruel surprises, things she could never have foreseen throughout those years of growing up, of loyal marriage, and devoted motherhood. And few resources in her background could have prepared her for it. Realities like poverty, failure, ugliness, and crime had been kept at arm's length, a part of other people's lives. Now she was forced to see that they might be inescapably a part of hers as well. She had made an unspoken bargain with life—she had always tried to do everything right—but the bargain had not been kept.

But of course it was not fate that had failed to reward her as she deserved, but Jeb Magruder. She had loyally followed him, adjusting her wishes to his with unswerving devotion. She had tried to find the entire meaning of her life in her marriage and her family. As for an independent existence, her furthest flight of liberated speculation was the suggestion that it might be fun someday to own "one of those cute little gift shops." She had trusted Jeb to provide a meaning for her sacrifice, to justify her dedication, yet in the end it was his miscalculation that brought them to the disaster of Watergate.

Worse still, it had been demonstrated that she hardly knew the man she was married to. Though she bravely insisted that Jeb had never lied ("I don't feel he ever did lie on this to me, he just didn't tell me, he just didn't open up"), the whole world knew that the Gemstone file was far from the only thing her husband had kept from her. Despite her weekly presence at the CRP office, she never had a notion of the nature of his job. More painful yet, she can hardly ignore the fact that throughout Jeb's period of indecision, when he was agonizing over whether and what to tell the prosecutors about Watergate, he never shared his feelings with her.

The conclusions the world has drawn about her husband can hardly please her. The man for whose sake she has suffered a good deal has been widely dismissed as a superficial, lightweight, trifling sort of fellow. Once such a favorite of the press, he is now compared with John Dean, largely to his disadvantage. His old teacher, the Reverend William Sloane Coffin, who professes to be friendly, has subjected him to lofty public analysis, characterizing him as "a good guy but not yet a good man." Even his own confessional book (soon to be followed by another, yet more intimate memoir) fails to project a very admirable or even likable image.

Gail Magruder, totally innocent of any wrongdoing, has been harshly punished. It would be surprising if she did not feel that life has been unfair. Yet, wholly committed as she is to her role as perfect wife, she cannot blame her husband. She cannot even allow herself to harbor the disloyal emotions—the rage, the self-pity, the passionate resentment of a woman cheated—that might shatter the tranquillity of their life together. And since there is no way she can express them, she continues to push away such feelings, prevent them from ever reaching the surface, by emphasizing and reemphasizing how wonderful Jeb is, how much she loves him, how happy they will be together.

On January 8, Judge Sirica ordered three major Watergate figures freed—John Dean, Herbert Kalmbach, and Jeb Magruder—and reduced their sentences to the time already served. As the *New York Times* reported: "At the suburban Maryland home of Mr. Magruder, a bare cherry tree in the front yard was festooned with yellow crepe-paper ribbons. This was done at the request of Mr. Magruder's wife, Gail, in reference to a ballad about a man returning from prison who tells his girlfriend to 'tie a yellow ribbon round the old oak tree' if she still loves him."

Tricia Nixon Cox

Malicious rumors, charges of wrongdoing—
unsubstantiated by any kind of proof . . .

It was not until the spring of 1974, far along the road to resignation, that Tricia Nixon Cox, choosing her father's favorite weapon, the yellow legal pad, joined battle in his defense with the hostile forces then crowding him close to the edge of political disaster. She produced a 1,500-word essay entitled "My Father and Watergate." It was not her first try—previous efforts had been suppressed by the White House as entirely too shrill—but this one was considered suitable, and it was offered free to two magazines. Both thought they had it exclusively, and there was a minor flurry in the press when they discovered that the White House had misled them.

Though Tricia is described by intimates as a gifted writer, this was her first published work, and she stipulated that not one word was to be omitted or altered. "Accusation without proof, accusation by unnamed so-called sources, accusation by rumor, is often a license to libel and lie," Tricia's essay begins, and goes on to explain Watergate as a politically motivated attempt by "accusers" (never identified further) to force Richard Nixon out of office by means of "malicious rumors, charges of wrongdoing—unsubstantiated by any kind of proof—and out-and-out character assassination." Those nameless accusers, Tricia continues, wanted to rid themselves once and for all of Richard Nixon in order "to satisfy their own jealousy of a man who by his accomplishments reminded them of their own ineptitude and failure." The conclusion she carefully builds toward is that "the people who are now crucifying him for his principles and ideals are using the Watergate caper as their vehicle."

"My God," said one Washington journalist on reading the essay, "it sounds like the President himself when he gets mad. I didn't know she was that much like her father." Perhaps he had forgotten that it was Tricia who once wrote to Georgia's Lester Maddox congratulating him for electing to close his Pickrick Restaurant rather than submit to integration. It was Tricia, too, who admired Spiro Agnew for so vigorously belaboring the press. "It's amazing what he has done to the media," she said then, "helping it to reform itself. You can't underestimate the power of fear."

Such stern sentiments hardly fit the public image of the ex-President's daughter. Dainty and feminine, Tricia is, as she frequently says, the tiniest of the Nixons. And her manner is altogether that of a proper little girl: sunny, demure, unfailingly polite. Appropriately, she neither drinks nor smokes. She has never fancied the bizarre or reckless in dress or deed. Rebellion against authority must baffle one who, explaining her reluctance to leave her parents' home, said, "I really look forward during the day to visiting with them at night." Since her marriage, she has telephoned them once, if not twice, each day.

Small wonder, given this closeness, that her parents see their own personalities mirrored in Tricia. Discussing her two daughters in 1969, Pat Nixon confided, "Tricia and I are the more quiet and introverted ones." A year later, the President evinced similar possessiveness. Tricia "does not like the limelight," he explained. "She has a passion for privacy—like me."

The image of Tricia most indelibly stamped on the public memory is one of utter, if traditional, perfection, on the day of her wedding in the White House Rose Garden. A few minutes behind schedule—time allowed for rain clouds to roll past—the Army string band struck up the "Trumpet Voluntary," and the shining bride moved forward on her father's presidential arm, to join her "first and last love," Edward Finch Cox, at the outdoor altar.

The four hundred guests were predominantly middle-aged, including Cabinet members and their wives, old Nixon friends like the Robert Abplanalps, Billy Graham, the Jack Drowns, and others from the upper echelons of U.S. industry and politics. Martha Mitchell was there, a vision of antebellum enchantment, contrasting nicely with the unsmiling Ralph Nader for whom Eddie had worked the summer after his Princeton graduation. Adding an acerbic touch to the proceedings was Washington's octogenarian *enfant terrible*, the dauntless Alice Roosevelt Longworth. All the elaborate arrangements and calculated simplicity of the occasion seemed lost on her. Asked if the wedding didn't remind her of her own White House marriage in 1906, she glared at the reporter. "It doesn't bring back one goddamn memory," she said.

But for millions of others who took a deep interest in the wedding and yearned toward Tricia as the ideal bride, it was the stuff of daydreams. For some people there is something ineffably satisfying about a White House wedding—a mixture of emotion and splendor, familiar words and all those famous faces—that appeases a secret yearning for royalty. No detail is too small for those avid commoners to seize on and treasure, and for their sake more than five hundred representatives of the news media swarmed the White House grounds that day.

The press had already headlined the choice of china (Blue Tree, by Lenox) and silver (Lunt's Eloquence), subjected the six-foot ten-inch wedding cake to a crumb-by-crumb analysis, and speculated at length over the guest list. Now, two and a quarter hours after Tricia and Eddie had been pronounced man and wife, they could record for posterity the scene of the newlyweds leaving the White House—not through the window by which the spirited Longworths had made their escape sixty-six years earlier, nor even by the secret route Lynda Bird Robb had archly recommended in print not long before—but openly dashing through a shower of flower petals to the waiting limousine. It was Tricia's ultimate gesture, her legacy to her public, offering the country this last, definitive glimpse of the image she wanted them to remember.

But Tricia's life had not been one big glowing pastel portrait. She and her sister Julie had, in fact, grown up in surroundings their mother tried to make as normal as possible. The girls set the table, made their beds, played with Checkers (who has since found peace in New York City's Bide-a-Wee cemetery). They went first to public school, then to Washington's Sidwell Friends; called on their mother's help in homework, her wardrobe for dressing up. Tricia was a Girl Scout, Julie a Brownie. During those years, Pat Nixon stitched up her own slipcovers and did almost all the housework. "I think it's important for the girls to grow up knowing that women do these things," she said, but somehow her theory never bore much fruit. Tricia not only never learned to sew but found cooking an arcane mystery. Just before her marriage she bemusedly confessed that "bacon is one of the hardest things to learn to cook. To do it just right and not have it greasy is real gourmet cooking."

Of course, all this effort to achieve a reasonable facsimile of a Middle American childhood was not being conducted in the secure anonymity of Main Street. Tricia Nixon, born just nine days after her father launched his first political campaign, has spent her whole life in the public eye. And it was not the discipline of table setting and Scouting that produced the strength of will, the loyalty, and lonely courage that mark the Nixons. Ironically, what brought the family close, toughened their spirit, and welded them into a fighting unit was Richard Nixon's disaster-prone career. As Nixon himself explained it, the secret of bringing up children successfully was "a strong family life," and "what helped keep us close together were my defeats."

As the Nixon girls grew up, they saw their father run a gantlet of hurt and humiliation. The press was not averse to taking cruel jabs at a man who had found his political footing in the witchhunts of the fifties; cartoons were often brutal. Even when he had achieved the eminence of the vice-presidency, embarrassing stories of Eisenhower's personal distaste were widely circulated.

The 1960 campaign was a torture for Tricia, who had to suffer an assortment of vicarious humiliations at school. Julie, always more dramatic, wept every night at home, attracting everyone's sympathy, as Tricia suffered in silence. On election night the girls were sent off to bed at eleven, promised that in the morning everything would be all right. Of course it was not, but Kennedy's margin of victory was so narrow that its validity was questionable, and it is no surprise that the girls were certain from that day forward that the Democrats had stolen the election from their father. Nixon, declining to contest the result on the grounds that to do so would imperil national unity, convinced his daughters beyond question that his loss of the presidency constituted a moral victory, and they admired him accordingly.

Tricia had always been protective toward her father. When his motorcade was stoned in Caracas in 1958, Tricia, first to hear the news, called his office. Although her mother was also present in the melee, she cried, "What are they doing to our daddy?" Now, in addition to her resentment at seeing her beloved father continually harassed by enemies, she had conclusive proof that he was morally superior to all of them. Right was on the Nixon side, and she yearned for public vindication.

When Nixon was making up his mind to run for the governorship of California in 1962, he called a family council to weigh the pros and cons. Pat Nixon and Julie declared that it was entirely up to him; they would abide by his decision. But Tricia, by then fifteen, was anxious to see justice done at last. "Let's show them, Daddy," she snapped. "Let's run." For a girl who saw things in these terms, the humiliation that followed, including Nixon's famous "last" press conference, must have been devastating.

Tricia had more personal difficulties, too. Even her parents' interviews over the years have hinted that her nature was not composed entirely of sugar and spice. "Tricia has a very strong personality," her father once confessed. "When I say 'Let's go to church,' sometimes Tricia says no. And she doesn't go." He also revealed that during the 1958 congressional campaign Tricia had complained bitterly at being at the mercy of the Secret Service and the press whenever the Vice-President got off at airports. "She didn't like being shoved around back there," Nixon explained. "So we changed things."

One suspects that was by no means the twelve-year-old's only complaint, either; that while jealousy and pain, boredom and fear have no place in the glossy prose of political public relations, they were very much a part of Tricia's growing up. A classmate of that era remembers her as "just a plain girl with a funny nose. She was regarded by almost everyone as very quiet. And scared. She never smiled." Tricia has since blossomed into almost a beauty, a fragile blue-eyed blonde whose artfully augmented flaxen hair tumbles past her shoulders. But the pain of those years still shows. It has taught Tricia to be on guard, to live defensively.

After the California debacle, Nixon decided to move his family to New York, thus offering them what they publicly claimed was just what they wanted: a truly private life. During those politically arid years, the Nixon women were said to be finding happiness in cultural pursuits, making friends, and living a normal life. But a girl whose most burning desire was for her father to "show them" could hardly have been content in what amounted to the luxurious semi-retirement of failure.

The Nixons' Fifth Avenue apartment—its very address signaling a new prosperity—was only blocks away from both Chapin, the sedate girls' school where Tricia spent her senior year, and Finch, the college from which she graduated with honors in 1968. Finch has the reputation of a finishing school where more emphasis is placed on manners and morals than on the pursuit of learning, but recent graduates claim it has kept pace with a changing world. And they resist the suggestion that Tricia is representative of Finch alumnae. One ex-student government president even proclaims, in huffy insistence on dissociation, that "Tricia Nixon is probably one of the most insignificant students who ever passed through these halls."

Tricia's best friends would hardly contend that she exerted a significant influence on the school, either socially or intellectually. Hers seem to have been the less colorful virtues of dependability, loyalty, civility. When there was a job to be done and Tricia was asked to do it, it was done. She was never unpleasant to anyone. Each year the class was invited to the Nixon apartment for a Christmas party. Tricia was, as one classmate said, "the kind of person that is so nice to everyone they can't be anything but nice to her." The technique evidently got results: she was elected class president in her junior year.

By her senior year, her father was on the campaign trail once again and asking for her help. Tricia, who had always hated politicking, balked at presiding over Virginia's Azalea Festival, and her father had to talk her into it. "Look," he admonished her, "they want you. This is a good state; we carried it twice." Tricia went, despite a strep throat, surviving four taxing days of social rounds with stoicism and grace. It was a performance to make her father proud, and one that enchanted local residents. "Oh, I just love your azaleas," enthused Tricia, touring Norfolk's oldest house. "Oh, I love that birdcage. Who gets to polish all the silver?"

Then at last, after what must have seemed to Tricia a lifetime of effort, her father won the presidency. The family honor was vindicated. With Richard Nixon firmly ensconced in the White House, Tricia retreated from public view, as if to say she no longer had to try so hard, to be so nice to everyone, to do everything right, to win acceptance. That was all taken care of by her new position. She held the expected school and hospital visits to a minimum and skipped official dinners; "Tricia will be busy privately" was the usual notation on the family schedule issued to the press. Julie referred to her sister as "the Howard Hughes of the White House," and even Pat Nixon occasionally seemed stumped. On being asked Tricia's whereabouts, she once replied, "If you can find out, you're better than I am."

Of course, Tricia's interest in fashion was unflagging, though it was the fluffy, ruffled, unfashionable kind of fashion that moved *Women's Wear Daily* to call her "one of the best-dressed children in America." To assemble an extensive size four wardrobe and her vast collection of purses ("One of the greatest I've ever known," as her indulgent father described it) was obviously a time-consuming avocation. One member of the White House staff explained that Tricia slept the mornings away and then "putzes around . . . spends a lot of time on her hair." True enough, she never appeared publicly in less than the blondest, most daisy-fresh condition. Still, there were whole days spent, awake or asleep, up in that pink-walled, pink-carpeted bedroom, with the Mary Cassatt, on loan from New York's Metropolitan Museum, and the Dresden figurines. It puzzled the most seasoned observers of White House life.

By her own admission, Tricia was almost totally unathletic, and she rarely exerted herself in the name of public service. Her much-touted stint at tutoring ghetto children was brief, and worthy groups—anxious to upgrade Washington's cultural landscape or free its streets of crime—received little more than Tricia's smiling approbation. "It's a shame," said one local activist. "I just think it's sad that she does nothing. The youth of America are so desperately looking for young leadership to follow. She could have worked with paralyzed children or the mentally retarded. But above all, she could have set some example for the young. Instead, she's nothing but a pretty little girl."

It is hard to imagine the rebellious young lining up to enlist under any banner held by Tricia Nixon, and she herself has been tactful enough to restrict herself to very limited statements about her own generation. It is a "very idealistic" one, she once said, adding the hopeful suggestion that if "any student at any university in the United States has an idea on how to bridge the gap between students and government, they should write it down and send it to the White House."

From time to time, Tricia emerged from seclusion to play the part of perfect hostess. She entertained England's visiting Prince Charles and seemed, in contrast to the grumpy Princess Anne, a radiant example of outgoing American girlhood. She graciously guided CBS newsmen Harry Reasoner and Mike Wallace, together with millions of viewers, on a television tour of the First Family's second floor.

Despite her poise, Tricia on this occasion volunteered a number of things that not only cast light on her father's private life but revealed a good deal about her own uncritical attitude toward him. One picture she offered was of her father coming upstairs after a speech or news conference and heading straight for the telephone to initiate a series of calls to his staff, Julie and David, and various other family members, "to see how they thought he did." Then she gave the world the surreal vision of Richard Nixon relaxing to background music by Mantovani, air conditioning turned to its maximum to make a wood fire bearable, as he gazed out the window toward the Washington Monument.

It is on occasions like this that Tricia is at her best, and Wallace announced himself "completely charmed" after his eight hours with her. But though she was capable of charming guests, she rarely played White House hostess. The one large party she organized during her White House years was—appropriately, many newsmen thought—a masked ball. Tricia's date for the evening was Barry Goldwater, Jr., and a fellow dancer, mesmerized by the sight of the senator's son leaning down to press his cheek against Tricia's, reported this exchange:

Barry: I think you're beautiful.

Tricia: Thank you very much.

Barry: You have the prettiest blond hair I've ever seen.

Tricia: Thank you very much.

Barry: I'd sure like to show you California.

Tricia: I've seen California.

Young Goldwater may have been captivated, but at least one member of the band was not. A long-time fan of the Turtles, Tricia had asked the group to provide music for the evening, but apparently her admiration was unrequited. "She was wearing organdy and stuff," lead singer Howie Kaylan later scoffed to a *Rolling Stone* reporter. "She rustled when she walked by like a fucking redwood. She had big, fat earrings and was perfumed to the gills." That was hardly a chivalrous response to the thank-you note Tricia had sent Kaylan the day after the ball. "Dear Mr. Kaylan," it said, "You started the ball rolling on just the right note."

Meanwhile, the private life Tricia kept so firmly in the background was going well. When Richard Nixon announced the engagement of his daughter to "Edward Cox of New York," the young couple had known each other for more than seven years and been secretly pledged to marry for more than two, yet not even the Nixons had known of the engagement until the previous Thanksgiving when Eddie, "white as a sheet," had formally asked the President for his daughter's hand.

Eddie was an eminently proper catch, a tall, quiet young man who had grown up in the moneyed WASP world of New York and Long Island. Everyone liked him, though he was considered more presentable than interesting, more dedicated than brilliant. The only criticisms anybody seemed able to adduce were that his mother, spurred by social ambition, might have engineered the match (though that seemed unlikely as the socially superior Coxes did nothing to cement a friendship with Tricia's parents) and that his nickname, Fast Eddie, might be an ironic reference to an excessively leisurely tempo. All in all, Ed Cox seemed the perfect Prince Charming for the postcard princess in the White House.

Officially engaged, Tricia obligingly emerged from seclusion to hold her first press conference since her father had won the presidency. In a white wool dress and elaborate coiffure, she perched on the edge of a large wing chair, her dainty feet barely touching the floor, and proceeded to reveal the details of her romance.

What Tricia most admired about Eddie was, it appeared, his sincerity. They shared an interest in jigsaw puzzles and the poetry of Keats and Browning, which they sometimes read aloud. What they did not share was Eddie's athletic interests. "When he plays squash or tennis," she confessed, "I cheer and get out the pompoms. I'm very unathletically inclined."

It turned out that Eddie had made his first impression on Tricia when they played a word game during an intermission at a Christmas dance in 1963. "His word was so incredibly esoteric," marveled Tricia. The word, a confection of Eddie's own, and intended to mean a lover of underdogs, was infracaninophile. Tricia misspelled it for her audience with a "k" and sighed, awed by the brain that could put it together correctly, "I think Eddie is more intelligent than I am." It was at that same press conference that she admitted for the first time to wearing a fall and announced, after some hard thought, that "the most important thing in marriage is love, but love is so intangible."

Tricia left the White House transcendent. Her father was President; she herself was groomed to within a hair's breadth of perfection; and she was embarking on a new life. Yet for all the storybook romance of the White House wedding, there were still those who did not soften to the young couple. Many Americans continued to regard both Tricia and her new husband as distasteful representatives of Nixonian politics and resented them accordingly. One hot night midway through the summer of 1973 Tricia and Eddie were among the 15,000 fans at Yankee Stadium to watch the home team trounce the Kansas City Royals. When the scoreboard lit up with the greeting WELCOME TRICIA NIXON COX AND EDWARD COX, the stands resounded with raucously enthusiastic boos.

Tricia and Eddie were not truly welcome even amid Eddie's former circle. They appeared uncomfortably at Eddie's sister's freeform wedding, a sunny, almost incidental finale to a weekend of partying in Westhampton. Fellow guests were surprised to see them, and there were whispers about Watergate. The Coxes looked oddly out of place amid the jeans, sandals, and granny dresses of the other guests—he conservatively suited in gray, she in flounced hot-pink chiffon—and they disappeared as soon as the vows were exchanged, leaving the others to their unconventional revels.

Tricia and Eddie seem most at ease at home, a four-room twenty-eighth-floor apartment on New York's Upper East Side.

Tricia, whose taste, like her mother's, tends toward soft colors and Louis XV, planned the decor herself, and her efforts have been rapturously praised by sister Julie, who proclaims herself awed by Tricia's decorating talents. The whole place reflects togetherness. In the entrance hall is a green hand-painted trunk, a wedding present from "The People of Delaware." It depicts a young man and woman, evidently Tricia and Eddie, standing by a tree on which is carved a heart bearing their initials. The apartment is strewn with music boxes, the favorite a carousel with moving animals that plays "their" song, "Somewhere My Love" from the movie *Dr. Zhivago*.

But even this cozy retreat could not shut out the cold winds of the outside world. By January 1974, rumor had it that the Cox marriage was foundering on the rocks of Watergate. The President and Eddie, it was said, so disliked each other that by common consent they avoided meeting, Tricia taking her father's side. All this seemed borne out by observable fact. Clearly, Tricia was in close and constant touch with her parents. The young Coxes had Christmas dinner at the White House but next day Eddie was back in New York while Tricia accompanied her family to San Clemente for an eighteen-day vacation. There she saw the New Year come and go, and even after the Nixons returned to Washington she lingered an extra three days at the White House before finally returning home. Aides explained that Tricia was simply spending extra time with her father during a difficult period because "He likes to have a daughter around," but by now trouble in the Cox family was Washington gospel.

"If it's printed," said Tricia, "it's a lie. It's nonsense." She explained that Eddie had returned to New York after Christmas only because "he has a job as a lawyer. He had been at the law firm for only a few months and he couldn't take off for a vacation." Eddie supported this interpretation by putting his shoulder to the Nixon wheel at a rally with Tricia, where he loyally called John Dean a coward and condemned the charges against his father-in-law as "one of the most vicious witchhunts in American history." To clinch things, Tricia, sophisticated in the ways in which the press can be helpful, invited a sympathetic Washington newswoman into her home to discuss the situation.

One by one, the hateful rumors were dismissed. Not only was Eddie Cox convinced that his father-in-law was handling Watergate splendidly, but he wholeheartedly endorsed the way he was running the country. Despite news reports that had questioned the way the

President and his "unrecorded partner," Tricia Nixon Cox, had
handled a profitable Florida land transaction, perchance to minimize
the taxes paid, the Cox tax returns proved the young people arith-
metically and morally pure. Tricia's unexplained hospital visits were
not the result of Hodgkin's disease; nor was she as unathletic as of
yore. "Trish is a good swimmer," Eddie declared. "She has a beautiful style. She is very coordinated and learns very easily." In fact, he
went so far as to claim that he had taught her how to roller-skate on
their honeymoon.

Above all, their marriage was a model of blissful domesticity.
Tricia filled her contented days with cleaning, cooking, and dishwashing (this last, in deference to the energy crisis, without the aid of
her electric dishwasher). Eddie, keen as ever on physical fitness,
bounded up twenty-eight flights of stairs each evening to join her. It
was a minuet, each in turn advancing to the other's defense,
gracefully bowing to the other's accomplishments. At last Tricia
turned to face her husband and summed up their marriage: "I've
never spent a boring day with you, Ed."

Not everyone sees it quite that way. Some suspect that rumor had
it right the first time, and that the marriage is faltering. Eddie, after
all, comes from a line of active people; the indolent Tricia, whose
time slips away without accomplishment, must be almost as much a
source of bafflement to him as she once was to White House
reporters. Her lack of social ease is said to be another source of
disappointment. Though Tricia manages well at large gatherings
where she can avoid the demands of intimacy and rely on conventional gestures and chitchat, she shrinks in smaller groups. Then too,
acquaintances speculate, there is the impact of Watergate.

Yet after the initial shock of her father's resignation, Tricia must
have realized that this triumph of evil forces over good was just what
she had expected all along. It was certainly a crushing blow, yet it
was, after all, only one more in a series of what she saw as the unfair
and undeserved defeats that have always afflicted her family. And
Tricia, who throughout her life has attempted very little in the way
of independent action, has always experienced her father's defeats as
her own.

Tricia, as her essay makes clear, knows beyond argument that
people who try to do great things will be hurt, misunderstood,
laughed at, rejected, traduced. The inescapable conclusion to be
drawn from her observation of her father's career is that to play an
active part in life, to take responsibility—even, one might suggest, to

grow up—all that is frightening and possibly disastrous. How much more pleasant to resist involvement, attempt nothing difficult, take no chances.

Tricia now, as before, resists change and disorder, searching for comfort in material things, manageable things. She is seen from time to time in Saks and Bergdorf Goodman, a small, unconfident figure in the crowds—"rather pathetic," as Alice Roosevelt Longworth once described her. And she clings to her trinkets, her reassuring little collections. Among all those Dresden and Meissen figurines is a prize piece, Tricia's favorite, a seesaw with two little girls, one brunette, one blond, playing with a small spotted dog. The President gave it to Tricia one Christmas. He called it "Tricia and Julie with Checkers."

Suzanne Krogh

I think it'd be lovely if Mr. Nixon said
he was sorry.

"It's for the wife's protection as much as anything," says Suzanne
Krogh, explaining why a U.S. government official engaged in
undercover work would bring no problem of importance home.
"If someone then puts pressure on the wife, she can say in all honesty, 'I don't know.'" And since for Egil (Bud) Krogh the summer
of 1971 was a period of crucial decisions—the time when, as leader of
the White House Plumbers, he would send Hunt and Liddy flying
off to the West Coast to burglarize the office of Daniel Ellsberg's
psychiatrist—Sue can understand his silence. She speaks sympathetically of his anxiety, the inner conflict that friends read upon his
face. But at the time, as Sue says now, "I didn't know if Bud wasn't
talking to me because he couldn't ... or if he wasn't telling me
because we weren't together. I just didn't know."

The Kroghs were separated for almost two years, from 1970 to the
summer of '72, and Sue has never made a secret of the fact that the
marriage almost sank. It was all, she says, a failure in communication, a flaw in their life together from the very start. As one who
firmly believes that straight answers deprive the curious of those
enticing mysteries they seek, she has even chosen to discuss the
matter in print. For all her candor, however, it is as difficult to
imagine Sue Krogh tied to the stove and uncommunicative as it is to
picture her as Government Wife, pumped by undercover men for
secret information.

Who is Sue Krogh? Well, to start with, she is a small, nice-looking
young woman in the medium range of pretty, and in no way out of
the ordinary, except perhaps in her extreme and noticeable normality. She has a pleasant rather than a striking face, is slender rather
than voluptuous. All in all, there is a reassuring impression of order-
liness, cleanliness, nothing in excess. Sue Krogh is *safe*. She would be

a nice mother to walk down the street with if you were a child, a good teacher to hire if you ran a school, a wife to count on when the going got rough—and you would never have to worry that she would make a wrong move, embarrass you, make a scene, cry, get angry, drink too much, or fail to put her litter in the trash can.

The Kroghs' house is predictable, in a section of very similar houses. These are the areas for the upwardly mobile whose dreams are not of inexhaustible wardrobes and sports cars but of a color-coordinated kitchen and two perfect children. Bushes and trees bloom on the lawn; there may not be much land around the house, but what there is is attractive, well tended, and clearly there for show. The houses are two-story brick, not cheap—but it is clear at a glance that they are intended for young families.

Inside, the living room is like its owner, pleasant, not striking, in no way unusual. It is papered in a blue toile pattern; the shag rug is gold. Some further decorational step, whatever step would be needed to make this combination work, has not been taken. Perhaps it suits the Kroghs better just as it is.

Two large and not entirely housebroken Siamese cats roam the house, and two handsome boys—nine-year-old Peter and Matthew, who is five. But everything is neat and ready for inspection. Sue says that the situation is not as good as it looks; the stereo does not work, the piano has broken strings, and the upholstery fails, in some un-specified and invisible way, to measure up to her standards. The Kroghs are living less lavishly now, since for some time they had to get along on Sue's teaching salary at St. Aidan's, a Montessori school, plus what she made writing two articles for *Redbook*. Bud Krogh was unemployed for many months, and on February 4, 1974, he entered Allenwood, the minimum-security prison farm in the hills of central Pennsylvania, sentenced to serve a six-month term. With time off for good behavior—and Bud was, as he announced before entering he intended to be, good—he was out in four months, rejoining his family on June 21.

The Kroghs can now make a fresh start and, with all the in-gredients of the American Dream in lavish supply, they should be able to begin anew, do everything right, and end up living happily ever after. This will not be their first fresh start: they have had two others. One was when they met and married; the other when they decided to resume that marriage.

The first picture of Egil Krogh (pronounced Egg'll Krogue) and Suzanne Lowell belongs in the annals of wholesome romance: they actually met at the Christian Science church where Sue was ushering and where Bud, a Navy officer ashore for a few days, had immediately headed while his shipmates were off seeking more secular pleasures. That they were both in Tokyo seems improbable for two such mainstream Americans, yet their being there was readily explainable in the most all-American terms.

Bud Krogh was born in Chicago in 1939 and grew up in a prosperous middle-class home. His father, Egil Krogh, Sr., was a vice-president of Chicago's best-known department store, Marshall Field. But as his was a career that moved the family back and forth across the country, Bud was placed in Principia Upper School in St. Louis. He went to Principia College, another small, expensive Christian Science school, where he was athletic (on the track team) as well as devout.

Bud's father had been a self-made man, a Norwegian immigrant who brought up his three children to expect success, to be ambitious, patriotic and religious. (Disappointed in his hope of serving his country in World War II, he had his small son dressed in military uniforms.) Converted to Christian Science himself when Bud was fourteen, Krogh, Sr., asked his boy to pledge that he would neither smoke nor drink. This compact was sealed with a handshake that is still in force.

Clearly, a father of such strong-willed dedication is no easy force to withstand, and it was his example that Bud followed; he even entered the school of business at the University of Chicago, just as his father had done. But in Bud's case it did not lead on to a business career. Within a week he decided that that was not for him and dropped out to enlist in Navy officer candidate school.

In 1962, three weeks before Bud's O.C.S. graduation, Egil Krogh, Sr., died; within months Bud lost his mother as well. It was during his three and a half years in the Navy that he met Sue.

Sue herself was in Tokyo because she, too, was trying to establish some kind of independence, rather than simply follow the expected path. She had grown up middle-class in Oak Park, Illinois; when she was ten, her parents moved to Miami, where Sue and her younger sister Leslie were to finish school and go on to Florida State College. Tomboyish, rebellious, competitive with her sister, Sue was brought up by a mother she now describes as "a lady's lady" to be a very feminine girl with domestic accomplishments. The reason for the family move was twofold: the father was tired of the urban rat race and the mother's health was poor. Settled in Florida, Mrs. Lowell had a series of operations—all apparently unsuccessful. And then, when Sue was about twelve, her mother discovered Christian

Science. The bottom shelf of her closet had been well stocked with medicines; now they were all discarded, even the insulin for her diabetes. From that time on, she trusted God to take care of her health, and He apparently has not failed her. She became a Christian Science practitioner and is still active in that vocation.

Sue believes that people must choose their own religion, that no matter what their upbringing may have been, they must eventually find their own answers. She declares that she decided Christian Science would be her religion not when she saw her mother miraculously transformed from chronic invalidism to radiant health, but only much later, after college. In fact, she cannot remember being aware of the decision that revolutionized her mother's life at the time it was happening. Only later, she says, did her mother explain it to her. It seems odd that anyone going through such a profound change would keep quiet about it and avoid proselytizing, but then perhaps Sue was resistant to such messages. She seemed better able to accept her mother's attitudes when at some distance from home.

Whatever subterranean rebellion was working itself out within that seemingly placid young woman impelled her to leave friends, family, and country in search of adventure. As she puts it now, she decided she had studied enough history of the Far East; it was time for her to make some. She tarried a year in Hawaii, working in a travel agency, and then she heard of an opening at an international school in Tokyo, teaching second grade. She applied for it and ("probably nobody else applied," she explains) got the job.

She was living, then, as conventional a life as such exotic surroundings would permit; she had a fiancé, and was an usher at the Christian Science church. But, to assure the continuance of nomadic excitement, she was considering a teaching post in Germany. As she describes her situation, she was determined not to get married until she was thirty. She wanted to live adventurously—and was sure that marriage would put an end to all that.

When Bud Krogh walked into the church she noticed him immediately. He was clearly the best-looking man who had come there in months. There were two doors after the main entrance, and Bud chose the one presided over by another usher. But Sue refused to abide by this decision of fate; after the service, she sought him out and introduced herself.

And then did they go off together? Did they make another appointment? Nothing of the sort. Sue went off for a date with her fiancé, and Bud returned to his ship. They might never have seen each other again. But fate, as it always does in hindsight, decreed that what has happened should happen.

On Wednesday evening Bud appeared at church again, this time with the commander of his ship's air squadron, who happened to be married to a good friend of Sue's. He immediately decided Bud and Sue were meant for each other, and made sure they all went out for something to eat afterward. The relationship had begun.

By one of the most unconvincing coincidences ever alleged by a participant, Sue had—she says—decided to break her engagement the day before, so by the time she saw Bud for the second time on Wednesday, she was free. Another odd coincidence, of course, is that of two engagements in the life of a young woman so firmly opposed to the idea of marriage. But against the promptings of better judgment, ambition, or wanderlust, the new romance prospered. When Bud returned to his ship, he and Sue exchanged long letters. Three months later, Bud was back, and at the end of the school year the young couple left Tokyo for Seattle so Sue could meet Bud's two sisters, Joegil and Letitia; and then on to South Miami to meet her parents. In July 1963 Sue and Bud were married at her parents' home—after, by Sue's count, fourteen dates, including the rehearsal dinner.

It is hardly fair to tell the story of the Kroghs' marriage chronologically, because in hindsight Sue Krogh sees it differently. What she felt about it then is lost in her new concept of what really underlay the apparent good times, the apparent adjustment. And yet her own account does not work either.

The outer story is that they started out lightheartedly in Long Beach, California. There Bud's ship would remain in drydock for a year and a half, and Sue taught school. After that, she followed Bud around the Pacific, meeting in Japan, Hong Kong, or Hawaii, a period Sue looks back on as one of unalloyed pleasure. She had not entirely lost her suspicion that marriage represented the end of all fun and adventure, but Bud promised her that their life together would not be dull. Apparently he kept the promise well—so well that, Sue says now, they felt as if they weren't married at all: they were having too much fun. And yet, she feels, they were laying the groundwork for later problems. In fact, she now recalls, they even said at the outset that if things did not work out they could always get divorced—surely an odd statement for two devoutly religious and conventional people to have made, if they ever meant it seriously.

This chapter in their married life was followed by another, almost equally idyllic, yet, in Sue's new interpretation, faintly grim. It has the young Kroghs returning to Seattle in time for their first child to be born. Bud is discharged from the Navy. That September he enters the University of Washington law school in Seattle. These three years seem to have been crucial. Bud had a trust fund to pay for his education, but to supplement his income he sold hats in a local department store and clerked in John Ehrlichman's law firm. This meant, presumably, long hours away from home—not to mention his studies, which did not go swimmingly. Sue says the first year of law school he watched a lot of television and the second year he saw a lot of movies and the third year he went to Vietnam for a few weeks to work on "land reform"—and the fact that this took place at Christmas was far from her own choice.

On the surface, however, things were smooth. Bud graduated and was admitted to the Washington State bar, starting work full time now at the Ehrlichman firm. (Ehrlichman knew the Kroghs because his wife Jeanne was best friends with Bud's older-by-twelve-years sister Joegil, and the Kroghs and Ehrlichmans are still close.) The Kroghs bought a boat. They had two cars. They had a baby boy. Bud supported the family. Sue stayed at home. (She had suggested working but Bud wouldn't hear of it.)

Then, just three months after Bud had joined the firm, Richard Nixon was elected President. Ehrlichman went to Washington as counsel to the President—and he asked Bud to come to the White House as his administrative assistant. According to one account, Bud considered this offer for ten seconds before accepting it. Sue is sure that she and Bud discussed the decision together. Whichever way it happened, both were eager and excited about what lay ahead. The Kroghs were off.

They found a small apartment in downtown Washington, stayed there for a year, then bought their present house in the suburban area that hugs the Maryland-District line. Beyond that, there seems to be more than one way of looking at their life together during that first year and a half in Washington. Sue remembers no loneliness, although, like other Administration wives, she rapidly discovered that Nixon people were expected to keep a low social profile. Not, she adds, that she had been looking forward to gala official functions or was terribly excited about them when they took place. What Sue docs rcmcmbcr with pleasure is casual, last-minute entertaining at the apartment after a call from Bud to announce that four or six old friends had just arrived in town. As Sue says now, "That's the way we like to do it, anyway."

She never felt excluded from Bud's work. It was simply a matter of logistics, she explains. With that "abominable" White House telephone inside the house, people would continue to call Bud right through the evening. And Sue thinks that she knew a lot about what he was doing at the White House just because of that.

On the other hand, Sue Krogh can become very firm when it comes to a wife's responsibility to make a life for herself. A husband, in her view, has made his own decisions, but that does not mean that he is relegating anyone else to a miserable existence. Sue wastes no pity on the woman who sits at home, jealous of the glamour of her husband's daytime life. In fact, she says, if she has ever found herself not getting on, not finding time for what she wanted, not enjoying full-time care of children, she has always felt it was her job to figure out another way of doing things.

One solution is to go to Europe. And that is exactly what Sue did in 1970, trundling four-year-old Peter off for a summer in Spain and the chance to learn another language. She was pregnant with Matthew at the time, but Sue routed the trip home via London and Paris so that Peter could see the places pictured in a beloved book of his. "In that particular year, I *was* feeling left out," she remembers. "And that was what I did about it."

It may surprise some that anybody pregnant and with a four-year-old in tow would opt for the European tour, but not those who knew the Kroghs. "Sue was always independent," says a close family friend. "Bud was so busy, the demands of the White House so great. They did a lot of things independently."

But by that September, the Kroghs had separated. According to Sue, the break was inevitable; they had both clung for so long to the idea that marriage was "fun" that there was no room for anger or pain, disappointment or threatened pride. The real trouble had started in Seattle, says Sue, where small resentments accumulated, almost unnoticed, and the issue of her working was never discussed. Bud's schedule in Washington may have contributed to their separation, she concedes, but in no way did it play a major part.

Others in Washington remember it all in a slightly different way. With his chiseled good looks and air of sincerity, Bud Krogh had dazzled more than one woman at the White House and, at the time of his separation, he was seeing a good deal of one of Dwight Chapin's secretaries. The liaison elicited a good deal of laughter, since Bud usually radiated piety. (As one colleague recalls, he and his closest friends at the White House, all Christian Scientists, "practically constituted a small religious community.") According to this version of the Kroghs' separation, it was clearly Bud's idea. "He's a straightforward person, very decisive," says one old friend. "He felt to continue on in that situation would be living a lie and it was more appropriate that they separate and see what would develop."

Sue agrees that it was absolutely the right thing to do. "It wasn't easy," she admits, "but I think we each took time to find out who we were as individuals and then put ourselves back together. It couldn't have been better." With the two children, still very small, at home, Sue got her Montessori degree, a nine-month course, and a start on a master's in early childhood education; she ran the house, with the help of a Venezuelan babysitter, managed a social life, and remained friendly with Bud when he stopped by to see the children. "Oh, we had the divorce papers all ready to go," she says now with a laugh. "We just never got around to signing them somehow."

Apparently, it was a more profoundly disturbing time for Krogh. For him, the marriage had not been working. And yet he deeply missed his family. Burdened by responsibilities, under pressure at work, in need of strength for what friends now call "the difficult decisions," Bud Krogh returned to his religion. He began work on it after he and Sue had been separated for just about a year, and the following June he went through what Christian Scientists call class instruction—two weeks of intense concentration on the faith, and close study of the "inspired writings" of Mary Baker Eddy. (One precept friends consider especially applicable to Bud's problem: "Get personality out of personal relationships.")

From all accounts, this is a powerful experience for a Christian Scientist, a step that can be taken only once in a believer's life. Right after Bud's two weeks, the Kroghs were reconciled. "It was very much a prayerful thing," explains a fellow Christian Scientist, "not a personal or physical or human reasoning type of thing—the right move for both of them."

Sue remembers the day in July 1972, when she was suddenly called out of class at the University of Maryland. An urgent phone call, she was told. It was Bud, en route back from a trip to the West Coast, asking her to meet him in St. Louis. She flew out next morning, and they decided—practically at the airport, according to Bud—to try again. "The next day," he adds, "we went to a jeweler in downtown St. Louis and bought new wedding rings. I haven't had mine off since."

The following February, thirty-three-year-old Bud Krogh moved from four years of presidential service to the undersecretaryship of the Department of Transportation—thus becoming, as Sue likes to say, one of the youngest Cabinet officers in U.S. history. And the trappings of power came to suburbia: the chauffeured black limousine that arrived each morning; the flurry of invitations; official trips that were distinctly more leisured than those he had taken for the White House.

Occasionally Sue accompanied him, and when in April 1973 Bud was scheduled to make a speech in Florida, they decided to turn the trip into a family vacation. Trailing sand into the motel room one afternoon, Bud turned on the TV set. And it was then that the news flashed across the screen. John Dean was naming names and, as the floodgates broke, out came the details of the break-in at Dr. Lewis Fielding's office. Egil Krogh was identified as chief Plumber and tour director. The Ellsberg trial, said the commentator, was in sudden jeopardy.

Sue by that time had been told of the burglary and professes deep understanding of "the pressures and intensities of the situation that had caused Bud to make his decision." Since the start of the Ellsberg trial, she claims, her husband, weary of his secret, had sought permission from the White House to reveal his role in the affair; the request was turned down for reasons of "national security." Apparently it was these instructions that had prompted Bud, just a short time before, to tell the prosecutors' staff that he knew nothing of the travels of Howard Hunt and Gordon Liddy.

Once back in Washington, they knew, Bud would have to take the stand. Rather than following the example of Dean or Magruder—who had already agreed to implicate others in exchange for immunity—Bud turned penitent (or began, as one man from the special prosecutor's task force was later to put it, "the long dark night conversion of the soul"). He submitted an affidavit to the prosecutors, in which he took full responsibility for the break-in.

Sue has described in print the days of toil that went into its preparation: the few close friends who were called in for consultation; the grilling to help Bud remember names and dates and attitudes once held; the Christian Science precept "injure no man" firmly kept in mind. "Bud asked me to collaborate with him in writing the affidavit," Sue explains. "He said that the project was too important for him to do alone."

For Sue, the summer of 1973 was a time of waiting, the pleasures of having Bud at home marred only by a "vague uneasiness that something we were doing was wrong." Apparently, it took Judge Gesell to tell her what it was, to bridge that gap between moral "wrong"—that Bud was ready to embrace—and the simple illegality of commissioning a burglary and then lying about it in a court of law.

That a lawyer, even one of scant experience, should be in need of such enlightenment may seem surprising, but its impact was profound.

Or perhaps it was, as both of the Kroghs now like to suggest, a Thanksgiving in Williamsburg that changed their thinking. They went down there in the Volvo, bicycles hitched on the back, and, from what Bud says, the very sight of the House of Burgesses brought home to him how much the United States has always done to protect the individual. "Here I was—a man under indictment in two different places, and still I was free—free to speak and to travel, to meet with my friends and, most importantly, to pray." While still in Williamsburg, Bud made up his mind to plead guilty to the charge of conspiracy to violate the civil rights of Dr. Fielding.

It was a decision that was to open up the gates of Allenwood just two months later—and one that elicited Sue's intense admiration. "At last I understood, too," she wrote in *Redbook*. "Bud's willingness to go to prison wasn't based on feelings of guilt, but rather on the idea that 'for reasons of national security' is not a valid excuse for a man's actions if it denies others their individual freedom." She learned from Bud, she says, to put away her fears, knowing that from then on they were headed in the right direction.

Today, there is something almost detached about Sue's observations on Watergate. Perhaps it is because she makes no link between the Los Angeles break-in and the one that took place in Washington just ten months later. ("People keep putting us into Watergate," she protests, "and really we weren't part of it at all.") Or it may be, as she says, that a history major always tries to put things into historical perspective.

She theorizes that the vast amount of power in the Executive branch, built up over many years and by successive Administrations, brought Watergate about. Looking back, she feels that "it was almost inevitable." On the other hand, it seems equally plausible to her that the morality of Watergate reflected that of American business life, where the whole mystique of corporate loyalty blinds staff members to the "greater right," and "each individual considers only whether he's doing the right thing in the corporate picture."

Whatever salutary effects Watergate may have on the country—and Sue tends to view them as short-term—she is certain that one lesson has been learned. "I think," she says firmly, "it's the responsibility of those who were involved to become part of what some columnists have called the healing process." She sees Bud as having assumed just that kind of responsibility on his recent lecture tour.

(To one group of audiences, he spoke on the perils of government service for the young and inexperienced; to another on prison reform.)

The Kroghs are said to feel that Richard Nixon "would be freer" if he, too, could come to grips with the full implications of what he did. And it may have been this concern that prompted Bud to visit San Clemente on August 24, 1974, two weeks after Nixon's resignation and before the Ford pardon was announced. It has been implied that on that occasion Bud suggested a guilty plea and was rejected. The former President could visualize only one result: thirty years in prison. On being asked, "Do you feel guilty?" the man in exile answered, "No." Bud's parting advice: "In that case, don't do it." Sue might have persisted. Months later, she says with feeling, "I think it'd be lovely if Mr. Nixon said he was sorry." Evidently, she agrees with a Christian Scientist who concludes that "Nixon hasn't reached the point that Bud has."

That certainty still radiates from Sue. Guilts, if they were there, have been expiated; any pain or loneliness is behind her. Despite an unclear future (Bud has yet to be reinstated in the Washington bar) and financial burdens (legal bills totaled a hefty $135,000, only $65,000 of which has been paid off with the help of a defense fund), Sue Krogh is clearly a contented woman. Her husband is back home. And their relationship is on a brand-new footing.

As Sue says, any crisis has to affect a marriage. "It just doesn't leave you where you started. It can't. And Bud has shared absolutely everything with me from the beginning, and any decisions he's made to plead guilty or to defend himself or *whatever*, we've made the decisions together." Friends agree that the Kroghs are now "tremendously close." One of them looks back at Bud's role in what came to be known as Watergate and at the man he was then—bright, tough, immensely attractive to many women—as a chapter closed. "At the time Bud made the critical decisions," he explains, "he was away—away from Sue and his religion."

Patricia Ellsberg

I feel they were taking my country away
from me.

The Pentagon Papers case was hailed as an epic constitutional trial, a historic courtroom clash between the great issues of national security and the people's right to know. As it turned out, the case was argued on far more modest points, and even those were eventually swept away in the mounting tide of evidence of government misconduct.

But the case had an additional significance unguessed-at at the time. Only later did it become apparent that if there was any one event that can be said to have set the complexities of Watergate in train, it was the publication of the Pentagon Papers. For it was in response to the publication of those top-secret government documents that the Nixon Administration, already obsessed by leaks, began systematically to break the law in the name of national security, setting up its own paralegal forces to deal with what it persisted in seeing as the dangerously threatening forces of the left.

Daniel Ellsberg, who had turned over the Pentagon Papers to the *New York Times*, seemed a most unlikely radical threat. Possessor of impeccable establishment credentials, he had believed in the rightness of the Vietnam war until 1968, and had even seen combat there. Yet, as a belated convert from hawk to dove, he had made his decision to break the law in a dramatic effort to halt the war.

This surprising turnabout was widely credited to his wife, Patricia. Pat Ellsberg today disavows so decisive an influence on her husband's thinking. "I was one ingredient," she admits, "but I was clearly not the woman behind the change of mind." At the time, however, it was generally believed that it was her early refusal to marry him because of their disagreement on the war that brought about the startling change in Dan Ellsberg.

On the eightieth day of the Pentagon Papers trial—April 29, 1973—it at last crossed paths with Watergate. It was then revealed

104

that over the Labor Day weekend two years earlier, G. Gordon Liddy and E. Howard Hunt, Watergate's own odd couple, had broken into the Los Angeles office of Dr. Lewis Fielding, Dan Ellsberg's psychiatrist. Disappointed when two CIA-prepared psychological profiles proved too tame to enhance Ellsberg's "prosecutability," Egil Krogh (and behind him John Ehrlichman) had authorized Hunt and Liddy to search the psychiatrist's files for something juicy and scandalous. They failed to turn up Ellsberg's records, but their attempt nonetheless constituted a first-degree felony on the government's part.

And that was not all. The presiding judge, William Matthew Byrne, Jr., created a second sensation—and a second Watergate link—by admitting that he had been summoned to the Western White House by John Ehrlichman, who had there offered him the directorship of the FBI and even introduced him to the President. Though Byrne maintained that there had been no impropriety—on his side, at least—on May 11 he put an end to one of the oddest proceedings in the history of American jurisprudence. After five months, 22,691 pages of courtroom transcript, and the expenditure of millions of dollars, the judge announced, "I have decided to declare a mistrial and grant the motion to dismiss."

The courtroom, jammed with visitors and press, rose in a body and applauded. One of the defense counsels brought forth a big cigar and lit it. And Patricia Ellsberg rushed over to her husband and was heard to inquire, "Haven't you got a kiss for your girl?"

Pat Ellsberg had traveled a long way to that Los Angeles courthouse—a long way both literally and figuratively—from Scarsdale and the sixteen-acre "place" where she grew up. Her father was Louis Marx, a toy manufacturer successful enough to be referred to in print as a "millionaire toycoon." His first wife died when Pat was only five; but he saw to it that she had a suburban princess girlhood, complete with the most lavish of Christmas toys, the best of boarding schools.

Pat was no unappreciatively rebellious daughter. She had a close, admiring relationship with a father who had a good deal more in common with Louis XIV than his name. Marx had been hobnobbing with Army generals since the days, more than half a century ago now, when he first began distributing free toys to the troops at military bases. The five sons of his second marriage were all named after military heroes, each with the appropriate general as godfather: Bedell Smith, Emmett O'Donnell, Omar Bradley, Curtis Lemay, and Dwight Eisenhower. Marx was a warm admirer of J. Edgar Hoover, and Eisenhower once painted his portrait. Pat herself would never seek such associations, but in those days she had no quarrel with her father's ways. As she was to say years later, "You don't worry about Santa Claus's politics."

After graduating with honors from Radcliffe in 1959 and a summer of piano study in Paris, Pat Marx settled in New York. She soon had her own radio program, *Patricia Marx Interviews*, which could be heard every Tuesday night from 1961 to 1969 on New York's municipally owned station, WNYC. A writer there who remembers the program well was deeply impressed by the knowledge Pat displayed about a wide variety of fields as she questioned guests ranging from Ralph Nader to Georges Balanchine. Toward the end of the sixties she branched out into television.

Pat Marx was a very successful young woman. She was attractive—tall, slender, dark-haired, with large, almost feral, hazel eyes. Home was a bachelor apartment on Sutton Place, its large windows overlooking the East River. But like any young woman so fortunately situated, she had her detractors. They said she was artificial and snobbish; that she loved being around famous people. They called her a rich, indulged young lady who wanted to be in the swim. "You couldn't get to know her," one less than friendly friend recalls, "because it was like going through marshmallow—you could never get to the person."

Even truer friends admitted that she was still very much a product of her careful, conservative upbringing. She was exceedingly patriotic; she felt it was wrong to criticize the United States. She was a bit prudish, too. She had heard Lenny Bruce with no reaction but distaste and, when the subject came up, was apt to dismiss it with "We've heard all those words." Friends noticed, too, that though she was surrounded by an aura of good intention, she seemed animated by no very passionate conviction.

During those years Pat Marx's most frequent escort—and her only serious romance before Dan Ellsberg—was John Simon, the film and drama critic. His special mixture of pedantry and vitriol might lead one to expect a certain lack of warmth, but his friends testify that he was always extremely helpful to Pat on her interview show, suggesting questions and editing the tapes. One even claims that Pat was "not very good as far as writing goes" and needed Simon to "make something out of it."

All agree that Simon was in love with Pat and very anxious to marry her. It was she who was unwilling. Simon has since implied that Pat and he would be man and wife today had it not been for the narrow-mindedness of her family. "We talked about marriage many times," he told an interviewer. "But her family didn't like me. They were very conservative people." He could not resist adding that now, "compared to Ellsberg, they would probably adore me." Looking back on it, Pat says lightly that if they discussed marriage, he was doing more of the discussing than she was. "I love John. He was a wonderful person," she says fondly, "but a very difficult man to be married to, I should think." Yet the relationship persisted, on and off, for seven years.

Perhaps those qualities in Pat that troubled her friends—a hesitancy about committing herself, a certain finicky reserve—were what kept the relationship so well contained. But Pat was changing. She was reading omnivorously and talking to people of widely differing viewpoints. She herself explains that it was during this time that she evolved from the rather passive Eisenhower Republican she had been in college to a person who felt that serious and radical changes must take place in society. But though she chooses to explain the change in purely political terms, political change does not take place in an emotional vacuum. Clearly, she sensed that there was something beyond the safe and pleasant path she had been on all her life.

John Simon, who says now that he knew her "before she was political," had no idea that the staid and privileged Pat was talking about real, irreversible change. He saw her desire for commitment as simply an interest in benevolent power. He realized that "she somehow felt" that the arts were not really accomplishing good on a global scale, and, later, he concluded that that was part of Ellsberg's appeal to her.

During those years Pat's job took her periodically to Washington, and it was there that she met Dan Ellsberg in 1964. He came recommended by a friend as someone who would interest her—brilliant, handsome, and dangerous, a man forever breaking women's hearts. A young woman seeking a more adventurous life could hardly hear anything more calculated to interest her. "My ears perked up," she remembers. In their first brief meeting they were immediately attracted to each other.

On her next visit to Washington, a full year later, they had their first real date—a curious one, considering the fact that Daniel Ellsberg was working for the Department of Internal Security Affairs at the Defense Department at the time. It was his first Saturday off in months, but Pat Marx was planning a day of work, covering the April 1965 peace march. He went along with her, carrying her tape recorder as she conducted on-the-spot interviews with the marchers. The dangerous man and the safe, successful woman "very rapidly" fell in love.

If Pat was looking for intensity, she found it in Dan Ellsberg. Her life had progressed at a leisurely pace, his at a run. Blazing like a forest fire in the groves of Academe, he had collected all kinds of honors and distinctions, with particular emphasis on things military. At the end of his Harvard senior year he married the daughter of a Marine Corps general and enlisted in the Marines in 1954, moving smartly up through officers candidate school. He extended his tour of duty by a year in hopes of combat, and was not discharged as a first lieutenant until 1957. But this was by no means the end of his preoccupation with military life. Returning to Harvard, he enlarged his scope from economics to political science and decision theory. His doctoral dissertation was in games theory—a way of analyzing strategies by plotting out the various possible consequences in terms of both cost and risk—a newly popular tool in military planning. With these credentials, he was able to join California's Rand Corporation, the famous think tank where games theory was applied to defense matters.

In 1964 he moved to the Defense Department. His departure for Washington marked more than a change in jobs. Carol Ellsberg and their two children remained in California. "My wife told me she'd never loved me," Ellsberg told a reporter years later. "I wish she had remembered to tell me that a little sooner. Like before we got married."

But one of the most significant events in Dan Ellsberg's life had taken place years before he met Pat Marx, and was neither academic nor military. When Dan was fifteen, his father apparently fell asleep at the wheel when driving the family home after a Fourth of July celebration. Dan's mother and sister were killed; Dan himself broke his knee; his father escaped with minor injuries. One change this brought about in Dan's life came home to him suddenly as he lay in the hospital recovering from the accident: his mother had always insisted that eight hours of daily piano practice was his responsibility to his talent, but now he need never play again. Dan did not in fact stop practicing until he went to college; as he has said, it was then that he discovered an extra eight hours in each day.

The significance of the accident story would later be emphasized in the CIA psychiatric profiles that interpreted Ellsberg's entire career in Oedipal terms. The CIA psychiatrist suggested that Dan, resenting his father for killing his mother and injuring him—and even for not accepting him in his mother's place and for marrying another woman—thenceforth transferred that resentment to other men and all those in authority over him. In fact, the CIA profile said that when Ellsberg spoke—as he frequently would, apropos of later events—of the dangerous power of the Executive, it was really his father he unconsciously longed to destroy.

When Pat Marx met Dan Ellsberg, however, he was still very much a part of the establishment. His association with generals must have reminded Pat of her father, in a way at once reassuring and disquieting. Yet despite the political evolution that had been taking place over the past ten years, she still had no very strong convictions about the war in Vietnam. She was thinking about it. Dan, too, always interested in reading and research, was learning all he could about the theories supporting American involvement. At that time he was a protégé of General Edward Lansdale, then in charge of the American pacification effort. Pat saw Lansdale as an idealist who felt that communism must be combated by democratic reform rather than by force, a view with which she could sympathize. And when Dan went to Vietnam with Lansdale, Pat visited him there.

In the euphoria of that trip, during which she and Dan took a swing around Southeast Asia, to India and Thailand, there was little time for political discussion. The two were now "tentatively engaged." It was not until the following summer that Pat, visiting Dan again, began to develop her antiwar convictions. With Frances Fitzgerald, who was in Vietnam on assignment for the *Atlantic,* Pat Marx picked her way through the back alleys of Saigon. She had a chance to see for herself the hospitals, the schools, the U.S. and South Vietnamese bureaucracies. And as she saw what the war was doing to the people, she was increasingly appalled.

Dan, meanwhile, was committed to American involvement. Those who knew him then remember that early in his tour he approached the job with Boy Scout enthusiasm, and Ellsberg himself has said that in those days he considered it a good day's work if he could leave an antiwar visitor "confused." One who was subjected to the treatment remembers his awe at the moral superiority that radiated from Ellsberg on such occasions. "He sent me away feeling ashamed of myself," he wryly confesses, "for being such a facile left-wing antiwarrior."

Pat remembers Dan's position as more thoughtful and humane than that; she considered him "the voice of reason" on his side of the issue. Yet they deeply disagreed. She would return from her explorations of Saigon to long discussions of the war. "We didn't yell or scream," she recalls, "but it did get intense. Dan would usually win with all the facts he had, but I would still know I was right, that the war was wrong, morally and politically." Looking back on it, she ascribes her earlier insight to an advantage Dan, so long in Vietnam, had missed: she had been exposed to all the revelations and criticism about the war then available from newspapers and television back in the States.

But the argument between the two was intense enough to be noticeable, and when Pat left Saigon she and Dan were no longer engaged. One member of the Saigon press corps traced the rupture to a specific quarrel that supposedly took place at a farewell party for correspondent Neil Sheehan. According to his story, Pat's tone, as she argued the immorality of the war, was more accusatory than Ellsberg was prepared to tolerate, and she left Vietnam in anger.

But this explanation of the ending of their engagement is simplistic. Conceding that Dan did take personally her "horror at our whole involvement, of which he was a part," Pat explains that politics were "only a contributing factor" in their decision to part. There were, she firmly says, "a lot of personal reasons." What those personal reasons were she does not specify, beyond saying that "it was really Dan who broke it off as much as I did." Describing her state of mind as she departed from Vietnam, she says: "I didn't think we'd broken off forever, nor did I think we would get together. I guess I was really open to what would happen." It was clear to them both that they loved each other, but they were by no means ready to get married.

From the way the two spent the next few years of separation it is possible to guess at what some of those unexplained personal reasons must have been. Pat describes those years as a period of limbo for them both, and for her it was a time during which she retreated into her old New York life, returning to her job and even—though now that relationship was greatly diminished—to John Simon.

For Dan, on the other hand, it was a period of experimentation, a restless search for new experience, a time of stretching the boundaries of his life. Returning to the United States and Rand (after a brief but intense affair with a Eurasian girl in Saigon, a good deal of combat, and a bout with hepatitis), Dan found the exotic and permissive atmosphere of California just what he was looking for. Tony Russo, who would eventually share the honor and obloquy of the Pentagon Papers with him, remembers the Ellsberg of those days as "eager, square, sort of sweet actually," a person who "just hadn't been onto anything that was happening."

Ellsberg, a respected eminence at Rand, consultant on a vast Defense Department study on the origins of the Vietnam war, and holder of no fewer than eleven different security clearances, now began, by Russo's account, to spend his evenings getting stoned, listening to Joan Baez on the record player, and saying such things as

"Well, I guess I'll have to lead a life of poverty now." By his own account, Ellsberg was also experimenting with group sex, nudist camps, and orgies. He would later downgrade that interlude as "really a rather short period" and not one "of very great liberation." But he did offer an interesting explanation of it: "I was a bachelor, and I'd always been very uninhibited about sex, but hadn't had a chance to express that during my marriage." He did not point out that the marriage had ended five years earlier.

Sexual experimentation did seem to go hand in hand with political change. Though Ellsberg never embraced a life of poverty, the secret documents he was reading in the course of his work on the origins of the Vietnam war were, in his words, having "an enormous effect" on his thinking. Before long, he totally rejected the idea that the gradual escalation of the war had grown out of miscalculation and misplaced optimism. His reading convinced him that Presidents from Truman to Nixon had all been well advised of the bleak outlook but chose to commit the United States to each successive upward step because they feared domestic political repercussions if their actions suggested weakness.

Meanwhile there was little communication between Dan and Pat. Divided by a continent, they were going their separate ways. Pat had begun work on a book which was to consist of a series of interviews with scientists, in which she planned to explore the social implications of the biological sciences. In preparation for this, she had a great deal of reading and studying to occupy her, in addition to her radio and television work. She saw Dan only occasionally, when he came East, and, as she explains it, "There was a distance between us."

Yet Dan was evidently settling certain conflicts in his own mind and, as time passed, the change in him became apparent. Both had been in analysis (for him, an intensive four days a week for eighteen months) and because of this, Pat says now, "somehow we're much more able to be open with each other and very trusting. It was very different when we got back together again—there was so much trust." In the late fall of 1969, they were close to renewing their engagement—after a hiatus of more than two years—and it was only then that he told her that a few months earlier he had begun, with Tony Russo's help, to copy the documents that would later be known as the Pentagon Papers. Dan was passing them on to Senator William Fulbright, hoping that they might be aired in a congressional hearing; neither he nor Pat could then foresee that the papers would eventually erupt into national headlines.

Pat and Dan were married the following summer at her older

brother's house in North Salem, New York. Louis Marx, Jr., is, if anything, to the right of his father politically, but the groom was still at Rand, apparently still a proper part of the establishment, his antiwar activities not yet overt, and all went smoothly at what Pat describes as "the last lovely family gathering we had together." The bride wore white, with flowers in her hair. It was, she says, "a very loving time."

The first year of their marriage was a chaotic one. By the end of 1970 Dan, increasingly preoccupied by the moral issues of the war, had left Rand so he could "speak to the public about his views." In theory he was a senior research associate at the Center for International Studies at M.I.T., but more frequently he was on the road, at peace rallies, or mass meetings in behalf of draft resisters. Pat, in their Cambridge apartment, was still at work on the book she had started before her marriage and was taking a science course at Harvard in preparation for it.

But, distracting as some elements of their life together were, their happiness was beyond question. A friend who first met them as newlyweds in New York remembers affectionately that "Pat was dancing on tiptoes that night on Seventh Avenue." The photographs Dan took as a hobby consisted sometimes of ethereal shots of blossoms, leaves, and fields, but more often had Patricia as their subject, posed in a waterfall, in bed, with a white kitten on her shoulder. When he was in California and she a continent away, he would hold the telephone outside his window so she could hear the Malibu breakers they both loved. And they made no secret of their delight in each other and the marriage. Dan was as likely to mention casually to a reporter that he had first fallen in love with Patricia's eyes as she was to beg a married woman of her acquaintance for advice on how to become a perfect wife.

But headlines were soon to dispel the Ellsbergs' rapturous privacy. Met by nothing but silence from Washington in response to the steady stream of documents he had dispatched there, Dan decided at last to bring the truth about the war to the public by releasing a 7,000-page top-secret Pentagon study to the *New York Times*. After weeks of clandestine meetings, checks, and double checks, *Times* lawyers finally gave the go-ahead, and the story splashed across the paper's front page on June 13, 1971. Just seventy-two hours after the first installment appeared, Dan was identified as the man who had provided the documents. The press converged on Cambridge, only to discover that the Ellsbergs had disappeared.

Reporters traced leads to California, Martha's Vineyard, the Manhattan headquarters of Louis Marx. To this day, the Ellsbergs have not revealed their hiding place, though Pat mentions losing weight because "there wasn't much food there." Their continuing absence triggered so much interest that it was almost a disappointment when, ten days later, they arrived arm in arm at the Federal Courthouse in Boston and Dan gave himself up to U.S. authorities.

During the months that followed, Ellsberg was investigated by two grand juries and indicted on two counts: unlawful possession of government documents and converting them to his own use. But with the dawn of 1972—an election year—the charges were revised sharply upward, and the Justice Department implicated three other people, Anthony J. Russo, Jr., plus two "unindicted co-conspirators." Ellsberg's fifteen counts now added up to a conceivable, if improbable, 115 years in prison. Suddenly the name Ellsberg was, in many circles, a synonym for traitor. He was a man who had betrayed his country by failing to keep her secrets.

The inevitable reaction elevated him to martyr status among the antiwar left, and Ellsberg—intense, complicated, yet somehow vulnerable—seemed made for the role. He had little time free from peace demonstrations, fund raising, and legal strategy sessions for his upcoming trial. FBI men were everywhere, paying visits to friends Pat had telephoned long distance, following people to whom she had written personal checks. The Ellsbergs were convinced that their phone was tapped. If they had needed anything to draw them even closer together, it would have been the situation in which they then found themselves.

Not only was Pat's father so outraged by what Dan had done that he refused ever to see him again or contribute a penny to his legal defense, but everyone who had known Dan at Rand, the Defense Department, or in Vietnam seemed to have turned away from him. "I never got a letter, never got a call," he explained later. "None of the old friendships survived." To add to the Ellsbergs' isolation, Dan felt it was his duty not to call anyone, since a call from him might lead the FBI to a friend, or, at the least, cause embarrassment. He dedicated his book *Papers on the War*, published in 1972, to his wife, calling her "my partner, lover and closest friend." Pat could have been his closest friend in any year; in that particular year, she was almost his only friend. Dan told reporters that she was probably the one person in the world who really understood him.

After months of false starts and repeated delays, the Pentagon Papers trial opened in mid-January 1973. Though most people thought of it as the Ellsberg trial, Dan Ellsberg was not being tried alone: his former Rand colleague, Tony Russo, was co-defendant. In fact, for some reason—newsmen suspected a crafty government attempt to prick Ellsberg's vanity—the official name of the case was *United States* versus *Russo and Ellsberg*, or, as the morning clerk would sometimes intone, "*U.S.* versus *Russo et al.*"

There was deep division among the defense, with resentment on both sides. Pat says now that the defense *was* unified, that "they really *did* stay together," and minimizes the abrasions most observers at the trial found so obvious. But it is hardly surprising that there should have been Russo and Ellsberg factions, in view of the differences between the two men. They had been an unlikely pair from the start: Russo large, rumpled, and bohemian, a self-proclaimed radical who sometimes followed the federal prosecutors through the halls chanting "There go the pigs"—and Ellsberg, coolly self-possessed, politically sophisticated, trig in a tweed jacket that matched his blue-gray eyes.

Their wives were equally mismatched. Russo's wife, a painter, kept her maiden name, and thus had to be introduced always as "Catherine Barkley, Tony Russo's wife." Inviting the judge's displeasure, she was a lively figure in the courtroom, selling organic food sandwiches to the defense staff, press, and spectators. Pat, who stayed close within her husband's orbit, dressed expensively and sat quietly in the courtroom's second row. In court the Ellsbergs gazed lovingly at one another; between sessions they strolled the corridor arm in arm; at lunchtime they hurried off together. Countless photographs taken of them at the time show them side by side, Pat's uptilted face alight with adoration as she gazes up at Dan. Reporters on the scene acidly noted that Pat, at five feet six almost as tall as her husband, was fully aware of any camera trained on them. At the precise moment when the shutter clicked, they said, she bent her knees, tilted her head, and smiled. "She wanted to do the right thing," one of her friends explains, "to help the cause. And if that included posing for photographers or smiling gently at the jury, then that's what she did."

In addition to the mutual mistrust provoked by antithetical life-styles, there was disapproval and jealousy between the two camps, Ellsberg partisans considering Russo people irresponsible, Russo adherents accusing Ellsberg forces of snobbishness. Ill feeling was by no means confined to superficial areas: matters of legal strategy, too, provoked dissension. When the Watergate revelations surfaced, their first result was to touch off bitter argument about whether the defense should press for dismissal (Ellsberg) or take their chances on vindication by allowing the case to go to the jury (Russo).

The Russo faction resented the fact that, though Russo had actually spent six weeks in jail for refusing to testify before one of the grand juries investigating Ellsberg, the headlines were all Dan's. They joked sourly that when Russo testified on his own behalf some newspaper would headline the event RUSSO TESTIFIES AT ELLSBERG TRIAL—and indeed that prediction proved accurate. Russo's wife so much resented the fact that her husband—who, after all, was risking a $30,000 fine and 25 years in jail—was being ignored that she almost stopped coming to the trial at all.

Eventually, a great deal of this floating resentment came to focus on Pat Ellsberg, who was held accountable for many of the slights the Russo faction had suffered from press and public. It was not anything she had done but the attitude she embodied—the attitude of those who were incapable of seeing value in any action not committed by Dan Ellsberg personally, those who could not allow anyone to share Dan's limelight for fear it might somehow diminish his credit, or dim the glory of his sacrifice.

The idea gained currency that Pat controlled her husband, that she was somehow to blame for whatever shortcomings might be perceived in him. Russo, for one, was convinced that this was so. "His politics, his life, everything," he told a reporter, "is bounded by Pat. He can become more radical in the sense that he might edge a little closer to the door. But he can only take one step before Pat realizes where he's headed and snatches him back to reality." He went on: "I can call Dan up and Pat will answer. She'll say, 'And now, here is Daniel Ellsberg, who is tired and has laryngitis.' And then she'll hand him the phone and he'll say, 'Hi, I'm Dan Ellsberg. I'm tired and I have laryngitis. But, uh . . . what's happening?' "

A number of reporters made similar assumptions about the Ellsberg relationship. One recalls being with them in a hotel, where, in an uncharacteristically festive mood, Dan suggested that the three of them get together later for a drink. Pat then moved in close to her husband and a few murmurs were exchanged, after which Dan announced, "I'm really pretty tired. I guess we'd better skip that drink." Another reporter, midway through an interview with Dan, was sufficiently irritated to tell Pat firmly to stop whispering in her husband's ear.

It is the same people who see Pat as controlling Dan's every move and thought who give her credit for reversing his views on the war, a theory Dan's friends reject with surprising vehemence, as if it would be somehow discreditable for him to be influenced by his wife. "Dan is much more open with women than he is with men," says one, "but the idea that Pat influenced his thinking is ridiculous. He is a very strong, a very complicated man, and the idea that a woman could change him would mean the reverse. He's a lot of things, but he's not weak."

The truth seems to be that far from trying to dominate her husband, Pat is dominated by him. Friends agree that he depends on her devotion. "He looks around the room to find her," one says, "and you can see him relax once he's spotted her." Another mentions an evening spent with them during which "Pat spent all her time bringing Dan cups of tea. And he wants that." All this should please the CIA psychiatrist who theorized that Dan Ellsberg had always disliked the submissive qualities in himself and constantly sought reassurance (through what the report called "blatant sexual activities with different women") that he was his own man.

And Pat publicly accepted her submissive role from the very beginning of Dan's involvement in the peace movement. She devoted herself entirely to the cause—and the cause was Dan Ellsberg. When she made speeches or greeted people at rallies, she did it competently but modestly, staying in the background whenever possible. She borrowed $75,000 against her trust fund to contribute to his defense. She was completely submerged in the role of hero's wife.

Ironically, it was this very adulation that backfired. Because she truly believed in Dan's unique superiority and wanted others to see and appreciate him as she did, she was resented. Those who did not share her feeling found the clear implication of their own inferiority insulting. They were annoyed by her humorless approach to a man who did, after all, have human failings visible to outsiders. And they unerringly detected the trace of complacency implicit in this exaggerated admiration. Not that the genuineness of her feeling was in question—as one observer said, "She is convinced that she is in love with a great, Gandhi-like American"—but the temptation to jeer at the Ellsbergs and their love became irresistible.

And then came Watergate. Its first effect on Pat and Dan, of course, was to put an end to the trial. Then the Ellsbergs—so much a part of the public landscape for so long that they had begun to seem public property—disappeared into private life.

Asked what he would do when the trial ended, Dan Ellsberg had announced his intention "to make love to my wife in every climate of the world." That promise has not yet been fulfilled. Though Dan has emerged from time to time to remind the world that the war still continued its deadly hemorrhage unnoticed in Vietnam, the Ellsbergs live for the most part unnoticeably in Mill Valley, California. Dan's friends explain that he is catching up on his studying, his self-education and writing. There was talk for a while that he was considering running for Congress, perhaps from New York with its large liberal vote, but Ellsberg denies that the suggestion was his.

Word has circulated, too, that he might be interested in a university post. One recipient of that suggestion unkindly joked, "No college that has a Xerox machine," a reflection of the price Ellsberg is still paying for the public sacrifice of his membership in the power elite: a still widespread residual feeling that however courageous his decision may have been, however noble his motives, he himself is somehow not quite trustworthy.

More than her husband, Pat seems to have set herself firmly on a course leading away from political activism. Nowadays she is much more interested in achieving inner change than dedicated to bringing about changes in the larger society. She has been deeply influenced by Arica, an eclectic mix of Zen, yoga, and meditation, put together by a Chilean named Oscar Ichazo. Described by one writer as "the perfect post-LSD religion," and by another as "rich people's religiosity of the newest kind—and terribly expensive," Arica's teachings are said by friends to be "an enormous amount of help" to Pat.

She is also enrolled in a Ph.D. program in psychology at San Francisco's Humanistic Psychology Association and is currently at work on a book she will submit as her thesis. Though she declines to be specific about its subject, she describes herself as "very happy about it and very excited." And now, since for the first time in their married life the Ellsbergs are really settled down, the subject of children is, she says, "very much on my mind." They plan to have one child of their own and then perhaps adopt a second.

Pat Ellsberg speaks of Watergate as if it had no special significance in her life, much as any other concerned citizen might, though perhaps with a more than usual emphasis on its implications for U.S. foreign policy and a more than usual knowledge of the Pentagon Papers case. She sees the central problem of Watergate as essentially one of governmental secrecy, an infringement on the people's right to decide the issues for themselves on the basis of complete information.

"Watergate," she says, "reveals what happens when the Executive overreaches in abuse of power, and it reveals the kind of conspiratorial behavior that secrecy and unchecked power lead to. It was an absolute parallel to what the Pentagon Papers show: that foreign policy has been conducted in secret and it's been done with total contempt for the democratic process, contempt for Congress, contempt for the American public. Finally, this was introduced into the domestic political process, where it's unacceptable."

She believes that the same kind of scrutiny that unraveled the tortuous strands of the Watergate scandal must be carried over into foreign policy; still deeply suspicious of the inner workings of the Executive, she says, "I feel they were subverting the democratic system—and still are, where it comes to foreign policy." She invokes the debacle in Chile. And then, quite simply, Pat Ellsberg, who has always been, in her own way, a patriot, sums up Watergate: "I feel they were taking my country away from me." And one believes her.

Yet there is a great deal that she does not say, but it is impossible to believe she has not felt. Pat Ellsberg has long believed that the question of central importance in American life was the Vietnam war, and that her husband's act in releasing the Pentagon Papers represented the one best hope of putting an end to it. Then, suddenly, the Pentagon Papers case, its issues still unresolved, was hustled off the stage of history, to be replaced by Watergate. Far from having led to the serious, radical changes in society Pat had envisioned so long ago, it had been relegated to the backwater of ideas whose time has passed.

It is hardly possible that the woman who invested so much of her own effort and emotion in her husband's unique crusade can turn her back on it without a pang. Of course she cannot afford to think of those days with regret, because that would imply that the Ellsbergs' present life, lying as it does in the lee of history, is somehow less valuable. Of course, too, no one can live forever at such a pitch of intensity. But she must occasionally miss the exhilaration of being at the center of what seemed then a gathering and a reaffirmation of the forces of the American spirit.

Julie Nixon Eisenhower

I know my father's not involved because
he says he's not involved.

During April of the Watergate year of 1974, a press conference called
by Julie Nixon Eisenhower spelled front-page news. Reporters responded en masse, crowding into the East Garden of the White
House to await her arrival. The 1,254-page transcript of the President's secretly taped conversations had been released just ten days
before, and the capital was awash in rumors that Richard Nixon was
about to announce his last farewell.

Not so, said Julie, her voice trembling with conviction. She stood
before the reporters, David at her side, and declared that her father
would carry on his fight to stay in office "constitutionally, down the
wire," as long as there was one friendly senator to back him up.
Barraged by questions, Julie maintained her composure until one
newsman asked why the President was not out speaking for himself.
"Now if the media has a hang-up," she lashed back, "an obsession
about resignation and feels they must be reassured by members of
the family . . . I feel as a daughter it is my obligation to come out here
and say 'no, he is not going to resign.' "

Then, turning to the TV cameras, Julie Eisenhower explained
that important issues were at stake. "It would be a bad precedent to
set up for a President to resign unless there were criminal action," she
insisted. "It's just not the American system of government."

If anyone else had been crisscrossing the country making so many
speeches and appearances, guest-hosting this show and guest-speak-
ing on that, shaking so many hands, and holding so many press
conferences, it would have looked for all the world like a politician
traveling in search of a constituency, assembling, piece by hard-
earned piece, a political base.

Yet politicians tend to emphasize themselves and their virtues;
Julie is modest and self-effacing. Politicians suggest that they might,

119

if allowed, provide answers for some of the country's troublesome questions; Julie presumes to offer none, skirting most substantive issues. Politicians want something for themselves, and audiences must be on their guard; Julie has always made it clear that she wanted nothing whatever for herself. She was wherever she was only for her father's sake, since he was too busy running the country, too deep in diplomacy, or, finally, too deep in trouble, to speak for himself.

Julie first made headlines as her father's Watergate defender in July 1973 when she revealed that the President had played devil's advocate in a family discussion at Camp David about whether he should perhaps resign. "We have talked about it," said Julie. "But. the whole family says: 'What would be the good of it?' The way my father looked at it for a while was that 'I want to do what is good for the country. If resignation would be good for the country, well . . . ' But all of us feel that wouldn't help the presidency. We feel that he has a lot to give the country still, and he should continue." Next day the White House Press Office issued a denial that Richard Nixon had ever considered resignation, but the public was free to doubt that any mere press office could know as much as the President's daughter about what went on in intimate domestic conclave.

Julie's father, in her view, needed a lot more of just the kind of publicity she was uniquely qualified to provide. She was convinced that the public did not know the real man, the man behind the presidential façade. To counter the widely held notion that her father was a cold and calculating machine, she related anecdotes to illustrate his human, thoughtful side. He was, she said, "the man who got up at 3 A.M. one morning when the POWs were about to be released and jotted down a thought: that each wife or mother should have a corsage from the President when she first greeted her prisoner of war."

In another revealing story, Julie was en route to a friend's wedding and mentioned it to her father as she left. By the time she got there, she found that the President had already called to congratulate the bride. "He startled her," Julie admitted, "but imagine how pleased she felt!" Evidently she takes it for granted that others share her high regard for any presidential gesture.

Julie was always at pains to point out that none of her efforts on her father's behalf had been undertaken at his request. He had never asked her to go out and take questions on Watergate, she said; he never wanted her on the firing line or to experience any pain for his sake. It was her own idea, she insisted, undertaken because she thought she "had a story to tell," and she was "very eager to do it."

On the other hand, he never asked her to stop. Perhaps it was because, as David Eisenhower has since explained, the President had always viewed politics as a joint venture, a family matter. Accordingly, the idea of a member of the family going out and getting politically involved was, in his view, "just kind of natural as the sunrise in the morning." In plain fact, however, daughter Julie was the only Nixon sun when she started speaking up on Watergate: her father had avoided the press for months; Pat Nixon kept herself sequestered from reporters; Tricia was leading a resolutely private life in New York.

From the beginning Julie protested her father's innocence. "I know my father's not involved because he says he's not involved," she announced firmly. Even after two years of Watergate revelations have deluged the nation, she explains that "he was running the country when all of this crap, so to speak, was going on. He didn't have time to sit down and listen to the tapes. He's still finding out what subordinates were doing." Her father's eclipse, she is certain, will be only temporary. She assures reporters that his morale is "darned good." Any talk of mental imbalance is "just crazy." She admires her parents' resilience, explaining that they can still laugh, that they are not bitter, and that "Daddy is planning his future." She was first to suggest publicly—evidently passing along her father's own suggestion—that he might become a "roving ambassador or top-level adviser." After all, she earnestly points out, "When you look back in history, the net worth of the man is going to far outweigh the mistakes."

Clearly, Julie is devoted to her father. The official White House photograph of the two tearfully embracing on the eve of his resignation sums up the quality of that relationship. One can readily believe that she sees Richard Nixon as an undervalued national resource, and she may be helping the country to share that belief.

Julie's admiration is returned. Recently Nixon confided to a friend at San Clemente that he plans to groom her to enter politics. "After all," he proudly noted, "she is both a Nixon and an Eisenhower."

Julie herself has recently taken every opportunity to disavow all interest in a political career, but certainly she was born and bred in politics. As she herself likes to say, "I was a political baby. I learned to walk in the House . . . talk in the Senate." And, as her father recognizes, her marriage, the confluence of two presidential traditions, adds the final touch of Republican rightness.

Despite its appearance of inevitability, the Julie-David marriage was no cradle arrangement. As children the two were barely acquainted, and if Julie had followed Tricia to Finch or David had gone, as his family expected, to West Point, the story might have had a different ending. As it was, he entered Amherst in 1966, the same year that Julie was starting at Smith. At his grandmother's suggestion, he hitchhiked the seven miles to Northampton. "I was just as curious about her as everyone else," says David. "Why should I avoid her just to avoid the jokes?"

Once engaged, Julie waited for just the right moment to break the news to her father. Nixon greeted the announcement with a mild "Oh, that's nice," a reaction that distressed her deeply. But when Pat Nixon passed Julie's complaint along to her husband, Nixon was able to set matters straight by slipping a note under Julie's door. Quoted from memory by Pat Nixon later, the note said: "How lucky you both are to have found each other. Even though you must expect some ups and downs, I am sure you will have a wonderful life together. I am also sure you know just how much happiness I wish for you both." Pat Nixon, too, professed herself delighted with Julie's choice, describing David as "a clean-cut and wholesome lad."

Julie became an Eisenhower in New York's Marble Collegiate Church a few days before Christmas in 1968, with Norman Vincent Peale officiating before five hundred friends and relatives. Former President Dwight Eisenhower was a patient in Walter Reed Hospital at the time, but he was able to watch the wedding on closed-circuit television and send the young couple the message that "David is the luckiest man in the world to get such a girl as Julie." Yet Julie, even at the altar, was still more Nixon than Eisenhower: before embracing her new husband, the bride turned to kiss her father.

From then on, she did her best to entwine the Nixon and Eisenhower traditions. When Julie and David returned to college in 1969, they were two very visible hawks on campuses where antiwar feeling was running high. That same winter Nixon told a *Newsweek* reporter that he saw his daughters as "front-line troops" in the battle to reestablish the traditional virtues—hardly a statement to endear Julie to her classmates. Small wonder, then, that they were glad to see the year end; and when demonstrations over the Cambodian "incursion" forced the President to skip Julie's graduation, she and David decided not to attend the ceremonies either.

Marriage never divided Julie and her parents. Indeed, it seemed to strengthen family ties and give her the very credentials needed to become its most visible spokesman. During college, the young Eisenhowers had spent vacations in a third-floor suite at the White House, and after graduation, with David slated to enter the Navy, it was to Pennsylvania Avenue that Julie retreated.

Calling David's departure "the end of an era for us," Julie

mourned their separation by having her hair cut. "We both knew he'd have his head shaved," she explains. "The day of his haircut, I went into my salon and shocked everyone by saying: 'Okay, cut it off, all off.' " But she adjusted to her newly intermittent married life by keeping herself thoroughly occupied—as student at Washington's Catholic University, where she earned a teaching certificate; as frequent White House hostess; and as tireless campaigner for her father. It was at a Kiwanis rally in Columbus, Ohio, that she announced that she would be glad to lay down her life to save the Thieu regime in South Vietnam.

When David was stationed in Florida in 1971, Julie went to join him there, to live in typical newlywed style in an apartment over a garage. She announced plans to teach in a local elementary school. Alas for typicality, a freak collision with a book wagon on her second day at work broke Julie's toe, and on advice of White House doctors she decided against resuming her job. Before she gave up the post, other teachers had been complaining about Julie's assignment to a non-ghetto school only four blocks from her home, while they had to drive miles to less desirable assignments. The superintendent of schools, a Nixon family friend, refused to comment on these charges of favoritism.

Julie later told the story differently. She had been criticized, she said, for taking the job when other recent college graduates were having a hard time finding employment. "I was offered jobs for $20,000 a year," she protested, "and didn't take them because I felt they were offered because of my name. But I did feel qualified to take a $6,000-a-year teaching job." She went on to compare herself with the Roosevelt children, who, she had read, did not care if they were criticized for such things, while she, on the other hand, had always been extremely careful, "because I wouldn't want anything to reflect on my father." Two years later she accepted an editorial job that allowed her to work at home.

In the spring of 1973 David was released from the Navy and, just three days before his twenty-fifth birthday, he arrived back in Washington to join his wife. It was the week John Dean had warned Nixon of "a cancer within, close to the presidency." Neither David nor Julie knew this at the time, but they sensed the oppressive gloom of a White House under siege. And, in their desire to alleviate the tension, they made several decisions that, in retrospect, they see as ill advised.

David took a job as summer baseball columnist for the *Philadelphia Bulletin*. Though the editor said he did "surprisingly well," not everyone agreed, and David found it a rather humbling experience.

Another mistake was the decision to rent—from Nixon crony and Julie devotee Bebe Rebozo, and thus, scoffed the press, at something well below the going rate—a large and lavish white brick house in Bethesda. Julie still justifies it as having been "so secluded, so good for my parents," but clearly the young couple had not yet found their own direction.

Advice was being offered from all sides, and David's future was a subject of special concern to Nixon, who urged him to run for Congress from his old home district of Gettysburg, Pennsylvania. David's father disagreed, advising him to "get a law degree, do something substantial" before reaching out for a political career. Finally, some of David's possible constituency decided the question for him by informing him that they would vote for him out of loyalty but would have to hold their noses to do so because he was "too darn young." David entered George Washington Law School that fall.

The campus had never been a Nixon stronghold, and in the law school that September there was a special sense of outrage. Faculty, classmates, and the student newspaper chorused their suspicion, indignation, and disappointment. Even among David's small circle of friends, vocally anti-Nixon Democrats argued the issues of Watergate.

Apparently some of it took. After the resignation, David told reporters it had been inevitable: Nixon was "losing on the evidence." For a while he had hoped that Congress might settle for a vote of censure and allow the Nixon Administration to continue. But then he read the transcripts and, as one of his classmates says, "he saw the whole thing coming."

Julie, just as surely, did not see. She had made more than 150 public appearances in 1973 alone, answering questions about Watergate, defending her father, and, along the way, winning golden opinions from all sorts of people. By December of that year, she hit *Good Housekeeping*'s list of "the world's ten most admired women" (where her mother was already entrenched in the No. 1 spot), and a few months later was named "outstanding young woman of the year" by the Women's National Republican Club.

In addition, her job at the *Saturday Evening Post* had expanded, now requiring her to fly out to company headquarters in Indianapolis once a week and work at other times in her own Washington office. She was not reading the transcripts or even talking to anyone who was likely to suggest that her father's troubles were not entirely the manufacture of hostile minds in the media.

David, in semibachelorhood, was to be seen almost every afternoon at the counter of his neighborhood Howard Johnson's, where he studied as he methodically downed his afternoon snack of two hamburgers, an order of French fries, and a piece of chocolate layer cake. Friends recall this as a very unhappy period in his life. As they tell it, David wanted to be at Julie's side "on the front lines." But considering his less belligerent position on Watergate, it seems more likely that he wished she would retreat from the barricades to join him in a noncombat zone. He started talking about going back into the Navy, transferring to the University of Chicago—anything to escape the pressure. Even his friends agree that he was worried that Julie might "spend the rest of her life trying to prove the bastards wrong." Inevitably, as Julie continued in that direction, the strains that were telling on their marriage became noticeable.

David explained to reporters that all those rumors of trouble were greatly exaggerated. Of course he and Julie had their little problems, as what happily married young couple did not, and he detailed just how trivial and commonplace these were in a long interview. Julie, he said, had "a tendency to take things too much to heart." As an example he offered the dishwashing problem: Julie, with her busy schedule, expected his assistance and sometimes did not get it. When that happened, "no matter how hard I try to reassure her that letting down on household chores doesn't mean I feel any less affection for her, I get the sense that she can't understand that."

Another area of contention was that Julie, who "wants to share everything," had a tendency to become impatient when he watched football or baseball on television, a pastime he considers a daily necessity. Then, "when she barks at me, I sulk." Throughout this display of the gee-whiz ingenuousness that had won him the sobriquet Howdy Doody among his detractors, there was no mention of their basic disagreement on Watergate.

Unrealistic as it must have seemed to David, who, after all, had read the transcripts, his wife's tenacity in defense of her father continued in the face of all the information available. "Julie would rather fight all the days of her life than have it end like this," explained an admiring White House aide who saw her as standing up "not only for her father but for a government and a country run by principles." It was not until August 7, the day Nixon conferred with his children in the EOB office—once with Tricia, Eddie, and David, once with Julie all alone—that she at last gave in. "I could only go along with whatever he intended to do," says Julie. "We all agreed."

Standing on the White House lawn as the helicopter lifted her parents away from their political past, Julie was stoic. Pat Nixon's press secretary remembers that last day, and how Julie threw her arms around Jerry Ford's neck saying, "I love you," and how she told Betty Ford, "If someone had to replace my mother as First Lady, I'm so grateful it's you."

Julie herself has described the ending of this chapter of her life. In the midst of packing the Nixon belongings, she says, she was crying over a billfold, five-dollar check still inside, that her grandmother had given her father for his birthday twenty-four years before, when she was informed that Ford was making his inaugural speech. "What touched me most," she later said, "was that he hoped this man who'd brought peace to millions around the world would find the peace he richly deserved."

The idea that her father "richly deserved" the peace Ford wished him was Julie's own addition to the speech and surely reflected a conviction that her father has been shabbily treated. Yet she has never openly expressed such a view, confining herself instead to emphasizing the positive aspects of his situation and suggesting that better things lie ahead. In fact, from the resignation onward, Julie has taken the lead in establishing and publicizing the happily Panglossian attitude that, despite what might seem to others a series of crushing blows and insurmountable obstacles, all is for the best in that best of all possible worlds inhabited by the Nixons and the Eisenhowers.

Two days after the resignation, a friend and his wife dropped in on Julie and David to find them rejoicing in their newfound independence. Julie went so far as to open a bottle of wine to celebrate not only the departure of the Secret Service that had guarded her as a President's daughter, but two gaping holes in her kitchen wall where the White House telephone had been. The end of the Nixon presidency, it was implied, was just what she had been wishing for.

Friends are not the only recipients of these artless confidences about the glories of the new freedom. Julie, previously so circumspect and proper, her skirts at knee level, exults publicly that now she can wear hot pants. David explains how much they enjoy their new life-style, which includes jogging along the Potomac, an occasional evening at the theater, or dining at that perennial Nixon favorite, Trader Vic's. Since they abandoned Bebe Rebozo's Bethesda brick, home has been a $409-a-month two-bedroom duplex in a new apartment complex not far from Watergate. The Eisenhower apartment is cheerful, with a mixture of furniture styles and a Grandma Moses hanging opposite another primitive, "Welcome to Gettysburg," signed by David's Sunday painter grandfather. There they enjoy having friends over for potluck suppers or a round of bridge. Julie raises African violets, while David, an aficionado of board games, alternates between playing Diplomacy long distance (by mail and phone) with brother-in-law Ed Cox in New York, and his second passion, a record collection of golden oldies. Every element necessary for the all-American good life is clearly present.

In addition to all this, Julie has her job, which keeps her increasingly busy. Her folksy writing style ("Love, family, caring about others, belief in our community, belief in our country. These themes strike a responsive note. They speak to young and old") has soothed *Post* readers since 1973. Now, with a new title (assistant managing editor) and boost in pay (up $5,000 to $15,000), she is juggling a variety of assignments. She is editing a set of condensed versions of popular books; she has prepared a collection of her favorite stories for children; the *Post* will soon publish a cookbook she has written; and she edits, reads fiction, thinks up ideas for articles, and works at layout.

Part of Julie's strength comes from her religious faith. During the last year of Watergate, at the suggestion of Billy Graham, she got in touch with Mrs. Elena Page, Washington leader of the Campus Crusade for Christ, a flourishing fundamentalist organization. She also joined a congressional wives' Bible study group. On more than one occasion since, Julie has sought comfort in her religion. Last September, on her first visit to her ailing father after his resignation, Julie telephoned Mrs. Page from San Clemente. "What verse of Scripture means a lot to you?" she asked. "Tell me." Mrs. Page instantly prescribed the first chapter of James, because, she explained, it deals with "trials and tribulations and how God gives us the strength to overcome them."

But above all, Julie's life centers on her husband and the relationship they have built together. Julie, who has said she would have been deeply moved by *Love Story* had it not been for the heroine's profanity, has always been willing to share her own romantic life with the public. One of their most widely published photographs shows her sitting on David's lap. She has also let it be known that she and David carry on the Nixon tradition of intrafamilial correspondence by leaving love notes hidden in each other's books. This can occasionally cause complications, as one Julie reminiscence demonstrates. One night Julie, exhausted from a speaking tour, announced that she was going to bed early. David, who had studying to do, stayed up. But, explains Julie, "I felt so guilty about deserting David that I wrote three love notes to him and dropped them on the rug leading to our bedroom." Next morning, on her way down to the kitchen to cook breakfast, she found the notes still there, apparently untouched, unread. Crushed, Julie accused her husband of indifference, but it was not David who had failed the test.

"He had turned the notes around and written me messages on the other side," Julie explains. "He's like that." Then, reflecting on the meaning of it all, she produces a rule of life: "When you're in love with someone, the emotions have to be renewed constantly."

Apparently David knows that. After six years of marriage, he describes his wife, in seemingly boundless admiration, as "energetic, creative, courageous, tenacious. And," he sums up, "we enjoy a lovely married life."

If Julie's life has been changed by Watergate, it has, by David's testimony, been for the better. "This thing," he says, has not discouraged her or slowed her down, because she has considered it "maturely," using it as an opportunity for growth. "She seized on her chance to stand up for her father," he says, "to go out and get a job and get involved in a profession. And build her life as well."

Indeed Julie has changed since she declared that "strident feminists" were alienating "a lot of women and most men" and asked the question, "What's more important than raising children?" These days she feels that "the image of the homemaker as a shrinking violet—as a mop holder and pot scrubber—is well on its way down the garbage disposal," and when asked about children of her own, she manages to change the subject. She and David say they would like someday to work together, perhaps in some editorial field. Other people suggest that she is a natural for television, and one of last winter's New York rumors had it that she was being offered a spot on a new morning news show. The *Post*, of course, gives her an outlet for her writing, and she says that someday she hopes to try a novel.

But Watergate has brought one big change to both of them: when David and Julie talk about their future, politics seem to have been ruled out. This, of course, represents a 180-degree turn in their posture of pre-Watergate days when David talked of running for Congress and both frankly admitted that they took a future in politics for granted. As recently as June 1973 Julie could say, "David and I will probably be involved with politics for the rest of our lives. We might be working for other candidates—or David might run." Then she added, "Or perhaps I will."

But nowadays Julie insists in no uncertain terms that she "would exclude politics as a career." She emphasizes the delights of a totally private life, the eventual novel; and David supports her, volunteering that the two of them have agreed to stay out of elective politics. "It's an agreement that we renew every so often," he explains, "because we're kind of terrified of it."

But despite Julie's impeccable tact, it is evident that this was a decision reached in the shadow of Watergate, and one very much subject to change. David, no match for Julie in discretion, concedes to a reporter that he is ambitious and that both he and Julie have what he calls "the power drive." After all, he points out, "You do not have the kind of background we've had and then be satisfied living the rest of your life lounging around. We want to be in the middle of things, influencing the course of events." In short, "Politics is in our blood, Julie and me. It's early in our careers, but we think we have a future there."

Indeed it is still early, though Julie once wistfully remarked, "When I was in school, I looked ahead and thought I'd have done much more with my life by the time I reached twenty-five." Even if Richard Nixon was right when he told a former speechwriter of his that it will be "a long, long time" before "some understanding and perspective" on Watergate can be achieved, it seems safe to guess that David and Julie will not be too old to set out along the road to political success. And if the question is, Have their chances been damaged by Watergate? the answer would seem to be no.

In fact, Julie's future may very well have been enhanced, rather than tarnished, by Watergate. Her sustained and vigorous defense of her father became a unique self-designed campaign; though Julie was not a candidate for any office, she came across as an idealistic, high-minded person with an appeal that transcended party boundaries, running on a platform of filial loyalty. It is hard to envision any set of circumstances more favorable to the honing of her skills, the display of her talents, and the winning of a broad and enthusiastic constituency. It might even be said that if there had never been a Watergate, Julie would have been well advised to invent one.

When his grandfather left the presidency, David left notes tucked away in various White House hiding places. "I shall return," they said. After his father-in-law's departure he let it be known that this time, too, there is a secret message somewhere in the White House. Perhaps someday he will return to reveal its contents. Or maybe Julie will.

Maureen Dean

My husband doesn't need any defense.

At last Sam Ervin's Watergate committee and the vast television audience beyond it had the witness they had been waiting for: John Dean, the man prepared to implicate the President himself in the Watergate cover-up. Behind him, throughout his thirty-hour week of bland, monotonous, meticulous testimony, as he piled date on place on name, sat his wife Maureen, a curvaceous ormolu Buddha by Chanel, bleached hair skinned back tight to emphasize the tip-tilted nose, the blue-green eyes, the thinly penciled brows. Once she passed a note to her husband. "I know you're trying to save your voice," it said, "but try to be as forceful as you can."

In the course of his testimony Dean admitted that he had been in possession of $15,200 in "pre-1968" political funds and had removed $4,850 of this amount from his safe to spend on his wedding and honeymoon in October 1972. He contended that he had replaced the money with his personal check and had the stub to "prove" it. Senator Edward Gurney, the committee's most dedicated Nixon loyalist, questioned every aspect of the transaction. "It seems like a lot of money for a honeymoon," he suggested. Dean countered that he was also having his yard done that day and thought he might have to pay for having dirt delivered. The patio, he explained, had been repaired. But, continued Gurney, why had Dean needed so much cash? Couldn't he have used credit cards during the honeymoon? "Well," said Dean, the very model of a frugal, serious, sensible young husband, "as my wife well knows, I try to use my credit cards as infrequently as possible, because I don't like to live on credit." As spectators laughed and Dean was observed to blush, Maureen, smiling sadly, shook her head and closed her eyes.

Most of the time, however, she sat impassive, occasionally sipping ice water, or daintily popping a wild-cherry cough drop into her rosebud mouth, maintaining the enigmatic silence that piqued the world's curiosity. Each day she appeared in a different exquisitely fitted ensemble, always perfectly groomed, always conscious of her effect. Pressed by insistent newsmen, she revealed almost nothing. "It's bad enough to sit here without having to talk about it too," she said. She grudgingly admitted that Los Angeles was her hometown, that she had worked there as an insurance broker before moving to Washington, where she had been executive assistant to the president of the by then defunct National Commission on Marijuana and Drug Abuse. She had met John Dean in California.

As Dean continued to drone out his description of life in a White House more besieged garrison than seat of government, Nixon partisans argued that he himself was, if not the prime mover of Watergate, at least one of its principal framers, now eagerly sacrificing the reputations of others in order to save himself; that all his improbable accusations rested on his unsupported word; that he was, in view of his own known past, a thoroughly unreliable witness; and besides, he was a turncoat. As Dean, unfazed, proceeded to detail his version of the truth, ugly rumors swirled about him. It took little imagination to suspect that they were the only ammunition the White House could lay hands on in an effort to discredit his testimony.

In order to check these stories and evaluate Dean's character for themselves, reporters delved into his past, where they found contradictions aplenty. John had grown up proper, his father an executive, himself well tended and well trained. He was remembered as both brilliant and mediocre, principled and opportunistic. Though his academic record was undistinguished, he was apparently able to write term papers for others (charging a small, unneeded fee) and guarantee any desired grade. College friends remembered that Dean, a Republican, watched the Nixon-Kennedy debates of 1960 with horror. Appalled at the sight of his man doing so badly, he groaned, "Oh, what an ass . . . he's making an ass of himself. Look at him now . . . it's crazy . . . it's stupid." He complained that Nixon would take two or three pages to say what should have been said in a single sentence. "It drove John wild," his old college roommate told a reporter. "He used to laugh at Nixon."

It was this same contradictory, ambivalent John Dean who went on to marry a senator's beautiful blond daughter (from whom he was quietly divorced in 1969) and join a Washington law firm, only to be fired from his first job as a result of what was officially labeled at the time "unethical conduct." A secretary nosing about in the young lawyer's desk drawer had discovered that though he was at work on a client's application for a TV license, he and some friends were simultaneously preparing their own application for the same UHF channel. A year later, when Dean was settled in a respectable government job (one most people assumed he owed to his wife's connections), his former employer softened the "unethical conduct" charge to a "basic disagreement over firm policies."

Aside from these surprisingly unconventional details, there were other touches of panache that sorted oddly with Dean's drab, puritanical public stance. He had apparently indulged himself in a boat, a motorcycle, a maroon Porsche. He wore $300 suits and Gucci loafers. His three-story, centrally air-conditioned white brick townhouse in Alexandria was furnished in Georgian replicas, but one Washington reporter who managed to sneak a look into the game room discovered a large, colorful sign that said FUCK COMMUNISM.

But, of course, John Dean's most interesting and luxurious appurtenance was the mysterious Maureen. Careful analysts of such meager clues as were offered promptly surmised that Maureen (or, as she preferred to be known, Mo) was not quite to the manner born. And sure enough, when reporters began to dig into her background, the story they pieced together was made up of only reasonably presentable scraps, with a good deal of inexplicable space between.

The consensus was that Maureen Kane had been born on October 10, 1945, and grown up in California. Her best Washington friend (Susan Goldwater, wife of Barry, Jr., who had been John's military-school roommate) told a reporter she "thought" Mo had attended U.C.L.A., but nobody else seemed to share that impression. On the other hand, American Airlines confirmed that Maureen Elizabeth Kane had graduated from their stewardess college at Greater Southwest International Airport on April 14, 1966. Her stewardess period lasted five months, and during this time she was also modeling a line of sportswear at the Dallas Apparel Mart. Her employer there later told a reporter that he had introduced her to George Owen, then on the business staff of the Dallas Cowboys, and that the couple had married in Las Vegas in 1967. Owen was director of player relations for the New Orleans Saints from the time they were formed in 1967 until November 1969 when—without Maureen—he returned to Dallas, where he is now in the real estate business.

Oddly, the enterprising reporter who had managed to illuminate this much of Maureen Dean's shadowy past was unable, despite some hard digging, to find any record of either a marriage or a divorce. Owen, now happily married and father of two young children, is reluctant to comment on any aspect of his relationship with Maureen. Though he clearly disapproves of John Dean's decision to bear witness against a President, he will say of Maureen only that she is "a nice girl" (but no different from hundreds of others) and he wishes her well. Unwilling to say anything that might somehow hurt or embarrass his family, he expresses a fervent wish to be "the forgotten man in the entire situation."

After this episode Maureen returned to Los Angeles. Her widowed mother, who always refused to speak to reporters, lived in Culver City until her recent death, and brother Ron Kane, equally taciturn about Maureen, runs a jewelry store in San Pedro. The next verifiable fact in Maureen's life is another marriage, to Michael Biner, a Los Angeles stockbroker, in 1969. His mother later explained, "I don't know much about it. They just came in one day and said they had been married." But that marriage lasted only a few months, and not long after the two were separated Biner was killed in an automobile accident.

The intervals between Maureen's marriages are hazy. Before Biner, she was briefly linked with actor Hugh O'Brian, and seemed to favor sports figures as friends. Meanwhile, or perhaps betweentimes, she is said to have worked as a real estate broker and in a bank.

It was generally agreed that Maureen met John Dean in California, though there were slight differences of opinion as to exactly how this came about. She was said to have been the girl friend of somebody or other (some people even suggested John Ehrlichman), but everyone agreed that Mo and John began their relationship in 1971 and that she moved to Washington in order to continue it.

Arrived there, she worked first as assistant to the director of the National Committee on Marijuana and Drug Abuse, then at the Justice Department's Bureau of Narcotics and Dangerous Drugs. Apparently she was responsible for scheduling training classes for the narcotics agents. This meant setting up programs, arranging for hotels, cars, and equipment in strange cities, and doing a lot of traveling. There were published reports that she had set up programs in foreign countries, too; one credited her with travels to no fewer than thirty-six. From all accounts she made friends, satisfied her employers, impressed people with her efficiency and attractiveness. She was said to "earn" her $10,470 salary.

Yet this job history is very dilute and intermittent. Her first Washington job lasted, as far as can be determined, only a couple of months; the second, eight or ten weeks on a part-time basis. Like the marriages, the friends, the cities she has lived in, every aspect of

Maureen's life seems to have been considerably more than the sum of its verifiable parts. As a history, it is not merely insubstantial and tenuous; it seems intentionally so.

As John Dean began his Watergate testimony, it was reported by a Washington gossip columnist that Maureen, accompanied by her friend Susan Goldwater, had spent most of the previous Saturday evening at Nathan's in Georgetown. Nathan's has the reputation of a gathering place for swinging young professional singles on the rise. Its front door, flanked by a discreet brass plaque that spells out NATHAN's and a blackboard announcing Irish coffee, opens into a low-ceilinged, paneled taproom where decoration consists of a series of framed posters from Paris art shows. There is a restaurant to the rear, but it is along the length of the bar and among the wooden tables tucked beneath small-paned windows that the would-be revelers gather.

Washington gossips promptly spread the word that while John Dean labored to prepare his Watergate testimony at home, Maureen was convivially mingling with new acquaintances at the bar. The bartenders at Nathan's admitted that Mo did come in "almost every night for a couple of drinks," and one, pressed for details, cut off further inquiry with a curt, "She's too good a customer for me to gossip about."

The other most enticing nugget of information about Maureen was unearthed by the same columnist who had publicized her night life. Managing to get a look at the Deans' marriage license application, she found that Mo had listed herself as a widow married only once before.

But the Deans were not going to permit themselves to be defined—and discredited—by a hostile White House or a skeptical press, and they had some extraordinary assets, chief among them Mo's appearance and John's public-relations skills. The efficiency once applied to containing the Watergate scandal was now used to wage an extraordinarily successful campaign on behalf of John Dean's own credibility.

From the beginning, John had made special arrangements with various reporters, leaking to them the selected facts and rumors best designed to protect him against counterrumors and to maintain a profile high enough for effective self-defense. The reporter with whom he established his most successful and productive relationship was Hays Gorey of *Time*'s Washington bureau.

Gorey is urbane, fortyish, and charming, well regarded as a writer. In addition to his work for *Time*, he is a prolific producer of books and articles. But the irony and sophistication of his presence tend to dissolve in his highly colored, dramatic prose. Many people—and reporters—approached the Deans warily in those days, but Gorey, from the start, was able to accept them, with no edge of distaste or suspicion, as two fine young Americans in love—a dose of syrup some found difficult to swallow.

In an early interview he presented John and Maureen at home, John describing their life together, Mo looking on. After a grueling day of testimony, John had arrived home to a dinner cooked by Mo, a review of the day's testimony, and the evening newscasts. After a hot bath and a rubdown by Mo, he planned to get to bed by eleven thirty and sleep well. Modest, eager, a Boy Scout come to lend a hand, John told Gorey he found the strength to testify ("Emotionally, the most difficult aspects were having to talk about the President of the United States as the truth demanded and having to involve former associates and friends") through his love for Mo. "I want to tell you," a fervent Dean continued, "the love of this woman has been one of the greatest sources of strength. You can't imagine how great." Love for Mo seemed, as John told it, inextricably linked with faith in a higher power. Each night, Dean confided to Gorey, the last thing before going to sleep, Mo and John were in the habit of asking each other, "Did you say your prayers?" And to counteract any lingering trace of skepticism, Dean quickly pointed out that he "almost went into the Episcopal ministry," an ambition unmentioned by Dean himself or anyone else in any context thereafter.

All this evidently appealed to Hays Gorey, and he became a family friend. "I'm really very fond of both of them," he says, apparently braced for a touch of dubiety in the listener. "I recognize their deficiencies, and I'm sure they do mine, but I do like them." It was natural, then, for John to think of Gorey when he had the idea that Mo should write a book.

John himself had an on-again, off-again history of negotiations for his memoirs dating back to his emergence as a Watergate witness. A figure of $250,000 was frequently mentioned, and a large piece of that may—depending on what story you choose to believe—have been paid to him and subsequently repaid to the publisher. When the federal prosecutors' office suggested that any book Dean might write could be subpoenaed and used against him, Dean had announced that he was postponing his book "indefinitely."

But a book by Mo would have no legal problems, and it was just after the Nixon resignation that John called Hays Gorey with his suggestion. Gorey was on vacation at the time and, hoping to prolong his holiday, demurred, suggesting that before discussing the matter further they try out the suggestion on Gorey's agent. The agent, unsure in turn, wanted to run it past a few editors. To Gorey's

professed surprise, "everybody was ecstatic." The vacation trun-
cated, the book was begun.

John admitted that one reason he had been inviting Gorey to
visit so frequently was to find out whether he and Mo could establish
sufficient rapport to work well together. It appeared that they had; so
much so, in fact, that they were able to strike a number of friendly
agreements. Gorey suggested that he would be perfectly happy to
give Mo all credit for their joint product, his name to be mentioned
only in a small-print interior acknowledgment. She generously insisted that his name must be on the jacket, and in print as large as her
own. Proceeds will be divided 60 per cent for her, 40 per cent for him,
and there will be large sums to divide. Gorey says it is impossible to
be specific about the six-figure advance, complicated as the contract
is with contingency clauses, but most published estimates call it
$150,000. Gorey certainly was in a position to arrange a more advan-
tageous split, but he chose 60-40 in a spirit of friendship. John Dean,
he explains, is "the most confident person in the world" and had no
worries whatever about making a living even after disbarment. "I
know of several ways to make a living," he had assured Gorey. But
Gorey was less sanguine. "I feel that they may have difficulties," he
said then, "despite John's confidence. And everything Mo can make
out of the book, I want her to make."

Since that time, of course, John Dean's confidence has been more
than justified with his signing of a contract for his Watergate book
that gives him an advance near $300,000, one third already paid. The
publisher predicts that he should make at least $1 million. And
Gorey's steadfast altruism, too, will be rewarded; he will help John
with the writing.

Maureen's book, which will be titled simply Mo, has been publicly praised by her husband. It was he who suggested that she begin a
diary in April 1973, from the time he began talking to the prosecutors, and he has read it. "She has a fine, perceptive mind, and she's a
good writer," he says. Her book, he promises, will "provide a side to
the story of Watergate that no one else could ever provide," and he
believes "she has something to share with other women, and with
men—something that may help others in time of crisis."

This idea of literature as public service is piously echoed by Mo in
her predictions of the book's eventual form. "There will be a lot of
vignettes," she explains, "my philosophy, what I've learned. I hope I
can impart some knowledge to young wives—all wives—of men in
power as to how to handle it and not get lost in the shuffle." She has
also said that "it will concern my feelings, my marriage, the conver-

sations John had with the President, the reactions from the press." It is about "Watergate and what has happened to our lives because of it."

When the book is mentioned in the press, it is usually described as "a love story," but one report says it will portray Maureen as "a once-archetypal swinging single," so much so, in fact, that supposedly "Gorey, a Mormon, is filtering out the raciest aspects of Mo's revelations." Among the materials made available to Gorey (but rejected by him) was said to be a snapshot of a topless Mo astride a motorcycle, her arms about a man other than John Dean. Mo has angrily denied the existence of any such photograph.

The book has also been widely mentioned as a very possible future film, an idea Hays Gorey and the Deans do not find displeasing. They have even argued about the eventual cast. Gorey considers Angie Dickinson a suitable choice for the title role; Mo dismisses her as too old.

Hays Gorey explains that only one chapter will be devoted to clearing up the mysteries of Mo's past, and from then on it will be simply Mo's account of what happened to her as a result of Watergate. In writing it, he refers to Mo's diaries and calendars, with occasional help from John's "phenomenal" memory ("Never saw anything like it," Gorey says). Sometimes, too, he has had Mo write down her feelings in a given situation. For example, when John went off to prison, Gorey explained that he did not want to be present, but "When you get through crying, I want you to sit down with a yellow pad and write what you feel."

But most of the writing is based on long, "incredibly candid" interviews, which sometimes last as long as five hours, and are not tape-recorded. Mo, Gorey insists, is always very cooperative; their common agent, on the other hand, admits that it is very difficult to get Mo to settle down to work.

Mo has been careful to reveal nothing specific about her book, coyly shunting questions aside with "If I told you, you wouldn't read the book." But Gorey is willing to preview a few tepid secrets of Mo's past. Stewardess college, it turns out, was not her only higher education: after graduation from a private Catholic high school, she had a year at Santa Monica City College. Her career in the business world does not interest Gorey much, but he can explain the Owen marriage. It seems that though Maureen thought she was marrying him, he was not divorced at the time, and she—though some might consider it supererogatory in the circumstances—had the marriage annulled. Her meeting with John came about because an aide of Barry

Goldwater, Jr.'s (who had dated her), suggested that if John wanted a date while visiting California, he should call Mo, the most attractive girl he knew. Dismissing the Ehrlichman rumor as nonsense, Gorey says that actually Maureen was an old girl friend of Barry, Jr.'s—though not, he carefully emphasizes, "a mistress."

Gorey seems uncharacteristically specific and detailed in his explanation of the Deans' finances, no doubt remembering that there has been considerable spiteful speculation on this point. Most stories about the Deans included questions about how Mo managed to be so well dressed and idle during the many months when they had no visible source of income. Gorey runs through the arithmetic on the selling of the Deans' Alexandria house to Senator Lowell Weicker and their subsequent purchase of a new one in Los Angeles. He insists that the Alexandria house was sold for $150,000, though all published accounts gave the figure as $135,000. Since the new house cost $110,000, the Deans, he explains, were left with a profit of $40,000, enough for them to live on for some time. What's more, he goes firmly on record, the Dean life-style is far from lavish; it has been widely misreported.

Even more so, by his account, is Mo's personality, and as he sketches it in, it is decidedly unexpected in light of her recorded past. He explains that she is shy and nervous, terrified of public appearances. From the beginning of Watergate, she was begged to appear on television, but she refused because she was frightened. She used to call him and ask him to accompany her to court when John was testifying, and escort her out. In short, she is a very dependent, fragile, old-fashioned woman, and the Dean relationship resembles that of stalwart oak and tender, clinging ivy. Mo, Hays Gorey explains, is totally unliberated and has no ambitions beyond marriage—and, eventually, motherhood.

This description does not fit the woman known by others around Washington. They can hardly believe that anyone could call Mo either shy or nervous. Rather she is seen as bright, independent, articulate, confident. One friend says, "Mo is not shy or nervous. She's exceptionally calm and placid, much like John. Not a nailbiter. She'd eat slow and talk slow. She doesn't get riled up at things."

She is said to be strong-willed, too, afraid of very little, a woman who rides a motorcycle with her husband and is well able to cope with the contretemps of everyday life. When a guest who had had a drink or two too many tried to kiss her at her wedding, an independent and unrattled Mo simply placed her hand firmly on his chest and administered a good, hard push.

Though she does housework and is conceded to be a good cook, she seems hardly an unliberated wife. A friend, describing the Deans' relationship, says, "They're very, very close. I wouldn't say either one clings to the other more than the other. It's an equal thing. One doesn't dominate the other. It's not like many marriages where the husband is totally dominant and the wife is subservient. She's pretty strong, too."

In general, Mo seems to relate better to men than to women. "It might be hard for women to be friends with her," one old friend concedes. "They might be jealous. And Mo is not a fuddy-duddy type of woman who likes to talk children, clothing, and the little things many women talk about." She has a sense of humor, he maintains ("She can banter with you if you start it"), and is not bookish or academic ("No depth conversations on politics and things of that sort"). She enjoys playing Ping-Pong, weekends on the boat, parties at their home, tennis. When Watergate first broke, she and John were planning a trip around the world. And she is indeed gregarious.

On that point Hays Gorey agrees with the Deans' other friends, all suggesting that there is a major difference between John and Mo, in that (as an old acquaintance says) "Mo loves to party and go out," while John is "introverted, selective in his friends, kind of a lonely person." Gorey explains that in his experience John is not a bit interested in going out, a very unsocial person; Mo, on the other hand, when under any kind of tension reacts by going out to dance and have a few drinks.

So from both sides there is some corroboration of the gossip columnist's account of the evening at Nathan's. They agree, too, that Mo has many male friends with whom she might well converse in a neighborhood place like Nathan's. But the implications of pickup aroused by the rumor they reject out of hand.

Certainly the Deans' feeling for each other leaves no room for speculation. Openly, demonstratively, unquestionably, they are in love. Hays Gorey admits he had his doubts on that score at first, but he has now had many opportunities to see them together, and their affectionate ways have combined with their intimate conversations to convince him that "they're very much in love." Friends supply additional support. The Deans, it seems, are uninhibited in their public expressions of affection. "She sits on his lap," says one person who has spent many evenings at their house. "He kisses her, hugs her, all that." At their wedding, which took place at the Alexandria house (Mo in a long, high-necked white dress, hair down, looked like "an angel," as one wedding guest recalls), John unabashedly toasted "the woman I love." Mo blushed and beamed. As one friend soberly explains, the Deans have "a very exceptional relationship. They're two people who are absolutely committed to the marriage, absolutely committed, that's the only thing in life. That's really how the reaction was with both of them."

When John went off to jail in September 1974, Mo began to grant interviews, chiefly to publicize a John Dean interview recently published in *Playboy*, but devoting a few incidental licks to her own forthcoming book. In person she did not correspond to either the Gorey version or that of her other friends, but combined elements from both portraits. She was certainly not timid or shy; indeed, she seemed exceptionally well poised and cool, and her demeanor put many observers in mind of the smoothly professional airline hostess she had briefly been. But though she dressed in today's mode, fingernails fearsomely long and sanguine, the words pronounced by that sweet little voice, an echo from an earlier, more innocent day, made Little Eva seem hard-boiled by comparison.

Yes, Maureen confessed, she had always been a very dependent person, first on her family, then on John. Her history was gently restated by Barbara Walters—a "tragic" life, Walters called it—death of father, death of first husband, terminal illness of mother. Maureen was brave, pointing out that sooner or later everyone meets tragedy. It was clear that she found her strength in her love for her husband. The "worst hour of my life" was the day he went off to prison, though she was sure that this ordeal would only strengthen the bond between them.

Asked by another interviewer if she had any regrets about her husband's decision to testify, Mo brought the conversation right back to their relationship with "I only regret that he's not with me right now." As she explained to a newspaper reporter, "I had become terribly dependent on John. We shared everything. Our thoughts were one. We were like one person. We were together twenty-four hours a day. Now, I hardly see him. It's just visits. We can barely hold hands. I just can't get used to it. And I'm so afraid I'm not dealing with it very well." Yet on another occasion Mo's adjustment seemed to have progressed; she told an interviewer that "I'm learning to have my own independence and deal with problems by myself."

But her attitude toward her husband was consistent. What she feels for John Dean is nothing short of worship. She unflinchingly refers to him as a hero, and can hardly believe that anyone could disagree. She has never, no, never, encountered one single person who had the least breath of criticism of John Dean. And what's more, she insists, neither has he. Every contact with the public, every approach, every letter, has been supportive, complimentary, enthusiastic. In fact, at the press conference *Playboy* called for her in New York, only one question marred the surface of her gelid charm. When a reporter tried to compare her speaking for her husband with Julie Eisenhower's defense of her father, Mo flushed angrily. "My husband," she tartly replied, "doesn't need any defense."

In all these interviews Mo was asked about Watergate, what she knew about it and when and how she learned it. That question had, of course, long since been answered. One of the very first things John Dean vouchsafed to interviewers during the period when he was in and out of hiding, discussing the possibility of immunity with the prosecutors and the Ervin committee, was that he had warned Maureen in advance. Looking back in the spring of 1973, Dean told a *Newsweek* reporter that "I told Mo just before we were married last October that I knew this story was going to break. I said it would be rough, but to hang on and we'd ride it out." Maureen, present at that interview, chimed in, "I didn't really believe it would be this rough." That was May. By June 26, John Dean was referring to the warning again, during the second day of the Watergate hearings. Then his story was that he had told his bride-to-be in September that at some point down the road "it's going to be a rough situation." This time, however, he said he had not explained why.

To the listener who wonders why, after such dire warnings, Maureen did not press for details, Hays Gorey explains that the Dean relationship is such that John (who has "a quality that appeals to a lot of women—gentleness") tends to protect Mo and do his own worrying. When John warned of "trouble ahead," Gorey assumes, he was not very specific; and he is sure Mo would never ask. From his analysis of her character, she is not the type to dwell on unpleasant things; she is able to banish painful thoughts from her mind. In short, she is an old-fashioned girl who trusts her man to shoulder all burdens and keep her safe.

The Deans were married on October 13, 1972, four months after the Watergate break-in. By that time John Dean had been managing the cover-up with total efficiency for four months. But in October the cover-up began to fray, and the Deans were actually summoned back from their Florida honeymoon so that John could devise an appropriate response to the *Washington Post*'s discovery of Donald Segretti's dirty tricks. Presumably, Mo evinced no curiosity even then, asked no embarrassing questions, dismissed any potentially unpleasant thoughts from her mind.

Maureen welcomes the opportunity to explain to sympathetic

interviewers how it could have happened that throughout the first six months of her marriage she had no idea what it was that was occupying so much of her husband's time and attention. She admits that she, as a newspaper reader and television watcher, had formed certain suspicions about Watergate, but she never asked John about them. "Had I asked questions," she maintains, "he would have answered. But he was so tired and he worked so hard, I felt, why bring it up? He'd get home after ten every night and he'd be hungry. I'd fix him dinner. We'd chat about light things. You could see he was not ready for the third degree." Summing it up, she says, in unwitting echo of Hays Gorey, "I have a facility to put things out of my mind that are unpleasant."

Hays Gorey and John Dean have both described the period between the wedding and the day John told Mo about the cover-up, and their accounts sound far less pleasant than hers. Gorey's published description of this time as seen from inside Mo's head tells of John's deepening involvement in the cover-up. "For his wife, the handsome Maureen," he says, "life became increasingly hellish. When John was home, which wasn't often, he was preoccupied, distracted, sullen ... Phone calls at all hours. Summonses to the White House just as guests arrived. All these mysterious urgent meetings. Ordered home from Florida on their honeymoon, even. All this could be endured, maybe. But not John's terrible blue funk. It was getting him, and now it was getting her."

In John Dean's telling, this was a period of agonizing reappraisal, trying to decide whether or not to talk to the federal prosecutors. "There were times after the 1972 election when I was incapable of doing my work," he reveals in the *Playboy* interview. "I would just sit brooding about it. The nights were very tough at home; I drank too much, and I had trouble sleeping. But ... there was virtually nobody I could talk to without getting him involved, and I didn't want to do that." And, speaking of Maureen's book, he says it will tell "how our own relationship underwent strain at times—especially during that treadmill period of cover-up, cover-up, cover-up—and how the experience we've gone through since then has brought us closer together."

The evenings of Ping-Pong, the boat on weekends, those jolly parties at their house—no such things figure in any of these grim reminiscences. But deliverance was at hand. John, after prolonged wrestling with his conscience, at last decided to reveal the truth, and Mo was first to hear it. Hays Gorey has told the story for several magazines. The President had suggested that John and Maureen spend a long weekend at Camp David, during which John could write that long-overdue report on Watergate. It was there—having tried and failed to write the report—that John made up his mind. In Mo's own words, "He sat me down at Camp David after he had thought about his decision for four or five days and told me he was considering stopping this cover-up by coming forward and telling the truth. He also felt the White House would try to destroy him and could I take it? I said, 'Of course, I believe in the truth.' "

Undoubtedly it will be a big scene in Mo's book, and even better in the eventual film. The young couple at Camp David, walking and talking, hand in hand in the piney woods. Spring, the perfect background for romance. But something is troubling the young husband. Something is on his mind. He broods. He goes off by himself. He takes long walks. He tries to write. And at last, after four—five?—days have passed, his mental storm subsides. He sits her down, glorious gilded girl, perhaps in a glade, beside a rushing stream, in that sylvan setting that has traditionally reinvigorated Presidents, and tells her he must decide whether to bring the cover-up to a halt.

Only Mo's book can provide an authoritative account of how she came to terms with this sudden inrush of new facts and insights, and then the somewhat slower process by which their marriage became closer than ever. (As Mo has since said, "The day John decided to go to the prosecutors was the day our marriage opened up.") Perhaps one of those promised vignettes from her philosophy will bring comfort to some young wife who realizes that her husband, longing for someone with whom to share his doubts, his fears, and his misery, has never considered her as possible recipient of his confidences.

Now that John Dean is out of prison, what lies ahead for him and Maureen? Surely not financial problems. In addition to his Watergate book, John has two others in the works, a book of essays on government and a novel, on which advances have been paid. His lecture tour, though he announced that he was curtailing it, seems to have made him very close to the $100,000 originally estimated. Mo has her book, of course, and is said to have turned down, among other offers, a movie contract, a TV commercial, and a public-relations job. Asked what she sees in her own future, she is vague but optimistic. "Husband and family," she says, changing the subject to what John will do.

Somehow it seems unlikely that the Deans will settle down in their Spanish-style stucco house to live happily but quietly ever after. John has frequently disavowed ambition of any and all kinds ("I'm going to have time to smell the flowers," he likes to say), but, as Hays

Gorey points out, John is confident. He is also energetic. Despite his protestations, it is hard to believe that Dean, once the personification of ambition, has now renounced it utterly.

Yet John's deepest ambitions, despite his flirtations with religion and authorship, industry and law, have always been primarily political. Old friends say that what Dean ultimately wanted was an ambassadorship. One, suggesting that "John is the type of guy who could run for the Senate or for governor—and get elected," says he always expected Dean would someday do exactly that. Jack Caulfield, the White House Plumber who specialized in Kennedyana, once admiringly told a friend that "John could end up President one of these days."

The only credible explanation of John Dean's decision to stay on in the White House even though he had good offers outside and was increasingly uneasy about the possibility of the eventual collapse of the Watergate cover-up is that the White House still had something to offer that John Dean wanted. And that something can only have been the hope, if the cover-up could somehow be salvaged, of a political launching pad.

And even after he had turned on the White House, in the darkest days of Watergate, when it still seemed that Dean might lose his desperate gamble for credibility, since there were as yet no corroborative tapes, he did not consider a political future for himself impossible. He rejected the idea, to be sure, saying to Hays Gorey, "I did, after all, rise to a very high position in the government. I've been there, and I have no desire to go back." But even then he assumed that the choice was his.

Perhaps he was right. Dean has always had his admirers. After all, deeply mired in Watergate as he was, and whatever his motives for deciding to speak out, he did tell the truth at a time when everyone else was lying. *The New Yorker* espoused that pragmatic view when it editorialized after Dean's release that he "shouldn't have been sent to prison in the first place, because he did more than anyone else to bring out the truth."

Maureen Dean is already dropping hints. "He could go back into politics. He knows government so well," she says admiringly. "He would contribute so much." Mo, of course, believes her husband is a hero. It remains to be seen whether the American people can ever fully accept him on those terms.

Barbara Jordan

> My faith in the Constitution is whole,
> it is complete, it is total.

Elizabeth Holtzman

> The fish stinks from the head.

When the House Judiciary Committee began its impeachment inquiry in June 1974 it seemed a lackluster group made up of anonymities led by a nonentity. By the time it had finished its deliberations and voted to impeach the thirty-seventh President of the United States, it was a roster of stars. It had brought controversy, instruction, and stirring debate into the living rooms of America, and, as its televised proceedings continued, even inspiration and a measure of illumination.

Among the brightest stars in this new galaxy were two previously little-known women, Barbara Jordan and Elizabeth Holtzman. Perhaps they stood out at first mainly because they were women, but that was by no means all there was to it. Both were unusually gifted and would have attracted attention in any company. Both were articulate and felt strongly on the issues; beyond that, they proved to have qualities of character that suited them admirably to the task at hand: they were tough, uncompromising, intellectually rigorous —and dedicated to what they saw as their duty.

Barbara Jordan, U.S. Representative from Texas' Eighteenth District, is an imposing black woman of formidable dignity and orotundity. Her eloquent statement of constitutional principles made during the committee's impeachment debate electrified a nationwide audience and earned for her almost overnight the kind of admiration and recognition most politicians strive for years to achieve and only infrequently attain. Since then she has been mentioned seriously as a possible future Speaker of the House, senator, Supreme Court Justice, and even Vice-President.

As a public figure, Barbara Jordan is serious, hardworking, and impressive, and, far more than most people, even most politicians, she *is* a public figure. She speaks very little about her personal life, and what is known of Barbara Jordan the private person comes mainly through observation and meager hearsay. Jordan is a large woman, five feet eight, and admits to indifferent health, probably related to overweight. Her frivolity quotient is very low and she eschews makeup and jewelry, except for a small wristwatch, but she does rise at dawn to have her hair done at 6 A.M. and admits to liking good clothes and to spending some time shopping for them. She is said to be good company at a party. One old friend, often quoted on this score, says that when Barbara comes down to Houston they get together for birthdays and "have barbecues and sing and sort of relive our childhoods." Others testify to the Jordan voice, said to be a rich contralto, and her ability to play "a good amateur guitar." Her reading tends to be professional. Aside from newspapers, it is confined to law, history, and political biographies. The women she most respects are Margaret Chase Smith, Edith Sampson, and Constance Baker Motley, because "each has made a significant contribution nationally as lawmaker or judge." The men she admires are Lyndon B. Johnson, Edmund S. Muskie, and Ramsey Clark, because "they are statesmen and great men." Asked what she would do if she were ever to retire from politics, she says she would "catch up on all the reading I would like to do, learn to play the guitar well, and write song lyrics and poetry." But then she adds, "After a long vacation, I would probably go back to practicing law and maybe even go into politics again."

Though she sometimes tells reporters that she does not rule out the possibility of marriage, she has also said she "prefers" to remain single. "Politics," she once told an interviewer, "is almost totally consuming. A good marriage requires that one attend to it and not treat it as another hobby."

Indeed Barbara Jordan seems so impersonal, so thoroughly professional, that it is difficult to imagine her in any ordinary human relationship. In fact, she is frequently brusque to the point of rudeness, and many people describe her as arrogant. A woman with no small talk, who usually fails to greet acquaintances in passing, Jordan is the subject of more than one cautionary anecdote. For example, some years ago when she was in the hospital the wives of the Texas state senators sent her flowers; she never responded by word or note.

Jordan is notoriously impatient, and though she says, "I always regret it afterward" when she is "more abrupt with people than I ought to be," she seems to make little effort to conceal her feelings. In Texas she was noted for rising in the state senate whenever someone made a statement she considered irrelevant, to announce resonantly, "That's a very amusing comment, but let's get on with the vote." She sneered at one opponent, "I have heard your statement and it is full of weasel words." And, with deft mordancy, she once told a fellow legislator who was talking too long about high fertilizer prices, "Congressman, it's refreshing to hear you talking about something you're really into."

Even among friends, her cast of mind seems irremediably sardonic. The day she first entered the Texas Senate, the only black face among thirty white ones, an uncle was there to watch. Congratulating her at the session's end, he said, "Barbara, we looked down and were so proud of you." Her acerbic reply was, "Well, Uncle, you didn't have trouble picking me out."

If she herself seems lacking in those warm human touches that help build an appealing political legend, her background is an almost ideal political asset. Barbara Jordan grew up in Houston's Fifth Ward, a typical black Southern low-income neighborhood—or, to put it more simply, a slum. Her parents were Benjamin and Arlyne Jordan; she was the last of their three children, all of whom were girls. Like their neighbors, the Jordans were poor, but, as Barbara describes it, "so was everyone else around us, so we did not notice it. We were never hungry and we always had a place to stay."

Arlyne Jordan seems to have been, if not oppressed ("No more than any other black mother in this era." is the way her daughter puts it), at least passive. She saw to it that meals were served on time, that clothes were ironed and ribbons tied. "My mother is very bright," Barbara Jordan once said, "but she never had a chance."

It was Benjamin Jordan whose influence shaped Barbara into the uncommon woman she became. He was a Baptist minister who worked as a warehouse clerk to support his family. Education was of great importance to him. He expected his daughters to go to college and become music teachers, as indeed two of them did, and he set high standards. "If I brought home a report card with five A's and one B," Barbara has said, "my father would point to the B and ask what happened."

No one in that household ever dared to question his authority. "My father was a strict disciplinarian," Barbara Jordan explains today, "and I always had to keep the lid on, no matter how angry I got. It did not have to do with his being a minister; it was my respect for him as a person. I had great respect. It was unthinkable to have a hot exchange of words with him, for me or my mother or any of us. So one does develop quite a bit of control that way. I suppose the kids now would say that was not good."

As young Barbara grew up, she longed to distinguish herself. "I always wanted to be something unusual," she recalls. "I never wanted to be run-of-the-mill. For a while I thought about becoming a pharmacist, but then I thought, who ever heard of an outstanding pharmacist?" It was not until she was in the tenth grade at the Phyllis Wheatley High School that she settled on a career, and when the decision came it struck with the force of religious conversion. A black lawyer (and later judge) from Chicago, Edith Sampson, came to address a Career Day assembly, and from then on there was no doubt in Barbara Jordan's mind that she, too, would be a lawyer.

Reaction to that decision has been variously reported. In one account, Barbara's homeroom teacher said, "Fine, fine. We'll see," and her mother said, "We won't worry about that at this point." But the man who was her homeroom teacher at the time has also told the story, and according to him he was alone in encouraging her. His story has a wealth of colorful detail, and the authoritative ring of fiction. As he tells it, Barbara's father appeared one day at the school to accuse him of "encouraging my daughter to become a lawyer. That is no place for a girl. I will thank you to stop." When the teacher asked Barbara later, "What are you going to do now, baby?" she is supposed to have replied: "I am big and black and fat and ugly and I will never have a man problem. The only way I will ever get to college will be if my father pays for it. So I will do exactly what he tells me until I am twenty-one years old and then I will do what I damn well please."

This tale collapses beneath the weight of the fact that it was Barbara's father who eventually spent his hard-earned money to send her through law school, and she herself provides a far more credible account. "It was my mother," she explains, "who was against my being a lawyer. She thought it was not the right thing for a girl. My father said I should do whatever I thought I could."

After graduation from high school in 1952 (she ranked in the top 5 per cent of her class), Barbara entered Texas Southern University, another all-black school. It was there that she lost her first election, for the presidency of the freshman class, but she did become a star debater, leading the T.S.U. team to a series of championships. Though she had already had some success in this line in high school, the T.S.U. debating coach likes to claim credit for burnishing the star. "I took her," he has said, "from a girl who couldn't do anything but read, to a girl who could stand on her own feet without notes. She suffered at the very idea of having to say something without writing it down first." (But no debating coach can claim to have taught her the mannered and elegant diction that so impressed the TV audiences of the Judiciary Committee hearings. A friend who has known her since third grade avers that Barbara has always talked that way.)

Debating was important at T.S.U., and, forbidden to compete with Southern white schools, the team was forced to prowl the North for its victims. Once they went as far as Boston University, and Barbara decided that eventually she would study law there. After graduation from T.S.U. in 1957, magna cum laude, she carried out that intention, earning her law degree from B.U. in 1959. Later that year, she was admitted to the bar in both Massachusetts and Texas. Apparently she hoped to remain in Boston, but since no attractive job offers were forthcoming, she returned to Houston. She had just enough money to have a stack of cards imprinted BARBARA JORDAN, ATTORNEY AT LAW; her office for the next three years would be her parents' dining-room table.

In 1962 friends urged her to run for the Texas House of Representatives. She ran and lost, but she did receive 46,000 votes. "I figured," she told an interviewer later, "anybody who could get 46,000 people to vote for them for any office should keep on trying," so she ran again, losing once more in 1964. Even this, however, did not discourage her. "I just thought I had run a very good race, and next time I would probably win," she concluded. In 1966 she ran for the state senate (against a white liberal), and this time, at last, she won. She was the first black woman elected to the state senate. Self-confidence personified, she said of her victory: "I didn't play up the fact of being a Negro or a woman. It feels good to know that people recognize a qualified candidate when they see one." Unopposed in 1968, she won a four-year term.

During this period Barbara Jordan accomplished a number of things, both legislatively and personally. During her first year in office she was named the outstanding freshman senator. In March 1972 she was chosen senate president pro tempore, an office which entitles the holder to assume the office of Governor for a Day on the traditional one day of the year when governor and lieutenant governor leave the state. She was becoming a power.

At the same time, a double view of her was gaining currency. Her admirers praised her brilliance, her ability to get things done, calling her an "eloquent spokesman against human injustices," as the conservative *Houston Chronicle* put it. On the other hand, there were those who were not so sure. Perhaps, they suggested, she was making deals with the powerful. Perhaps she had sold out to the establishment. By diluting the strength of liberal proposals to get them past the conservatives, was she not betraying the very causes she seemed to be upholding? One liberal state senator, assessing her political evolution with deep disappointment, said, "Maybe it goes back to the old tale of the talents. God gave Barbara so many talents, I expected more of her."

Bitter controversy surrounded her campaign for the House of Representatives in 1972. Her principal opponent in the primary race, Curtis Graves, black himself, charged her with "Uncle Tomism" and, even more cuttingly, with being "the best black congressman that money can buy." He based these insults partly on his charge that she had made a deal with a mainly white redistricting committee when she helped draw the lines for a new congressional district allotted Houston by the 1970 census. Though this was done in such a way as to include a large number of blacks (42 per cent), somewhere along the way a safe black state senate seat was lost.

Jordan refused to answer charges of this nature. As she told an interviewer at the time, "I can get things done. I've pushed a good deal of important legislation through the state senate. I'll run on my record." That record was good enough to bring her 80 per cent of the total vote cast in the primary, and she went on to win the election handily, running far ahead of George McGovern in her district.

As she went off to Congress, supporters and detractors alike waited to see what she would do. True, she arrived in Washington as a protégé of Lyndon Johnson's, and it was his influence that got her the place she wanted on the Judiciary Committee. True, too, she continued to refuse to ally herself with any specialized constituency of blacks or women. As she has said of herself, "I'm neither a black politician nor a woman politician. Just a politician, a professional politician."

Watergate gave her a chance to clarify her position before a nationwide audience. In the speech that would indelibly emblazon her image on the political life of the seventies, Barbara Jordan pointed out that when the Constitution was first written, she as a black was not included in that "We, the people" it spoke for. And yet, she went on, through amendment, interpretation, and court decision, she had finally been included. It was therefore within that proven constitutional framework that she intended to proceed. "My faith in the Constitution is whole," she said; "it is complete, it is total." And as she defended the wisdom and foresight of its framers, she was defending her own decision to form no part of any special-interest group.

When Elizabeth Holtzman entered Congress, she made two promises. One was to her constituents, that she would not stay fifty years. The other was to herself. "When you give up fighting and get too accustomed to the status quo and don't have the sense of outrage you did before," she explains, "you shouldn't be in government anymore. So when that happens—and hopefully it won't for a while—I'll leave."

As every viewer of the Judiciary Committee hearings knows, Liz Holtzman has a capacity for sustained outrage that is likely to endure, if not for fifty years, at least for the foreseeable future. In person it is still evident, though Holtzman is far smaller and less physically formidable than the implacable image of the television screen. Despite pleasant features, conventional dress, and careful grooming, the impression she conveys is cold, wiry, and tense. She does not participate in an exchange; when she replies to a question, she takes the opportunity to make a statement. She seems unwilling to extend herself, to charm or placate.

One begins to understand the comments of reporters who see Holtzman often in Washington. Yes, as reported, she does seem to have a chip on her shoulder. Yes, as claimed, she seems to be all business, a sort of caricature of women's liberation. One newsman explains his bafflement: "I keep thinking there's more to her than I see, and there must be. I admire her. I think what she does is terrific. But she's a very distant person. It's impossible to relax with her." Perhaps this harshness is what her friends refer to when they describe her as shy.

Like Barbara Jordan, Elizabeth Holtzman resolutely conceals her private self. She suggests that personal questions are somehow sexist, as if only women had private lives and no man had ever been the object of anyone's curiosity. Anything outside the confines of her job is almost unmentionable. She admits to wearing jeans and T-shirts at home (though as a trial lawyer she was "brainwashed against pants"). She says she enjoys tennis, sailing, music, riding. As if revealing an atomic secret she says, "I read a great deal." She goes so far as to add, vaguely, that "anything diverts me."

Asked what her underlying concerns are, what kinds of things she really cares about, she automatically limits the question to political concerns, the motivations underlying her career. "One reason I went into government in the first place," she says with obviously practiced ease, "is that I feel very deeply that the system of government should operate decently and humanely and fairly. And I care about the city I was born in and grew up in. I'd like to see that the kinds of opportunities I had would be open to other people."

Pressed as to what she more personally cares for, Holtzman balks. "I'm interested in other things too," she says defensively. "I like abstract intellectual questions. Talking with my friends about personal problems interests me. And there are a lot of things that engage my emotions." What those things may be, she does not say.

As for marriage, Liz Holtzman told one reporter, "I don't regret the life I've chosen." To another she said that she would like someday to marry and have children. It seems irrelevant. As one interviewer put it, "When she does talk, she talks so precisely and with such a straightforward tone that it's difficult to believe that she could ever talk much about anything personal."

It is not easy to find out anything about the private Holtzman from her friends, either. They have been discreet to the point of inanity, revealing such provocative tidbits as "She has a habit of pushing her glasses back up her nose," such illuminating character insights as "Until recently she had a weakness for pizza." Liz obviously resents having her friends questioned. "If people want to find out about me," she says firmly, "they should talk to me."

Her parents have been slightly more accessible. Her mother reminisces with obvious pleasure about a trip to Europe with Liz after her freshman year at college. "All the five-minute-tour guides were upset with Elizabeth," she recalls indulgently. "She wanted to take two and a half hours at each stop."

Liz's father beams with pride at the thought of his daughter's brilliance and accomplishments, even reaching for the recollection that she always went out with "very nice young men." Then, revealing that he knows his prickly daughter's nature well, he brings forth a doubtless well-worn joke. A very serious problem did arise with Elizabeth in her childhood, he announces. "There came a time when she didn't want to kiss me." He asked her why, and (foreshadowing her present self) she told him, "Daddy, be reasonable."

Both parents are Russian immigrants, successful in their adopted country. Liz's father, Sidney, is a trial lawyer; her mother, Filia, heads the Russian department at New York's Hunter College. Liz and her twin, Robert, now a neurosurgeon, went through school together. Robert is reputed to be a rather frivolous, fun-loving, gregarious person, but perhaps he only seems so by contrast with his sister. Asked if she would mind if Robert were interviewed, Liz Holtzman hesitates. "Uh . . . well . . . uh . . . the answer is yes."

Through the years the twins competed, now one ahead, now the other. In high school they ran for president (Robert) and vice-president (Liz) of the student body, their slogan "Win with the twins." The victory celebration at their home was an unforgettable event. "I think they had the whole school here," their mother says. "We had to have the police over and redo the grass."

Liz went on to Radcliffe, where she majored in American history and literature, graduating magna cum laude in 1962. She applied to Harvard Law School because—if one can accept the explanation she once offered a reporter—"the application was easy to fill out" and was accepted as one of the twenty-one women in a class of 539.

After two years as a litigating lawyer in New York, she became a mayoral assistant, liaison between John Lindsay's office and the Department of Parks, Recreation, and Cultural Affairs. Experience in city government was an eye-opening experience. As she later explained to a reporter, "The bureaucracy was all screwed up. The agencies just weren't responding to the public needs." She decided to enter politics.

In 1972 she zeroed in on Brooklyn's Representative Emanuel Celler, the eighty-four-year-old perennial who first campaigned and won office in 1922, during the Warren Harding Administration, long before Liz Holtzman was born—and had held that office for fifty years. Not only did she deplore his unavailability to his constituency (Celler kept no office in Brooklyn) and his congressional attendance record ("the second worst of any New York City congressman," she called it), but she heartily disapproved of his voting record.

She set out to establish an opposite image. On street corners, at meetings, in launderettes and supermarkets, anywhere she could find a voter, she buttonholed her quarry, shook hands, and introduced herself, politicking in the classic fashion practiced long before by Celler himself. In fact, Liz even appropriated his 1922 slogan, "Time for a change."

For some mysterious reason—perhaps because the district had a high index of older voters—Celler, along with many other supposedly savvy observers, discounted his rival's chances. She was a political "nonentity," he said, joking that she was "a toothpick trying to topple the Washington Monument." Overconfident, he campaigned at low pressure. Direct-mail literature, posters, and a few weekend appearances before friendly groups marked the limits of his endeavor. When Liz won the primary, which was tantamount to election, he had no excuses to offer. "My problem," he ruefully explained, "was that I didn't have any problems."

Representative Holtzman's first widely publicized achievement was her fight against the bombing of Cambodia; she originated a court action against it, claiming it was unconstitutional. But she was still not a national figure; it took Watergate to make her that. "Barbara Jordan and I," she explains, "were thrust into circumstances neither one of us could have predicted. I know I certainly couldn't." Both suddenly found that people recognized them in the streets and that they had become heroines to other women. "I can't quite picture myself in that position," Holtzman says now. "It's a tremendous responsibility. My judgment is that if I do my job correctly and do it well, people will respond to that. If you search out a way to be a role model or a heroine, I think it rings hollow."

She found little pleasure, either, in the actual impeachment process. If the way she did her job made an impression on people, "I'm pleased that it would happen in that way." But she refuses to recognize any such thing as an exhilarating moment anywhere along the line. "It was too . . . kinda horrible," she says. "The things we were dealing with weren't exhilarating. They were very depressing and very saddening and horrifying and frightening."

Approaching it in that sober spirit, it was no difficult question for her to decide whether to vote her conscience or try to allow for her constituency, as it was for some members of the committee. In fact, she concedes, "It was fairly easy for me. Most of my constituents voted against Richard Nixon in '72—as did I—and we both started out from that point of view." And as she listened to the tapes, she found her position hardening. The experience of listening, she points out, was very different from reading the edited transcripts. From the beginning, she had been, "frankly, very suspicious of a cover-up," but at the start of the inquiry she had been by no means prepared to say that she had any suspicion of Nixon's complicity in the original break-in. As she listened to the tapes, that changed. "When I finished this inquiry," she says, "I came to realize that Richard Nixon had an unremitting disregard of basic constitutional rights and that wiretapping and bugging political opponents was a way of life to him. And if somebody said now that the evidence showed that Richard Nixon ordered the Watergate break-in, it wouldn't surprise me in the least." What the tapes taught her, she concludes, is that "Richard Nixon was the master of that show. There's a saying, 'The fish stinks from the head,' and that certainly held true in this case."

Yet despite the committee's long investigation she believes that many important Watergate questions remain to be answered. "Some of the crimes," she points out, "I don't know if we even know about." Others have been identified but insufficiently studied. Methodically she ticks them off. "We don't know who really ordered the break-in originally. Nixon has to take responsibility for that, of course, but who gave the order? That should be discovered if we can. Then, there were wiretaps. We know that, and no indictments have been brought. I don't know why, since those taps were purely political and had nothing to do with national security. Then, too, the Huston Plan was authorized. To what extent was that put into effect? We still don't know. And there were personal improprieties of Richard Nixon that should be investigated further—for example, the various funds, and his connection with Bebe Rebozo. All those things should be fully explored."

She hopes they will be. "There may be more indictments," she suggests. Failing that, she still believes that someday more of the White House tapes will be made available, and from them it will be possible to piece together the rest of the story.

As for Ford's decision to pardon Nixon, it was "outrageous." Liz Holtzman takes it as primarily an affront to the Judiciary Committee. Her idea of the committee's main accomplishment was "creating a respect for the established procedures and for the rule of law." By the pardon Ford demonstrated to her "that he simply didn't appreciate what we had done." Moreover, she was offended by the manner in which Ford proceeded. She resented his suggestion that Nixon could not have had a fair trial. And failing that, she is convinced that an effort should have been made to obtain an acknowledgment of guilt from Nixon, as well as to delineate the extent and nature of the wrongdoing of Watergate.

And that she considers this wrongdoing a most serious matter there should be no doubt. "Richard Nixon," she says positively, "represented the arrogance of power, a total disregard for the limits of power established by the Constitution. The Founding Fathers tried to limit power because they knew the temptations that absolute power could have encouraged—and this is where temptation led Nixon. Signing the Huston Plan should be taken very seriously by every American. Civil liberties were infringed, and that's a serious wrong, especially if a President of the United States is involved." The people who have tried to excuse or defend Nixon's actions are, she suggests mirthlessly, "the very people who are first to scream about law and order. It's an irony."

Consequently, she is unable to imagine that Nixon can ever hope to return to a position of respect in public life. "The evidence is clear," she says evenly, "about the part Nixon played. I don't think he can rise like a phoenix from the ashes. Public knowledge of what he did will prevent it."

Yet she admits to having learned one surprising thing from her experience with Watergate. She discovered from her mail that "many people thought that the Plumbers' break-in at Ellsberg's psychiatrist's office was perfectly fine—because Ellsberg was a traitor." Shaking her head, Holtzman declares the idea that the ends justify the means "very foreign" to her own thinking. It had not occurred to her that anyone could think this way and she found it "a sad commentary," because, she concludes, it proves that these people "have no perception of what democracy is all about."

The idea that ends justify means might not seem quite so foreign to Barbara Jordan, that advocate of compromise in place of confrontation. Yet, as she says, "in the Watergate era, the kind of crisis we confronted did not allow room for compromise, because you cannot compromise on criminality. You cannot compromise on abuse of power. You cannot compromise on gross intrusions into the civil rights and liberties of people on the part of the chief executive."

This view of Watergate is very close to Liz Holtzman's. "Richard Nixon," Holtzman says, "was given a very sacred trust. Enormous power was given to him to use for the public interest. Instead, he used it to subvert the laws, to harm the people in this country, and for personal gain. This was an extraordinary wrong—and it helped to undermine the confidence of people in the system of government, which is not helpful to the health of the country."

Liz Holtzman has always been an uncompromising idealist, whose toughness on the issues has been called "crude" and "boorish." Barbara Jordan is a political pragmatist whose loyalties to party and patronage run deep. Yet Jordan is also the woman who once said, "All blacks are militant in their guts. But militancy is expressed in different ways." And on the issue of Watergate, these two very different women managed to establish a substantial common ground. Without hesitation and without uncertainty, they judged Watergate and condemned it. Both believe beyond argument that their conclusions are inescapable. As Liz Holtzman sternly says, "If you condone these things, I don't know what you can believe in."

Patricia Colson

Chuck feels, as a lawyer, that perjury
is a real no-no.

Back in the fifties, when she was a secretary in the office of Vermont's
Senator Ralph Flanders, Patty Hughes was one of the prettiest, most
popular, most vibrant girls on the Hill. Her black hair was prema-
turely threaded with gray, but lithe, slender Patty, who was known to
have dated Jack Kennedy, was a perfect choice for Vermont's Cherry
Blossom Princess. As an old friend wistfully recalls, "She had the
world eating out of her hand in those days."

Recently, in the faded seventies, many an old friend was dis-
mayed to see Patty on the *Today* show grown gray, stout, and
obviously ill at ease, clumsily hoisting the flag for her husband,
Charles Colson, the man who had boasted that he would walk over
his grandmother if necessary to ensure Richard Nixon's reelection.
Though he had formerly taken pleasure in describing his job as "chief
ass kicker around the White House," he had recently been the
subject of a much publicized—and widely questioned—religious
conversion. It was partly in consequence of this access of faith that
Colson, originally indicted as a conspirator in the Watergate cover-
up case, had finally arranged to plead guilty instead to one compar-
atively innocuous count of disseminating derogatory information
about Daniel Ellsberg, thus avoiding a full airing of his Watergate
role. Patty meanwhile was gaining a reputation as the tragic victim of
his career, a woman whose previously carefree life had been shattered
by the impact of Watergate, which had dimmed her personality,
whitened her hair, cooled her marriage, and driven her to the re-
frigerator in search of solace.

The truth, not surprisingly, lagged somewhat behind this dramatic report, but even Patty Colson's closest friends hardly recognized the woman they knew in the Barbara Walters interview.
Clearly agonized, Patty needed several tries to come out with the

statement that yes, she would *consider* writing a letter to the President asking a pardon for her husband. To another equally bland inquiry she replied, with a miserable smile, "That's a toughie."

A friend who was present that day describes this interview as a nightmarish ordeal for Patty. It was her first without her husband, who had just begun serving his one- to three-year sentence at Maxwell Air Force Base Prison in Alabama. Well-meaning friends, and Colson himself, had telephoned repeatedly in the past few days to advise her as to what she should or should not say on the air, and when the too-well-briefed Patty arrived at the Washington studio her nervousness was compounded by the conditions of the interview. She was placed, alone, at one end of what her friend describes as "a room the size of a football stadium" and questioned by the disembodied voice of New York-based Barbara Walters emanating from an invisible source. To add to the general malaise, Walters repeatedly cautioned her victim: "Don't be scared." Small wonder, then, that Patty was less than poised, confident, comfortable.

Yet in person Patty Colson is all these things—and extremely personable. Her short, curly hair is gray, and even Rubens might find her a trifle plump, but the overall effect is one of disarming prettiness in all-American cheerleader style. Her smile is frequent and radiant, and she exudes the cheerful complacency of the securely married. Even while her husband was in prison (where he would spend seven months), and with Watergate still casting its shadow on her future, she remained a candid, humorous optimist, hardly the pitiably dismal creature of the TV screen.

A glance at her past makes the present less surprising. Patty Hughes grew up with every agreeably banal attribute of normality in a happy middle-class Catholic family in Springfield, Vermont. Her father was in the machine tool business; her mother was a housewife ("but with good business sense") who devoted herself to raising Patty and her brother. Family life was close and, Patty notes today with approval, very strict, though it seems never to have prevented her from doing anything she wanted to. Patty was always popular, always one of the crowd, always having fun. She enjoyed all sports and, obviously destined by nature to be a cheerleader, in fact became one. She liked everyone and they in turn liked her.

High school finished, she continued on her pleasant path, taking the job that brought her to Washington at eighteen as Senator Flanders' receptionist. She avoided loneliness by living with an aunt and uncle who had four daughters near her age; their friends soon became her friends. Eventually she worked her way up from receptionist to secretary, and eventually, too, moved into an apartment shared with other girls. Flanders' office was unusually friendly and informal, and working there was a pleasure augmented by the fact that small states place no very rigorous demands upon their senators' staffs.

During this period Patty's brother, an FBI man, was killed in an automobile accident; her father died; her mother came to live in Washington, but she, too, soon died. Patty was then an orphan who might well have felt adrift and sorry for herself, but she continued her self-sufficient life. People who knew her then describe that as a "tragic period," but Patty now does not refer to this series of sad events unless she is asked; she tends instead to look back on those years as a time when she enjoyed her work, her freedom, her limitless social opportunities.

Having so pleasant a life, she was in no rush to marry. Patty had started work in 1948, and time was passing; but it seemed to pass invisibly, and she insists she was not conscious of any nervousness on that score. After all, she points out, most of the other girls on the Hill were not getting married either, and she had plenty of social life. Only once did she come close to marriage—with Goldwater aide Dean Burch, later FCC chairman and presidential counselor in the twilight of the Nixon Administration. But when that romance ended without rancor after three years (Burch remembers her fondly today as "a hell of a gal"), she was still content to wait for the right man to come along.

In 1958 Charles Colson came along. When Senator Flanders retired, Patty Hughes applied for a secretarial job in the office of Senator Leverett Saltonstall, where she was interviewed by a young fellow who prided himself in those days on being the youngest administrative assistant on the Hill. Patty remembers the interview vividly, but not because she was attracted to Colson the man: it was Colson the administrator who deeply impressed her as someone who knew how to get things done. He has since admitted to her that his reaction was somewhat less professional.

Colson in those days was obviously a young man on the rise. He had grown up lower-middle-class in Harvard-awed Boston, a fact that may help explain why he would later harbor feelings about that city's effortless Kennedy clan paralleling those of awkward, straight-haired moppets of the thirties toward Shirley Temple. Turning his back on a proffered Harvard scholarship, he chose Brown where he could be one of the biggest men on campus, and the Marines where he became the youngest—or perhaps *almost* the youngest—company commander in the Corps. Later, while working for Saltonstall, already married and father of three, he went through law school at night. Whatever he did, he tried harder, but his appeal to Patty Hughes surprised most people who knew them both.

"She could have had anyone on the Hill," one old acquaintance sighs, "but from the very first, Chuck Colson was what she wanted. It was hard for a lot of us to understand." Another explains that "everyone loved her but detested Chuck. He created a lot of dissension on the staff, which we had not been used to. At one point, the entire staff almost mutinied." But when co-workers warned her against him, Patty only laughed and said, "I always seem to go for the heels."

Colson is still a man who creates dissension, but his wife is convinced that his bark is far worse than his bite, and that even his bark is charming once you get to know him. "If he could just walk in here now and sit down and talk to you," she says earnestly, "I know you'd think he was the neatest guy you'd ever met." Their relationship is notoriously good, their friends' assessments generally ranging somewhere between the ecstatic and the hyperbolic.

They must have had their share of difficulties at first, considering that he was married at that time, with three young children, and she was a Catholic. In fact, one old acquaintance suggests that Catholic guilt about divorce may explain the change in Patty's figure from the "almost sylphlike" size eight of the late fifties and the more generous outline achieved in the first years of her relationship with Chuck. If so, it is the only noticeable sign of any flaw in the marriage. A former aide, who used to visit the Colsons frequently, describes theirs as a "honeymoon relationship." According to his account, they embrace fondly and frequently, wait on each other, share jokes and secrets, all in "a manner one rarely finds in a middle-aged couple." It is true, too, that on her birthday in 1974 he gave her the gold cross she wears around her neck ("And don't ask me how he managed to get it in prison," she says, delighted). On his birthday, her gift to him was a gold wedding band.

But this emphasis on sentiment makes Patty uncomfortable, and she is quick to undercut the apparent significance of her gesture. "We usually don't give gifts much," she explains. "We buy them together—a painting or something." Her choice of presents in this instance was determined by the unusual circumstances: prisoners, though deprived of most personal possessions, are allowed to keep their wedding rings. Chuck had never had one and, Patty explains matter-of-factly, "He just wanted something secure."

Security, in fact, seems the hallmark of the marriage as its out-lines emerge from Patty's account of their good-humored teasing routines. Chuck, she says, is fond of telling people, "My wife used to date JFK," to which she inevitably replies, "*Once!*" She happily debunks the myth of that memorable date: all they did, she explains, was go out to dinner and dancing at the Mayflower Hotel with another couple, returning in time for a late House vote. Yet she does admit to cherishing an inscribed ("For my old friend Patty Hughes") copy of *Profiles in Courage* and takes the opportunity to point out that despite his well-known objections to other Kennedys, Chuck has always had the highest opinion of Jack.

Patty's mock complaints about her husband are sometimes di-rected to him, as when she holds him accountable for her gray hair ("I owe it all to you") or teases him about the weight he gained when he quit smoking; more frequently, she fondly criticizes him to others, obviously enjoying the opportunity to demonstrate how lovably small his faults are. He is, she says, a terrible host who loves to talk all the time and gets so involved in conversation that he forgets his responsibilities to their guests. On these occasions she tries to attract his attention by grimaces or by kicking him under the table ("People must think I'm a spastic"), all to no avail. His favorite music is the Marine Corps hymn. She disapproves of modern movies and refuses to go, but he still loves them. He is a totally unliberated man and a "disaster in the kitchen."

In short, Colson has all kinds of little ways, and it is plain that his wife accepts them all. In return, he accepts hers. One friend says that if anyone hints to Patty that perhaps she should consider a diet, she is apt to respond by rushing home to make herself a couple of tuna fish sandwiches; but whenever she starts to worry about her weight, Chuck assures her that he doesn't care at all. "And," says her friend, "if he doesn't care, she doesn't care."

Both Colsons are devoted to the house they built a few years ago in McLean, Virginia, a wooded and expensive suburb they coin-cidentally share with several of the odious Kennedys. The plans were drawn by an architect, but Chuck himself planned the layout with the aid of his son Wendell, an architecture student, and enjoyed working on the place himself. Patty, too, spent months seeing to it that Chuck's long lists of orders were carried out, and eventually decorated the house (which was by no means finished when they moved in) in what everyone agrees is quiet good taste, if perhaps somewhat too full of symbolic Republican elephants.

Colson's three children from his first marriage, Wendell, Christian, and Emily, live in a Boston suburb with their mother but spend a good part of their time in McLean with Chuck and Patty—drawn there, Patty jokes, mainly by the swimming pool. Chuck has always maintained close ties with his children, and some friends suggest that Patty may actually understand them better than their own mother, Nancy, who is described as "rather a worry wart." Patty herself says Nancy is "a marvelous mother."

Within the McLean house, demurely Tudor on the outside, hangs Colson's famous sign WHEN YOU'VE GOT THEM BY THE BALLS, THEIR HEARTS AND MINDS WILL FOLLOW. And this solid suburban householder and father is the man who supposedly suggested blowing up the Brookings Institution and, when questioned about it, gleefully assured his interlocutor that indeed he had made such a proposal and had even followed it up by suggesting that the Washington Monument be put in orbit.

This sense of humor is not everyone's, and perhaps it is not surprising that people sometimes fail to understand. Though both Colson's grandmothers are dead, even his own mother protested the projected line of march toward victory. "Grandma Colson wouldn't appreciate that kind of publicity," she scolded. And Chuck, telling the story later, claims he suppressed the rejoinder: "How do you know it wasn't *your* mother I meant?" But Patty does understand Chuck's sense of humor and values it; above everything, both Colsons enjoy a joke, and the people they like are those who can make them laugh. "I don't think they *know* any serious people," one friend says. Another, asked what she and Patty do together, replies, "Oh, just laugh and giggle."

The Colsons have always lived an extremely comfortable life, and one that Patty describes as wonderfully exciting. Going to the White House meant giving up a six-figure income as a lawyer, and such amenities as a power yacht that slept nine, but it is those nearly four White House years that Patty thinks of when she looks back on how pleasant her life was before Watergate. Of course, Chuck's days were even longer than they had been before; he started work at eight, and only infrequently arrived home before eleven. During the day Patty lunched with friends; put in an occasional stint as political volunteer; did all her own housework ("vacuuming the pattern right off the rug—she loved it," one of her friends says); planned what to cook for Chuck's dinner. Whatever activity engaged her, she kept the television set tuned to the afternoon soaps; she only followed them with half her mind but well enough to be considered an expert by the girls in Chuck's office, who would call her for plot briefings or background explanations whenever they missed, or failed to grasp the complexities of, an episode. At night—sometimes napping before he arrived —Patty had dinner ready for her husband, and he, with television blaring and phone constantly ringing, filled her in on the events of his day. Even after that, of course, there was still the White House telephone, that unbreakable round-the-clock link to Nixon. As for social life, the Colsons could have been at the White House nightly, but rarely chose to go. It wasn't, Patty ruefully admits, as glamorous as she had expected it to be. In fact, she confesses, it was so formal it was downright stuffy—you just couldn't put your feet up.

It was at this period that the Colsons decided to adopt a child. In the early days of their marriage, when she was thirty-four, Patty had wanted children and expected to have them, but as the years passed that prospect began to seem remote. Near the beginning of Colson's White House tenure, they formally applied for adoption. Chuck, of course, already had three children, but he was willing to do whatever would make Patty happy. If she wanted a baby, she should have one.

At last her wish came true: the adoption agency notified Patty that a baby was available—and at that point Patty rethought her position. After all, she reminded herself, she was devoted to Chuck's three children; she was over forty; above all, it would hardly be fair to the unknown infant to adopt it unless she was absolutely sure that she wanted it. She had to admit that she was not quite sure. Eventually Patty called Chuck at the White House to tell him, "Call the lady and tell her I've decided the answer is no." She has never regretted that decision. As she says now, "I'd love to have had our own—we both would—but it just didn't work out." It will only happen "if that's what the Lord wants."

All this adds up, one might think, to just the life to make a wife droop and fret at the long hours of absence, the unfilled days; perhaps to feel neglected, or even to resent playing so peripheral a role. Yet Patty never did. She was far too good-humored to resent anything for long, and too sympathetic to a man subject to intense job pressure. Besides, she was happy.

Because Patty had so evidently organized her entire life around home and husband—with not even a baby to distract her—the Colsons' friends worried about what would happen to her when Chuck went off to prison. To make matters even more difficult, he would not be staying at Maryland's nearby Camp Holabird, where at least Patty could conveniently visit him. Chuck, who has a circulatory problem, had requested permission to serve his sentence in a warm climate and was being assigned to Maxwell Air Force Base in

Alabama. Of course, the concerned friends admitted, Chuck was as emotionally dependent on Patty as she was on him, but he was a man and, what's more, an ex-marine: he had already demonstrated the ability to endure solitude and hardship. But what would become of Patty, the dependent wife?

To the surprise of almost everyone, including herself, Patty did not pine, sigh, and fade. On the contrary, in trying to raise Chuck's morale, she discovered unexpected reserves of strength. Her schedule became hectic, her assignments onerous. Back and forth she flew between McLean and Alabama, taking advantage of every possible visiting opportunity, every available telephone. Apparently the Colsons' long-distance calls were costly enough to make it almost an economy for Patty to do her calling from an Alabama motel.

Between visits she had plenty to occupy her. She was Chuck's liaison with the rest of the world, carrying out his instructions on a variety of legal and personal matters. She read all his mail (he was averaging thirty letters a day), routing most of it to three volunteers who spent their full time answering it, and keeping the trickiest for herself. She kept up a steady stream of letters to Chuck; she began a diary; she took notes for a cookbook she might write. But, most important to them both, she dusted off her secretarial skills and became her husband's amanuensis.

Much of Chuck Colson's time in prison was spent dictating and revising the material that will eventually become two books. One is his "religious book," which will detail his conversion and prison experiences. The other, which in Patty's opinion is "a fantastic book," will be an account of his three and a half years in the White House.

In a number of interviews both before and since his prison days, Colson claimed that he would never consider writing such a book. He said he had turned down three offers to write books about his intimate daily contact with President Nixon, one of them including what he called "a considerable advance," because of his deep belief in the importance of maintaining presidential confidentiality. But this "fantastic" book seems, from Patty's description, to breach the principle of confidentiality as thoroughly as it could be breached. Because Chuck intends it as a historical textbook for students of the future, it will include everything—about war, foreign policy, his day-to-day dealings with the President, *everything*—that he learned at the White House. It will differ from other Watergate-related books in that it will be not merely inclusive but balanced, chronicling both triumph and failure, the mean and the sublime. The Colsons agree that this book should not be rushed to completion. They prefer to wait until those other Watergate books—all written, they believe, in a partisan spirit or "for the fast buck"—have been forgotten. Then, "at the right time," theirs will come out.

Of course, there was another, inescapably less positive, side to all these changes in Patty Colson's life. Her husband had, after all, been a central if shadowy figure in a national scandal; however courageously they might meet the problem, its impact on him and his family and their future was bound to be painful. Chuck's father, in the midst of planning a visit to his son in prison, died of a heart attack. Chuck's mother, embittered, blames her husband's death on Watergate.

Patty herself had to contend with a temptation to be bitter. Throughout Chuck's imprisonment she insisted that neither she nor her husband harbored bitterness or animosity toward anyone, describing a state of mind that others might have labeled "bitter" as simply "disappointed." She was ready to admit to disappointment on three counts: first, that her husband was in prison in the first place; second, that anyone could be convicted on so ridiculous a charge; and third, because Chuck's sentence was disproportionate to those of other Watergate defendants. (Chuck himself was in the habit of telling friends that he was serving half his sentence for himself and half for former Attorney General Richard Kleindienst, who had gotten off with a suspended sentence, a nominal fine, and a few comforting words.)

Chief among inequities, of course, was the Nixon pardon. Even this, however, never brought either Colson to a repudiation of Nixon himself. Patty manages to express a reasonably convincing happiness that that "terribly beaten" and "terribly sick" man was pardoned. After all, she points out, his current plight is "a tragedy" because he "had so much to contribute." Then, too, she can sympathize with the mental strain he has been under for so long; she understands, after going through all Chuck's difficulties, what that must be like. Just the strain of remembering what he said when . . .

Of course, Patty married into her allegiance to Nixon; however much she may admire all those wonderful things he achieved for the country, clearly Chuck's loyalty is a more personal one.He, after all, knew Nixon in a different way, and frequently saw him alone, as Patty never did. Chuck, Patty says, was always a person Nixon could relax with, and laugh with. Far from holding Nixon responsible for his own troubles, Chuck wrote the former President a letter on the day after the resignation. In it he tendered, as well as his "bitter disappointment" that the goals of the Nixon Administration would never now be achieved, his "great loyalty." And two months later Chuck received a reply expressing appreciation of his loyalty and the former President's certainty that a man of Colson's strength would bravely endure the hardships of his situation.

Any resentment, then, is carefully diverted away from Nixon and toward Gerald Ford. Ford must have known, Patty says acidly, that Chuck was in prison simply for following Nixon's orders; when he decided to forgive the ex-President, he most certainly should have extended a similar mercy to his followers. Though she *wasn't* bitter, she *could* have been: the grounds were there in Ford's decision to grant amnesty to the draft dodgers. "My husband served his country," Patty points out grimly, "and it's a *little* hard to take." To underline the irony of it all, it turns out that when Chuck arrived at Maxwell Air Force Base, he occupied a bunk just vacated by the first draft dodger to be pardoned.

Then, she recalls, to provoke further disappointment there was the announcement, made soon after the Nixon pardon, that Ford was "studying" the possibility of pardoning the others. Patty's hopes were high, only to be dashed in what she refers to as "the yo-yo bit" when Ford later announced that each case would be considered on its merits. Patty was convinced that Chuck's merits conclusively outweighed those of others, since he, after all, had never committed perjury ("Chuck feels, as a lawyer," she says seriously, "that perjury is a real no-no.") So she wrote Ford a letter. In reply she received what she calls "a cryptic note" from Philip Buchen, Ford's counsel, advising her that requests for pardon were to be handled through the Justice Department. Inquiries there produced no result, no one, apparently, having informed them that this was one of their duties, so Patty wrote again, expressing her "disappointment," only to receive another Buchen missive to the effect that he was sorry she felt that way. Patty does not know to this day if Ford ever saw her letters.

Finally, of course, Chuck was released on January 31, 1975, on the order of Judge Gerhard Gesell. Serious family difficulties" were cited as a major factor in the decision, but no specifics have been offered. Presumably they included the deterioration of Chuck's mother's health and the previous week's arrest of his younger son at the University of South Carolina on charges of possession of marijuana with intention to sell. Accounts published at the time suggested that Patty had been seriously ill, or even on the verge of breakdown, an idea her friends dismiss as ludicrous. Reports made much, too, of the weight she gained during her husband's imprisonment, but Patty, though she admits to dieting, refuses "to make a big thing of it."

In fact, despite the dislocation of her life brought about by Watergate, and despite its undeniably painful effect on the whole family, Patty considers her situation a fortunate one by comparison with that of other Watergate wives. It would be, she says, "a devastating disappointment" to find out only after the fact, as some of these wives did, what your husband had been doing. Worse would be the knowledge that he had not felt he could tell you the truth. This above all Patty hopes will never happen to her, because then "you'd lose a little respect for your husband—and I hope I never do for Chuck." She, unlike those other wives, was always in intimate touch with everything that was happening, with everything Chuck was doing at the White House; she was always wired in.

Since she was so fully informed about his activities, she could discuss his decisions with him and even, perhaps, disagree. She admits that she usually came around to Chuck's way of thinking ("He's always so persuasive"), and, of course, the responsibility for any action he eventually took was his, but she has always shared his political life. Just as she would later watch the Watergate hearings and read the transcripts, so she had always read two newspapers attentively. And why? "Because if you're in politics, you have to be on top of everything." When she read or heard something that would interest Chuck, she called him at the White House; he had to know what was going on in the world outside, and helping him with that was her responsibility.

Housework, cooking, and television were part of her life, but they were not its center. Other people might interpret Patty's role in light of the traditional wifely stereotype, but that was not the way she thought of herself. As she explains it, she never could have quit work after all those sixteen years to become just a housewife. "No way," she says. She never could have adjusted to it.

After all, Patty had been in politics ever since she first came to Washington at eighteen. It would be wrong, of course, to romanticize her job. She was, as she herself always emphasizes, just a secretary. Not an executive secretary, mind you, but a plain secretary. And yet, that admitted, she was contributing all that she had to give. Politically she was always, as an old friend puts it, a hired gun, in the sense that she worked for a senator and that was her politics. That is true of most people who work on the Hill. They are hired guns who must subjugate any personal political feelings to whomever they are working for; they are in the implementation business. Yet they at their level, like their senatorial employers at theirs, are undeniably in politics. And if Patty was in politics as a senator's secretary, she was no less so later as Chuck Colson's wife.

She had never been an originator of policy, a theorist, a dreamer of great political dreams. But she had a practiced eye for the means the theorists employed; she knew the ropes, understood the political realities—and her job was to help implement their policies. Throughout her political life she had had the good fortune to work for men she respected, whose decisions she may occasionally have disagreed with but in the main admired. Chuck Colson is no exception in that line. He won her respect at their first job interview, and he has kept it.

Patty looks down on those she feels are lacking in Colson's political savvy. Of Haldeman and Ehrlichman she explains, with some contempt, that "they had different backgrounds from ours." She clearly feels that Haldeman's background in advertising and Ehrlichman's in zoning law constitute inadequate credentials. Then, too, real political people have a grasp of reality, are in touch with the real world, the real people out there. They are not insulated and they are not naïve. "Coming from California, or wherever they came from," she explains, dismissing Haldeman and Ehrlichman from serious consideration, "you just don't get the feel you do in Washington. Sometimes they just didn't understand what it was all about." Chuck Colson, Patty knows, was the only one who always told the President the truth, not just what he wanted to hear.

Patty loyally resists any suggestion that her husband ever did those things people said he did. Asked about the phone call Magruder says Colson made to him, urging approval of Gordon Liddy's bug-and-break-in budget, she insists Colson had no notion of what that budget was intended for. And she points out that as soon as Chuck suspected that Mitchell might be involved in Watergate, he took his suspicions immediately to the President. Now, she says, he blames himself for not having made a stronger case for candor. She seems quite willing to accept the notion that it took the experienced, practical Colson six months to guess that CRP was implicated.

And yet, as Patty talks about Watergate and what was done, it begins to seem that all this recitation of when who knew what, and what who said to whom, is really almost a formality. It hardly matters to her exactly what happened, or exactly who was responsible, because she really does not believe—as clearly Chuck does not believe—that any of what was done was wrong. Chuck, after his celebrated conversion, announced that he had moral qualms about having disseminated derogatory information about Ellsberg, even though the President had repeatedly urged him to do so. His prayer group concurred in his decision to plead guilty to that charge. Patty, on the other hand, has never been able to see what was wrong with Chuck's action, feeling as she does that Ellsberg "belongs behind bars—for the security of our country." But beyond that one trifling disagreement, the Colsons are united in the assumption that Watergate is something that has befallen them, a wave that has inundated them—certainly not the result of any action taken by Chuck.

Their view is that Watergate was, pure and simple, a political purge. As Chuck explained it to Patty, other countries have had political purges in the past, and now there has been one here in the United States. "They went from the bottom to the top, or from the top to the bottom, whichever you want to call it," Patty Colson says, "and brought everybody down." She is resigned to its impact on their lives, because it seems to her that there was nothing either of them could have done to avert it. "How," she asks, "could Chuck avoid being brought down, how could he stand over to the side, having been so close to President Nixon for all those years? There's no way. No matter what he did right, it didn't matter. They were just out to get everyone, and they have." When Chuck went off to prison, both Colsons thought of him as a political prisoner.

The "they" who were out to get everyone were, in Patty's telling, the Watergate committee, the prosecutors, and the media. She rejects the idea that their actions in any way reflected the will of the American people. Outside of Washington, she says, there is tremendous sympathy, as she knows from the mail Chuck has received. There have been, in fact, only two hostile letters, and Patty threw them away. What the vast majority of the people really want, she says, is to forget Watergate.

She is convinced that it will in fact soon be forgotten—and rightly so. It may, she admits, have some mild and temporary good effects; she and Chuck agree that campaign funding has long needed reform. "There was just too much money floating around CREEP." But taking it all in all, there will be no real change. Politicians will fall back into their accustomed ways.

For the truth as Patty sees it is that nothing that happened in the entire course of the Watergate scandals was in any way different from what has always been the accepted mode of politics. As a person intimately involved over the years in Washington's political life, she feels qualified to speak with some authority. "If you go back in history," she says, "you'll see that there isn't one thing in Watergate that hasn't been going on for years and years on either side." She readily admits that it was "stupid," but insists that it was essentially unimportant and that the same thing could have happened to the Democrats. "The break-in itself," she says, "was nothing. It's so incredible—the breaking in of an office shouldn't bring down a government."

But looking back on Watergate is not something Patty likes to do. When she thinks back on it now, she thinks of it as simply a waste, a terrible waste of talent and devotion. "It's an awful price to pay for serving your country," she says sadly, "for the years and the hours that Chuck put in." It is not a part of their lives she and Chuck want to dwell on; they want, she explains, to get on to future things.

Perhaps, she suggests, there comes a point in everybody's life that is traumatic, a point at which things must be reevaluated, and this has been it for the Colsons. Their lives will be different now, because "Chuck thinks differently now." This change in Chuck's thinking, of course, was not brought about by Watergate but by the conversion that has altered his direction in life. Now, if Chuck is allowed to practice law again, it will be a different kind of law. Now he wants to change the penal system, and lecture, and, of course, finish his books.

As Chuck's changed thinking alters the direction of his life, it alters Patty's as well. As a devout Catholic, her husband's discovery of the consolations of religion so late in life has come as rather a shock to her. But it does her heart good, she says, to see what it is doing for him, and she has even tried a Bible class in an attempt to share at least a part of the experience with him. She tries her best to embrace his new decisions about their future, making them hers as well. Dutifully, she follows him on the newly discovered path of humility and social service. They are "doing wonderful things together now," she says.

Being the wife of a prisoner for seven months, she insists, has left a mark on her. If she had not seen prison for herself, she never would have known what it is really like. Now that Chuck is free she knows that what she really wants is to devote her life to helping the prisoners who are left behind, those men with no one to speak for them. "If it hadn't been for this experience," she says, "I never would have known. I would have *liked* to help, but I wouldn't have really understood. Seeing prison makes you realize that standing around with a glass in your hand . . . that's not where it's at."

As for politics, she and Chuck "will always have that interest," she admits, a touch of wistfulness creeping in. But because of Watergate they know they won't be in politics again "for a while." Resolutely looking forward now, Patty is ready, as she has always been, to follow Chuck into dubious battle, to make his cause, whatever it turns out to be, her own. He may think differently now, but he is still the man who won her respect so long ago for knowing how to get things done. And she is still, after all, a hired gun.

Jill Wine Volner

There'll never be another case like this.
It was the chance of a lifetime.

There was something almost theatrical about the Watergate cover-up trial. Maybe it was the crowd lined up outside, good-humored and expectant. They came each day at dawn, tourists and Washingtonians alike, the young in ponchos, the middle-aged clutching steaming coffee cartons, to sit in Judge Sirica's courtroom.

The spectators knew it was a momentous trial, with its testimony of misdeeds by men who had once been the highest officials in the land. There was an exciting sense of history come to life as White House tapes brought Richard Nixon's voice into the courtroom. And the scene itself was dramatic: the hunched-over figure of Judge John J. Sirica at the bench; the prosecution witnesses, suddenly sprung from prison to recite their litany of sins; the well-known faces of the five defendants.

The lawyers clustered before the judge. On one side were the seasoned establishment attorneys representing Mitchell, Haldeman, Ehrlichman, Mardian, and Parkinson; on the other, the young lawyers of the Watergate task force, working under Special Prosecutor Leon Jaworski. The defense was split into a series of separate constellations, but the prosecution team was united in constant consultation—passing notes, conferring on strategy, hissing suggestions to each other. They were out to prove a case that had been long and grueling months in preparation.

Among them, a veteran of those months of work, was a young woman, the assistant special prosecutor often referred to as the "No. 2 man on the task force," Jill Wine Volner. She had won headlines in December 1973 when she questioned Rose Mary Woods during grand jury hearings on the eighteen-and-a-half-minute gap in a crucial White House tape. In court, her style was simple, direct, without flamboyance; but with unfailing concentration she led her witness step by sensible, unhurried step, into one damning contradiction after another.

A woman lawyer is still a rarity in the American courtroom, a woman prosecutor rarer still, and Jill Volner quickly became a celebrity. Yet however professional her demeanor, however impressive her skills, most of the public insisted on viewing her not as a lawyer but as a woman.

Jill is a handsome young woman, blond, wholesome, and sturdy. Though she proclaims herself "a hopeless athletic failure," it is easy to imagine her as yesterday's diver or figure skater, rounded arms aloft, smiling with satisfaction as she performs a gracefully exuberant leap before an admiring crowd. Newspaper accounts were apt to mention her lawyerly prowess in passing, then to concentrate on her milk-and-honey good looks. Her hemline was usually her headline. Hardly a story missed the opportunity to estimate the number of inches of Volner thigh exposed by that day's court appearance. Eventually it began to seem that her full formal title must be Miniskirted Lawyer Jill Volner.

Leon Jaworski, the Texas attorney who succeeded Archibald Cox as Watergate special prosecutor, downplays the significance of Jill's abbreviated costumes. Pointing out that Judge Sirica never complained about the miniskirts, he adds, "I certainly wasn't going to, in this day of women's lib." Evidently he regarded them with a tolerance mixed with amusement and admiration. He enjoys telling an anecdote about the photograph taken of him and a miniskirted Jill as they walked together to the courthouse on the morning Rose Mary Woods was to take the stand. That picture appeared on the front page of the *Houston Chronicle* next day, and one of Jaworski's fellow elders in the local Presbyterian church rushed, brandishing the picture, to the minister. "Remember that prayer meeting we held for Brother Jaworski before he left for Washington?" he cried breathlessly. "Well, it's working! It's working!"

Jill Volner certainly did not grow up in a way that would lead any rational observer to suspect that she would ever break new ground or occupy a particularly unusual position. Her background was thoroughly conventional, and few careers have had a more haphazard start. Jill herself seems not particularly interested in surveying or analyzing her past. Perhaps it is just the lawyer in her laying out the facts, but she looks back with no special affection or enthusiasm. "It was a nice childhood," she says. "Nothing stands out as a trauma or as a wonderful experience."

Jill Wine was born in Chicago, raised in Skokie, Illinois, the eldest of three children. Her father was a C.P.A. with his own accounting firm; her mother "was very happy being a mother and was a great mother." There was always the expectation that all the children would go to college, and Jill explains that her father insisted on the importance of being a well-rounded person, active in extracurricular activities, even if it meant a drop in grades. An able student, Jill seemed to manage one without the other.

Although she always enjoyed writing, she had no flaming ambitions as she was growing up. One aunt was a professional woman and Jill can still remember the excitement of going to the airport to see her off on a business trip. "I thought that was neat," she says. But it was certainly a step removed from the life she knew.

At the University of Illinois, Jill plunged into sorority life at Iota Alpha Pi. But, though she later became its president, she found that most of her best friends were men. In general, she says, the women she knew were not interested in current events or politics; they "wanted their M.R.S. degree." She herself was engaged for a while to "a great college beau, the life of the party," a relationship that ended with no great distress in her senior year. *That*, she says, "would have been a stereotypical relationship."

Jill's college career had been eclectic, and, though she always expected to work eventually, she still did not think in terms of a profession. She had begun as an occupational-therapy major but, daunted by the realization that this would eventually entail the dissection of a cadaver, she switched the next year to education for the mentally retarded. Finding that unstimulating, she went into journalism. Suddenly in her senior year she found herself with no fiancé, no plans for graduate school, no real career. Journalism seemed to promise, at best, a job as copy girl. She had, however, taken law boards "as a lark" in a constitutional law class the year before, and when Columbia Law School accepted her, she decided to go. She had some vague intention of eventually applying a legal background to writing, and a more definite interest in living in New York.

Columbia was a shock, with its highly competitive atmosphere and student body. Jill, accustomed to success with little real effort, for the first time did not do well. "I did not love law school," she says carefully. As a matter of fact, the best part of that first year was Ian David Volner, then in his last year at Columbia Law. They met during orientation week, became engaged shortly after Christmas, and were married in August 1965.

It was Ian who persuaded Jill to return to law school after a year off spent at a somewhat unsatisfactory job as an editorial assistant.

She went back to Columbia to make the dean's list, was sparked by a course in trial practice where she discovered she liked being a prosecutor, and ended up winning a prize for the best brief in New York State in a moot court contest.

After her graduation in 1968, both Volners decided they wanted to work in Washington. That fall, Jill's résumé was sent to Henry Petersen, head of the Criminal Division at the Justice Department. She was hired, the first woman prosecutor there. By 1970 she was trying major labor racketeering cases in Detroit, Alaska, Boston, and St. Louis, amassing the trial experience that eventually led to her being tapped for Archibald Cox's special Watergate prosecution force. She jumped at the chance, signing on in July 1973.

Jill was assigned to the chief task force, the one charged with the investigation of the Watergate cover-up and direction of the Watergate grand jury hearings, headed up by the five-foot-five Richard Ben-Veniste, a thirty-year-old New York lawyer. Because of Jill's courtroom experience, Ben-Veniste chose her to assist him with the questioning of witnesses. The two of them handled it all in the months that followed, alike in their persistence and their passion for thorough research as they divided the witnesses between them.

Together they survived the Saturday Night Massacre, that convulsive twenty-four hours during which a desperate President forced the departure of Archibald Cox, Elliot Richardson, and William Ruckelshaus from government, bringing down on himself an outpouring of some three million protesting letters. During the weeks of insecurity that followed, "All of us," Jill says, "thought we had been fired or expected that if we hadn't we all would be very soon." Some members of the prosecution force resigned at that time in protest, but to Jill resignation as a moral protest seemed an empty gesture. "We felt very strongly—or I felt, at least," she says, "that what we began had to be finished. And that as long as we weren't fired or forced to do something that was unethical or immoral or in any way violated our own principles, we should stay. That that was the moral thing to do."

Within a month the Texas lawyer Leon Jaworski arrived in Washington to take over the investigation, and though the very fact that he was a Nixon appointee was enough to elicit doubts in some quarters, Jill reserved judgment. "We all felt he should be given a chance to show whether he was going to permit us to continue our work," she explains, "and to pursue investigations wherever they led." Her hopes were well founded. As she explains, "Mr. Jaworski turned out to be a quite strong man and to lead us as we had been before." Relieved, Jill Volner settled down to work.

If the media sometimes seemed to forget during the course of the trial that Jill was in court not as a model for some new brand of panty hose but as a prosecutor, fellow members of the legal profession did not. Miniskirted she might be, but her gifts as a lawyer were still noticeable. As Jaworski says, "Jill is all business in the courtroom. She has very, very good taste in the questions she asks." Calling her "a very talented lady who, I think, has demonstrated that a woman can perform successfully in the courtroom," he predicts that "she can well achieve what fame she wishes as a trial lawyer."

"I can still remember her memos," says the Columbia Law professor who hired Jill as research assistant her last year at law school. "I can still see her straight-up-and-down signature and her straight-up-and-down thinking." Even in those days, he adds, it was "obvious that she was going to make a hell of a lawyer."

The judge who presided at her very first trial agrees. He recalls being flabbergasted on learning that it was her first time ever before a jury. "She's an excellent lawyer," he says, "but the real significant thing is that she knows how to go for the jugular vein. She's an excellent cross-examiner and she knows how to destroy a witness."

Yet if some people did her less than justice by insisting on seeing her only as a woman, others were no less insistent on ignoring her professional talents to concentrate on her as a representative of womankind. As they observed Jill, a woman performing in traditionally masculine terrain, they waited, alert for slights—and found them.

In December 1974 Robert Mardian took the stand, and Jill conducted the cross-examination. Admittedly an impatient man at the best of times, Mardian showed utter contempt in court that day. "I'm not going to dignify that with an answer," he barked in reply to one of Jill's questions, then turned toward the jury, shaking his head in mock despair. He might, of course, have treated a male prosecutor to a similar display of rudeness, but most people believed that his scorn was directed at Jill's sex and that he was doing his best to involve the jury in sexist complicity with him. Judge Sirica evidently assumed just such an attitude when, tiring of the verbal duel between Jill and her witness, he finally told Mardian, "You never gain by arguing with a woman."

All along there had been suggestions that Judge Sirica himself could benefit from a little consciousness raising. Many of his listeners had not forgotten, either, that on a previous occasion, when Jill and Rose Mary Woods were disagreeing, he had concluded that witness and prosecutor were quarreling over a triviality and ended their exchange with "All right, we have enough problems without two ladies getting into an argument." Sirica admirers pointed out the extenuating circumstance that it was twelve thirty, arguing that perhaps hunger had led to uncharacteristic sharpness. But more were offended by the attitude implied, and they insisted that Sirica owed Jill an apology.

As a final example of sexism encountered by Jill during her Watergate experience, some people point to her selection as the person to question Rose Mary Woods. They seem convinced that the choice of a woman for that task, by any means other than pure chance, would constitute a sexist put-down. When such suggestions surfaced, denials were prompt and firm. Ben-Veniste dismissed reporters' questions with a joke. Jill had been assigned, he said, "Because she's my No. 2 man. We're all men here." Jill agreed: "This is a nonsexist office." On another occasion she protested, "She wasn't the only person I questioned. I don't think it was in Rick's mind to assign her to me because I was a woman." On yet another, she insisted, "It was chance."

Today, Leon Jaworski explains that chance had nothing to do with it. "I selected her," he says calmly. "It was a very sensitive situation, a touchy subject, and I thought it would be better, all things considered, for a woman to conduct the questioning." The implication is unmistakable that a man (perhaps especially Ben-Veniste?) would have appeared bullying and ungentlemanly as he bore down upon the wilting Rose. As Jaworski diplomatically puts it, "A man would have been in a more sensitive spot."

Jill herself is hardly a militant feminist. She tends to shrug off most slights or sexist comments that come her way, and is not at all eager to offer any examples or discuss her reaction to them. She has even told a reporter about one judge so eager to demonstrate complete fairness that he insisted on addressing her as "Sir." She did not react with anger to the incessant comment on her miniskirts. "My hemline is irrelevant," was her usual measured comment. Sometimes she explained with the faintest hint of feminine helplessness that she could hardly afford to buy a new wardrobe each time fashion decreed a new skirt length; sometimes she said that all her recently bought clothes had long, long skirts. To reporters who wondered why she did not switch to pants, she explained, "I've never worn pants to court and I'm not about to. I'm not here to revolutionize the courtroom."

Eventually she went so far as to admit, "I'm a little sensitive about people's comments on what I wear. They don't comment on what men wear into court." But she certainly does not insist on her right to conduct herself exactly as a male lawyer would. Comparing her own techniques to those of men, she explains, "I'm no less ambitious, but I'm not as aggressive or loud. It wouldn't be appealing to a jury, they wouldn't accept me. It's bad enough that I'm a lawyer and doing what they think a man should do—but if I did it the *way* a man would, they wouldn't accept me." And then she concedes, with just a touch of regret, "Besides, I don't think I'm capable of it. I'm just enough imbued with the stereotype."

Women's liberation is not an important concern of hers. She feels she has had to come to terms with the question on her own. As she puts it, "I was really there before there was a movement." But she did belong to NOW when she lived in New York, and she does credit the movement with making people more sensitive, more aware of the problem. "When you flash an angry look now," she admits, "people notice." She is quite conscious, too, of her own role as a pioneer. "Because of all the publicity," she points out, "I am much more accepted by male attorneys now, and hopefully I can set an example for other women who may aspire to be lawyers."

But though she is quiet about it, she does think of herself as a liberated woman, liberated by her own definition, which is "doing whatever you want to do." As she explains it, "My sister is as liberated as I am, because she's raising a family and that's what she wants to do. It wouldn't be liberated for me, because I don't want to do that."

In a good deal of Jill's publicity, however, her personal life is seen as something less than liberated. Even though her husband shares household responsibilities with her, and despite the fact of their two separate but equally successful legal careers, he is frequently pictured as a man who competes with his wife and resents her success. In this view, her struggle to liberate herself is a lonely one, made more complicated by her marriage.

Ian Volner is a large, casually attractive young man with frizzy hair and a quizzical manner. As he explains, "There have been several articles that said I resent her fame, notoriety, whatever. I've given up trying to convince people otherwise." This is ironic in view of the fact that Ian Volner has probably been the greatest liberating force in Jill's life.

Jill herself says, "I think the marriage that I have is a fantastic one based on mutual respect and a great amount of independence for both of us in terms of our careers and our thinking." This concept of marriage results to a great extent from Ian's expectations. As the Volner relationship has evolved, so have their individual roles. Jill's background, as she realizes, was based firmly on all the time-honored stereotypes about men, women, and marriage. Ian's was not. His expectations were modeled on what he had experienced growing up with a mother Jill describes as "a female chauvinist." Over a long period of time, Ian had had the chance to learn that fathers can do laundry, that mothers do not necessarily stay at home and cook the meals, and that though the children may at times feel deprived at not being the center of full-time attention, there are benefits for them, too, in such a situation.

Accordingly, Ian Volner has been flexible in the marriage, and those who see him as a man who prefers meek subservience or feels threatened by strength are quite mistaken. Ian's reputation as male chauvinist ogre seems to derive mainly from a newspaper interview he once gave, one which has caused both Volners some pangs of embarrassment. This interview was liberally spiced with such characterizations as "level-headed up to a point" and "a restless personality." He called Jill "a fairly vain woman" and described a "glorious battle" in which she struck him with a hairbrush. Friends have criticized him for this interview, Jill says, and "hit him about the head and shoulders." She herself still seems slightly hurt. "He says he was misquoted," she explains. "He was taken out of context. And I *hope* he didn't say those things, because that interview certainly doesn't speak well of our relationship."

The fact is that he probably did say all those things, but the impression that emerged from the published piece was a long way from what he had intended, and he has been leery of interviewers ever since. Jill was upset, he says, "and justifiably upset." As he explains it, the reporter assured him that "it was not going to be another of these damn 'miniskirted lawyer' routines." She told him she wanted to understand what Jill was like as a real person, "and I was trying to show that she is a real person. She is a *real* person." The title of the published interview turned out to be "A Lawyer in Miniskirts."

Having given a good deal of thought to the disastrous interview, Ian Volner has concluded that the writer had "a distinct bias." As he tells it, "She asked, 'Do you admire your wife?' I said yes. That never got in. 'Do you respect her abilities?' I said yes. 'Do you feel you're in competition with your wife professionally?' I said no and that never got in." He says he does not know the source of the reporter's bias but he is sure that "she resented Jill's fame and glory and wanted to make her look bad—through me. She made it look as though this woman's husband doesn't have a high opinion of her, and she did it by using things through which I was attempting to show that I have a very high opinion of her—but second, and equally important, that I recognize that my wife is a human being."

His worst mistake, he thinks now, was telling about the hairbrush episode, though, he adds in exasperation, "If there's any married couple who hasn't had a fight . . . !" What he was trying to demonstrate through the anecdote was "the strength of Jill's intellect and the strength of her sense of herself." He thought he had made it clear that in picking that fight in the first place, he was in the wrong. "I was being a wise guy," he explains, "and Jill took it up to a point—and then said no. She cut off that argument for good and sufficient reasons. She sensed that I wasn't going to change her mind and she sensed, probably correctly, that I only half believed it myself and it was futile and had to be brought to a halt. And I was very, very impressed by what she did, and I was trying to convey that I am very impressed with my wife's abilities. What I succeeded in doing was making her look like a buffoon, and that I did not want."

He has learned from the experience that he cannot adequately convey what the dynamics of their relationship are or what he thinks of Jill. From now on, he announces wryly, his official position will be that his wife does everything superbly, that she has nerves of steel, and that she is thoroughly and totally indifferent to how she looks. But then, less guardedly, he admits that such a position would be not far off the truth. "She does things awfully well," he says, "a lot of things. Everything she turns her hand to she does well. When she commits her considerable energies to something, she succeeds. I have never seen her fail at anything."

Clearly the marriage is working, whether he can explain its dynamics or not. "What can you say," he asks rhetorically—"that you love her? Of course I love her—what does that prove? Or that it's fun? Well, my marriage is fun. It's always fun because the unexpected happens, and the expected happens." And there is no question in his mind that "if she has an intimate, it's me—and vice versa."

Certainly there seems to be something competitive in the Volners' marriage, just as there is in a good tennis match, but it is a match between equals. Just as Ian recognizes and respects Jill's autonomy, he expects his own to be respected. He rejects the suggestion of subservience on either side, pointing out with some asperity, "I also have ego needs, I have aspirations, ambitions, professional responsibilities, and personal responsibilities." Decisions are made jointly, with care that neither one should oppress the other; both believe in compromise. And one decision that remains for them to make is whether or not to have children. They have discussed the impact that would have on their marriage, and they have not yet made up their minds.

Jill admits, "That has been a troublesome question for me." When she was growing up, marriage to her meant husband, home, and decorating. "I never associated children with marriage," she says. "I haven't resolved what I'll do. Will I reach my forties and be sorry I didn't have children? Or reach them and be sorry I did? I don't know. I enjoy my career. My husband enjoys my career. And having children without giving up work—well, I have all the normal guilt of the stereotype: you have children and you stay home, or you deprive them."

She does concede, though, that she is beginning to think that children can grow up well if the time devoted to them has quality, even if it lacks quantity. After all, she muses, most children have, in effect, only one parent, and "My husband loves children and he's willing to take more responsibility for children than I am . . ."

Ian, though he says he too is still considering the question, apparently leans toward the idea. He believes people have children for reasons very similar to those they have for marrying. "You know you like children," he suggests. "They have insights and something to offer. So the rewards plus the detriments, the pain, are worth the effort. That's what you say when you get married. You'll never know what having children is going to be like until you try it—just like marriage." And as for the lifelong commitment a parent undertakes, he adds, "I surely didn't get married on the assumption that if it didn't work out I could walk away from it. I got married on the assumption that it would be a near-disaster—but that it would survive." For life? "Yes." Trying to fit the whole question of children into the framework of his life with Jill, he describes their approach as "opportunistic." As he explains it, "where the opportunity exists to make a change in our life-style because one or the other of us wants something, and it doesn't create an impossible impediment for the other, I would suppose we would do it—and I'd include children within that."

Whether or not she opts for motherhood, the end of the Watergate conspiracy trial offered Jill the opportunity to stop for a while and consider her future. Few people, she realizes, have such an opportunity, a natural breaking point in their careers, for taking stock. She considered entering private practice, going back to the Justice Department, or perhaps a return to her original interest, journalism.

Now that she has resigned from the Justice Department, she has received a number of offers from various sources, but has made no long-term commitments. "I'd like to make a decision wisely," she says. As for journalism, she hesitates. As late as November 1973, she says, she was considering it seriously, but as the Watergate trial continued she realized increasingly "that I really do like the combat of the courtroom." Reporting, she says, is "a more passive kind of job. And while it's very important to report on what's happening, my main interest lies in doing what people are reporting about." But then, evidently still undecided, she adds, "Unless I got into something like investigative reporting, I would rather be a lawyer."

One thing she has no plans to do—at least in the immediate future—is to write about Watergate. "Oh, maybe later," she concedes, "but that's far enough off in the future that it's just something that will have to simmer—if I ever feel I have anything that can properly be told and that would be of value to anybody. There have been so many Watergate books, and I'm not sure that my insights are going to be better than anybody else's. And because of my obligations as a lawyer, the ethical obligations, it's a little difficult."

The Watergate trial dominated Jill's life for more than a year and a half. It forced her to work six or seven days a week, often until nine in the evening. Jill describes the work involved as "emotionally and physically demanding," explaining, "I've never been forced to make so many ethical decisions or spend so many hours at the office." It placed a strain on her friendships (what friends remained had to delay dinners in ovens, postpone their own plans, adjust to Jill's hours) and even her marriage (as she explains, in terms of household responsibility Ian had "what he would call the fuzzy end of the lollipop"), and it exhausted her. Yet there is no question in her mind that in accepting her job on the Watergate task force she did the right thing.

"There'll never be another case like this," she says with absolute conviction. "It was the chance of a lifetime to work on it, in a professional sense as well as a historical sense. And if you believe—as I do—that the legal system is the way to remedy any legal wrong, then it was philosophically a good place for me to be."

Jill Volner is a lawyer, a thoroughly professional one. Accordingly, she believes that "every man has a right to a defense," and she could conceivably have been on either side of this case. She might have found herself defending Haldeman, Ehrlichman, Mitchell, Mardian, or Parkinson. Yet she is reluctant to believe that she might have chosen that course of action. "When a trial becomes a political issue," she says thoughtfully, "I'm not sure if I could support *any* cause." But then, thinking it over, she concludes, "But if I had freedom to conduct the case as I wanted . . . perhaps."

The issues of the Watergate trial have clearly affected her. She has measured the extenuating argument that bad things may be done for good motives against her own convictions and discarded it. "If loyalty makes you do things which are wrong," she says flatly, "then loyalty is not a good thing." She has given some thought, too, to the Watergate wives, some of whom must have suspected that their husbands were involved in criminal behavior. "You would lose so much respect for your spouse," she says, "how could you go on living with him?" Her own experience with Watergate, she says, has taught her something important: "It has made me much more attuned to the importance of ethical values and taking responsibility for what you personally do. And what you personally do is not just what you do. It's also what you know is being done by your superiors as well."

The Watergate conspiracy trial found four defendants guilty. As Jill Volner points out, it is the function of a trial to determine whether a particular statute has been violated. Beyond that, however, lies the question, Did the legal wrong constitute a moral wrong? That is a question no court can judge. In the case of the Watergate defendants, the moral issues are complex. To decide whether or not any of the actions taken by the defendants throughout the course of Watergate constituted a moral wrong—and if so to define that wrong and assess its gravity—is, Jill Volner says, "for the country to judge."

The sentencing of Mitchell, Haldeman, Ehrlichman, and Mardian was to begin at nine thirty on the morning of February 22, 1975, and by nine o'clock those involved were gathering. Prosecutors and defense lawyers, defendants and reporters arrived, some aloof, some pleased to greet each other after a separation of nearly two months. At nine twenty-nine Judge Sirica entered, to begin the sentencing.

Jill Wine Volner knew that the sentencing did not mark the end of the Watergate affair; nor did it mean that the four convicted men would enter prison then or ever. Yet this day marked the end of her responsibility. In the courtroom were the spectators, the lucky ones who had begun lining up outside the courthouse the night before, waiting those long, dark hours to witness the ending of this historic trial. The judgment of the court was final now, but for these spectators, unofficial representatives of the American people, the process of judgment was just beginning.

Rose Mary Woods

I don't *know* if I left my foot on the pedal. I
am telling you what everybody *thinks* happened . . .

Richard Nixon once expatiated publicly on the role Rose Mary
Woods has played in his life. "Next to a man's wife," he said, "his
secretary is the most important person in his career. She has to
understand every detail of his job; to have unquestioning loyalty and
absolute discretion. On every count Rose measures up. I'm a lucky
man."

Even today, after she confessed to the most famous blunder in
secretarial history, Nixon still seems to value his association with
Rose Mary. For though he lives in lonely exile and reduced financial
circumstances, the ex-President continues to pay her a handsome
salary for performing what to the outsider seems a rather imprecisely
defined task a continent away. The world may never be privy to
Rose's thoughts about her new circumstances, or to her reflections on
Watergate—including those tortured hours when it seemed she was
being abandoned by the boss she had served so faithfully, as he
fought for his job. Rose continues the soul of discretion, turning
aside curious reporters' questions, her thoughts and actions filtering
only occasionally through friends and other third parties.

But that is hardly surprising in light of Nixon's long-ago description. Unquestioning loyalty and absolute discretion have always
been Rose Mary Woods' middle names. Not only did she understand
every detail of her boss's job, but she was probably a good deal more
important to his career than his wife ever was. Over their years
together, it must have been satisfying indeed, and deeply reassuring,
for him to see this woman bowed over her notebook as she took his
dictation. A man who lacks confidence in himself looks for unflagging
dedication from those around him; their zeal buoys his spirits, as-
suages his doubts, and infuses him with renewed resolve.

From the beginning of their association, a well-publicized lust for toil united Nixon and his secretary, twin saints of the work ethic. When he was Vice-President, she was hidden away behind an unmarked door in the basement of the Capitol, but it was known that she had five secretaries there to assist her, her desk was equipped with seven telephones plus an intercom, and she started work at seven. From that time on, she labored straight through the day, including lunch, during which the Vice-President was wont to dictate rapid-fire memos for the guidance of his staff while munching a sandwich. At night indefatigable Rose returned to her apartment, usually carrying a full briefcase and accompanied by another secretary to whom she would dictate during the evening. Even after that, there were phone calls from friends and strangers, all wanting something from Nixon.

When Rose Mary flew, she had her typewriter strapped on a table across her lap so she could type without interruption by take-off, landing, air pocket, or rough weather. And on the ground she was equally prepared for emergency. When Nixon reached her by telephone at a wedding reception in a Washington hotel to tell her Eisenhower had just had a heart attack and that he wanted her to make some calls for him, Rose calmly installed herself in a lobby phone booth and got down to work. Later in the day she notified government operators to switch the Vice-President's calls to her at the dinner party she was attending. Her hosts postponed the meal for two hours, but the telephone never stopped, and Rose Mary had no dinner that evening. More impressive still, she indulged in only an hour's sleep, as calls continued throughout the night.

As a secretarial high-water mark, there was the occasion when Nixon was summoned from the 1956 Republican Convention to the bedside of his dying father. He picked up Rose Mary in his limousine and, as they zoomed to the airport behind a police motorcycle escort, dictated to her the speech in which he would accept renomination to the vice-presidency.

Throwing in one's lot with so exigent an employer might not tempt every secretarial aspirant, but there were rewards. One was the salary, which would eventually climb to $42,000. Rose Mary could afford a two-bedroom co-op, professionally decorated in shades of beige and brown, in the luxurious Watergate complex. Her evening gowns were glittering and numerous; her jewelry, value unspecified, sufficient to tempt burglars to the Watergate.

Aside from that, the job offered a varied social life. Centrally, there was intimacy with the Nixon family. There was the opportunity to baby-sit for the Nixon daughters; girlish exchanges of clothing with Pat Nixon; jolly "just family" gatherings, such as the Camp David Halloween party after which Nixon had his mask sealed in an envelope for forwarding to the archives along with his presidential papers.

Rose had outside social interests as well. Not only was she a devoted aunt to her many nieces and nephews, and dear friend to a number of government secretaries, but she was much in demand at Washington parties. She loved to dance and stay out late and, according to friends, she sometimes drank a bit too much. That, they said, was the Irish in her.

In recent years, her most frequent escort has been Robert Gray, a perfectly groomed, extremely successful Washington lobbyist who for five years was part of the Eisenhower Administration. True, nobody seems to have considered for so much as a millisecond the possibility that Bob Gray might have any romantic interest in Rose. One friend described his role in her life as just that of a presentable escort with nice manners who "won't fall down drunk on a date and have to be carried home or anything." But as extra men go, Bob Gray is a prize.

As for a more intense and passionate love life, some friends and observers maintain that Rose Mary has had, or could have, such a thing. They repeat the story of an old hometown love, a high school basketball star, who died of meningitis before Rose could marry him. Others have heard rumors of a yet more ghostly presence, a businessman waiting patiently in Chicago for the time when Rose decides to settle down. One friend insists that Rose herself informed her that she and the mysterious Chicagoan will wed within a month of Rose's departure from the White House, but that prediction loses some of its luster with each passing day.

This putatively glamorous but certainly undemanding private life left Rose Mary free to play whatever part Nixon might design for her in his crisis-to-crisis progression through public life. When his vice-presidential motorcade was stoned in Caracas by what were generally described as mobs worked up to a frenzy by Communist agitators, Rose Mary, as usual, was on hand. Because, as she said, she wasn't going to let "those people" see her cry, she had put on her dark glasses, and she credits this move with saving her eyes when stones broke two windows of her car, leaving her with minor cuts.

This hardly amounts to a star turn on the stage of history, but at least Rose was demonstrably present among the supernumeraries, a fact that must impress some of the 4,500 people back in Sebring, the Ohio town where Rose Mary was born. Three of the five Woods children settled in Ohio, and Rose might well have been expected to do the same.

Sebring is a pottery town, and Thomas Woods came there to work as a potter at the Royal China Company, where he later became foreman, and eventually personnel director. The people of Sebring remember him as "a prominent citizen." It was from that "hot-headed Irishman" that Rose inherited her red hair; she thinks she got his temper, too. Her mother, Mary, though also Irish, was apparently the gentle one whose sweeter nature still struggles for dominance within Rose's soul.

Rose grew up in a pleasant shingled house across the street from the Catholic church in which her parents had been married. The placidity of her life was interrupted only once, by a bout with disease. She has described it simply as "a growth," and says that, wasted to eighty-two pounds, she was forced to drop out of high school for treatment. The growth disappeared, but Rose's friends still like to say she "conquered cancer." In any case, she was able to return to school, where she was proving a whiz at secretarial subjects. She won a prize, in fact, as the best all-round commercial student. In those days, she was taking shorthand at the impressive clip of 150 words a minute.

After graduation, Rose went to work in the office of the Royal China Company. The woman who managed it was an old family friend, but she denies hiring Rose as a favor to her father. "I hired her," she says, "because she was a very quiet girl and never a pusher. A model young woman, really." Rose lived up to that description fully for more than seven years; nobody would have guessed her life would take a turning that would eventually expose her to the Communist-maddened, stone-hurling mobs of Venezuela. But at that point her sister, who was working in Washington, D.C., was overwhelmed by some unspecified personal tragedy. Rose went to Washington in 1943 to console her, found a typing job in the same office, and started along the path that would lead her to Caracas and, beyond that, to Watergate.

Her third job in Washington was with a special House committee being formed under Christian A. Herter, then a Massachusetts congressman, later Secretary of State. Through this committee she somehow met Richard Nixon, the man who would become "The Boss." Stories vary. Perhaps she noticed his neatly typed and itemized expense accounts, so strikingly different from the indecipherable scrawls of the others. Or perhaps she met Pat Nixon at one of Herter's parties and was impressed by how nice and friendly she seemed and how kind the Nixons were to drive her home afterward. However it began, the generally accepted story is that Nixon offered Rose a job as his secretary in 1950 just after he was first elected to the Senate. According to this version, she asked for a month to think it over. After all, she knew nothing about politics and had never set foot in California. What should she do? Friends advised her not to let the opportunity slip. Nixon, they said, was a bright young man on the way up. She heeded their advice.

But one friend offers a rather different version of the Woods-Nixon connection. In this telling, Rose Mary presented herself as a job applicant. She was pretty sure she would be hired, but there were two confessions she felt obligated to make. The first was that she was a Democrat; the second, that she was a Catholic. Her friend explains the second reservation: "You see, Rose remembered a time, back when she was growing up in Sebring—well, she remembered a cross burning on her family's lawn one time, see, and she figured that might work against her being hired." When a reporter tried to check this colorful tale in Sebring, people there conceded under pressure that it *might* have happened, considering that most of Sebring was Protestant, but nobody could actually remember a cross burning.

No matter which version of the hiring you choose, the ending is the same: Rose Mary Woods became Richard Nixon's private secretary, and from then on she shared his fortunes, good and bad. From the beginning her ambitions for him were high—so high, in fact, that she wept as she watched him on television being chosen as Republican vice-presidential candidate in 1952. "It's such a waste," she told a friend. "He's so young. Why do they want to make him a nothing? They're going to bury him in the Vice-President's office."

Apparently she came to terms with the idea in time to commit herself fully to his campaign, during which she played a role in another of Nixon's six major crises. This one was occasioned by the discovery that Nixon was the beneficiary of a fund collected for him by wealthy businessmen. One newspaper headlined the story SECRET RICH MEN'S TRUST FUND KEEPS NIXON IN STYLE BEYOND HIS SALARY, and it attracted national attention, greatly to the surprise of Nixon and his political intimates, who seemed to consider it nothing out of the ordinary. Eisenhower, on the other hand, found it worrisome. He opined that Nixon would have to convince "fair-minded" people that there was nothing unethical about the secret fund, and went on to ask rhetorically, "Of what avail is it for us to carry on this business of what has been going on in Washington if we ourselves aren't as clean as a hound's tooth?"

When Nixon heard of this, he forced a disbelieving smile and muttered something; no one could understand, or at least no biographer is willing to reveal, exactly what. Mrs. Nixon exploded to a friend, "Why should we keep taking this?" Days of indecision followed—should he withdraw from the ticket or should he not?—before Nixon finally delivered the famous televised address in which he piously proclaimed that the fund was only his way of trying to save the taxpayers' money and, artfully shifting the focus away from that difficult subject, announced firmly that the one thing he would always keep, even if it *was* a gift, was that little black-and-white spotted dog six-year-old Tricia Nixon had named Checkers.

After this speech, thenceforth to be known as the Checkers Speech, Nixon gathered up his notes and threw them on the floor. He called his performance a flop and wept in his dressing room. When congratulatory calls began to pour in, he briefly "came to life," as his official biographers put it, only to languish again when it seemed that Eisenhower, the one indispensable convert, had not been won over. An inaccurate and incomplete news bulletin on the general's reaction dashed all Nixon's nascent hopes. Eisenhower, apparently, had not been satisfied by the speech; he demanded further explanations. A despairing Nixon called Rose and dictated a telegram, directed to the chairman of the Republican National Committee, announcing his resignation as candidate for the vice-presidency. As the secretary left the room, Murray Chotiner, Nixon's ever devoted campaign manager, sped after her, yanked the telegram from her hands, and tore it to bits. Faithful Rose said simply, "You didn't need to do that. I wasn't going to send it anyway."

Rose followed her leader through two terms as Vice-President, through the unsuccessful campaigns for the presidency and the governorship of California, and thence into moneyed eclipse in New York. Friends looked hard for a silver lining during this period of exile from politics and found it in what they thought was an expanded personal life for Rose. They were pleased to see her living in a cheerful apartment with a paper rose on its front door, giving dinner parties, dating frequently, going to the theater, making new friends. Yet others saw this period as more deprived than liberated. Rose, tucked away in what one visitor described as "a little cubbyhole office" at Nixon's law firm, was said to be unhappy. She missed the political glare and gossip, the sense of being at the center of things. Nixon's decision to try for a political comeback came as welcome news to her. She was still (until he hired a speechwriter) his entire staff, still in control of access to the candidate; and it was to her that important Republicans had to apply for a few minutes' talk with him. Eventually, a triumphant Rose sat in the House gallery and listened to President Richard Nixon deliver his first State of the Union message, typed by her own hands. "All of a sudden," she told a friend, "there he was—and there I was."

But, unfortunately, they were not alone. What should have been paradise for Rose was marred by the presence of a serpent—her rival and the President's new chief of staff, Bob Haldeman. There may be more versions of this epic struggle between the forces of Woods and Haldeman than of any other since Ormazd started slugging it out with Ahriman. Apparently Haldeman was determined to control access to the President, and he set about it by ousting Rose from her accustomed place directly outside Nixon's office. Without a series of notarized maps showing the layout of all White House offices and their occupants over a considerable time span, it is impossible to document this complex tale. Suffice it to say that there was conflict. A bunch of roses was or was not sent by Haldeman, followed by a request that she move. Rose Mary either did or did not go over his head to complain to the President. She was or was not the victor. Haldeman forces spread the word that Rose was drinking to excess; one of her best friends accepted this as fact, but suggested that she had been driven to the bottle by vicious persecution. Everyone had a comment, a footnote, or a reinterpretation to offer.

But Watergate brought Rose at least temporary respite. Haldeman was forced to step down as the President's S.O.B., and with the demolition of the Berlin Wall, Rose was elevated from "personal secretary" to "executive assistant."

Within twenty-four hours it was demonstrated that this was no empty title. The press discovered that Rose was custodian of the only known copy of the secret list of important cash contributors to the Nixon campaign, promptly dubbed Rose Mary's Baby. And as the roiling currents of Watergate continued to rise, Rose's importance became more and more evident. She was the only person so trusted that she was allowed to transcribe the White House tapes then in the "sole personal possession" of the President.

On November 8 Rose appeared in Judge Sirica's courtroom. She is five feet four, slimmer than photographs suggest. If the famous red hair seemed faded and somehow sparse, it was well coiffed, as proper as the discreet wool dress she wore. And under the questioning of prosecutor Jill Volner, Rose Mary demonstrated scrappy self-confidence. Asked if there was any possibility that she could accidentally have erased any part of a tape, she was curt. "I think I used every possible precaution," she snapped. "What precautions?" inquired the lawyer. "I used my head—the only one I had to use," Rose Mary replied caustically.

But two weeks later the situation exploded into absurdity. On November 21 J. Fred Buzhardt, then in charge of Nixon's Watergate defense, admitted to Judge Sirica that one of the tapes he had just been forced to surrender contained a gap of eighteen minutes and fifteen seconds. Instead of the conversation between Haldeman and the President about Watergate that Haldeman's notes had promised, there was nothing but a meaningless buzzing sound. And who was the last person who had actually listened to that tape? None other than Miss Woods. Indeed, as Buzhardt readily conceded, "It doesn't appear from what we know at this point that it could be accidental." Buzhardt suggested that Rose ought to "have time to reflect on this and she ought to have time to secure counsel."

She was allowed time for both, and the lawyer she selected conducted her case with effective theatricality. He commiserated publicly with poor Rose Mary, thrown to the wolves by other wolves. He muttered that he "could blow the lid right off the White House." Under his guidance, a still vigorous and unrepentant Rose told a new and different story. Basically, it was that after a miserable weekend at Camp David, during which she had transcribed for twenty-nine hours to piece together a conversation between Ehrlichman and the President from a tape almost incomprehensibly laden with background noise, clattering dishes, ringing telephones, and overlapping dialogue, she had returned to Washington to continue her labors with a different machine. This one, to simplify her task, had a foot pedal. Perhaps the taxing weekend left her exhausted and she was not at her best. Or it may simply have been that she was not accustomed to using a machine with a foot pedal. At any rate, she pulled the monumental boner that quickly became famous as Rose Mary's boo-boo.

She had finished the Ehrlichman segment, and, to check whether it was complete, she ran the tape a little further into the conversation with Haldeman, which, as she understood it, was not under subpoena. She heard a discussion between Nixon and Haldeman of Ely, Nevada, Pat Nixon's birthplace. And then the phone rang.

Removing her earphones, Rose Mary reached for the stop button but, as hindsight clearly revealed, hit the record button by mistake. Then she picked up the phone and talked to someone for between four and a half and six minutes. The length of that conversation was graven in her memory, but she had no recollection whatever of her caller's identity.

The machine she was using was a sophisticated one. It had been designed so that two mistakes would have to be made simultaneously in order to erase a tape inadvertently. Pressing the record button alone would have done no damage, so what could the other mistake have been? Miss Woods, questioned closely, decided that her foot must have remained on the pedal.

Of course there was no need to stop the machine by pushing a button; the machine would stop if the operator's foot left the pedal. And, in view of the relative positions of recorder and telephone, maintaining that foot on the pedal was a feat of almost superhuman endurance. The Rose Mary Stretch became an overnight joke.

Jill Volner induced Rose to re-create it in the courtroom and, in the midst of the reenactment, looked down and gently observed, "You lifted your foot from the pedal, didn't you?" Later, at a photographic session in her office, Rose Mary grimly insisted on demonstrating that it was at least physically possible to perform the stretch as described.

On her first day of testimony, Rose had seemed willing to concede that she might somehow have caused the entire erasure, since, as she said, "Obviously my judgment of timing is bad." On the second day, however, she insisted that she could not possibly have been responsible for more than six minutes of it. By the last day, she was on the verge of disavowing the whole incident. After all, she had never heard any words on that segment of the tape now covered by the buzz. Perhaps, she suggested, the suspicious hum had been there all along, as a consequence of some malfunction of the system. And, she reminded the court, her mistake was largely hypothetical. "I don't *know* if I left my foot on the pedal," she protested. "I am telling you what everybody *thinks* happened, or you are *saying* happened."

Rose's changing stories were not the only elements of confusion. Buzhardt swore he had succeeded in re-creating the mysterious buzz, using Rose's electric typewriter and Tensor lamp; nobody else could replicate his results. Rose said that when she had rushed, distraught, to inform the President of her "terrible mistake" and he told her not to worry because it was not a subpoenaed tape (though it quite clearly was), he was in his office alone. White House records showed she had seen him elsewhere and in company. Why had Buzhardt not investigated Rose's story when he had first heard it, supposedly weeks before? And why had Rose been so sure on her earlier appearance that all was well with the tapes? And then there were those tape experts testifying that the gap had been caused not by one but by many separate, inferentially intentional, erasures.

By this time there were so many inconsistencies piled atop impossibilities that the whole episode began to seem merely an entertainment designed to divert attention from more serious matters. There was no following any one account to its conclusion, so entangled were they all in contradiction; clearly there would be no satisfactory explanation of just how that buzzing gap had been produced.

What above all made Rose's story so difficult to believe was her own known character. How could she—able, brisk, and unflappable—possibly have behaved as she said she had? It was hard to escape the inference that she had not, that in fact everything she had done from the start, and all the stories she had told, were simply aspects of her professional skill. When a perfect secretary appears in public, clouding the issues, confusing everyone, and befuddling the minds of her employer's opponents, it seems fair to conclude that she believes, rightly or wrongly, that doing these things is part of her job.

Looking back on Rose's long career with Nixon, the most striking thing about it is the unspoken bond between the two. Observers of their work habits had often marveled at the "instant communication" they achieved while working at top speed, their "almost telepathic relationship." Often, Rose knew what Nixon had in mind before his sentence was half finished. As far back as her calm intention to change history in the making by suppressing Nixon's hasty resignation telegram in 1952, it had been obvious that Rose was far more than simply a capable secretary who could take action in a crisis without consultation. She was almost an extension of Nixon's will, so sure of the real intention behind his avowed purpose that she could disobey him in the perfect confidence that she was actually carrying out his wishes.

As for whether Rose had really caused the damage to the crucial tape, nobody seemed to care very deeply. Clearly, not all her contradictory stories could be true. But whether she was right when she said she had erased the tape or when she said she had not hardly mattered, since her motive was assumed to be the same in either case: to execute Richard Nixon's wishes. If she had erased the tape by accident, surely she could not be blamed. And if the erasure had been intentional, or if she was lying to protect someone else, most people assumed that she had done whatever she did at the spoken or unspoken behest of her master. No one condemned her. In fact, many believed (though no hint of a possible firing issued from the White House) that the faithful Rose had been heartlessly cast off by her boss, flung to the pursuers to keep them off his trail, and they pitied her even more.

Whatever had happened, Rose was accepted as the quintessential loyalist, and when her loyalty was talked of, it seemed simply another name for love. Plenty of witnesses stood ready to testify that Rose adored Nixon and always had, and they spoke of it in surprise and admiration. Rose, they said, was like a nun, and Richard Nixon was the church. For her, they said, there was nothing above or below the President. He was her whole life, really.

The passionate debate about the gap in the tape was soon overwhelmed by other disclosures and became simply one more lacuna in the great palimpsest of Watergate. Yet a few lingering questions remained unresolved. If Rose's whole life had been built around a silent passion for Nixon, how to explain her behavior after his resignation? There he was, sick and sad in California, while thousands of miles away in Washington a cheerful Rose Mary maintained a higher profile than ever before. "One might have thought," says one puzzled friend, "that she would have gone out to San Clemente to die with Richard Nixon, but she's not doing that."

Far from it. Though she is one of the few still securely on the Nixon payroll and has visited San Clemente several times, she neither hovers as ministering angel there nor settles in like a member of the family. Instead, she busies herself with mysterious chores in Washington (she is said to be sorting through old Nixon papers) and is frequently to be seen at parties and restaurants. The impeccable Robert Gray, once so eager to discuss Rose's loyalty and other fine qualities with reporters, now refuses all interviews, but he is still very much in attendance. And reporters still cluster about Rose, meeting with no encouragement whatever. "I've had fifty requests for interviews, and I'm not granting any of them," she coldly informed one would-be interviewer recently. Unwelcome persistence turned Rose's face lumpy and tight. "You better watch out," she warned. "You just watch out or you'll hear from my lawyers on libel."

If Rose's long relationship with Nixon had been based on simple, self-abnegating love, she could continue to serve him in devoted obscurity, untroubled by inquisitive reporters, in his San Clemente exile. But the truth is that her career was never really that of a humble handmaiden who wanted nothing more than to please her master. It only looked that way. The idea that she was motivated by love in all she did was an assumption based squarely on the fact that

Rose was a woman and Nixon a man. It rhymed as easily with assumptions about those two conditions as moon with June.

In plain fact, Rose's career depended on Nixon's in much the same way Haldeman's did. Haldeman in turn provided Ehrlichman with his link to power. And beneath them were a whole string of protégés. None of those relationships ever struck anyone as in the least touching and beautiful, though it is at least possible that there was more true feeling in the hearts of some of those protégés than there ever was in Rose Mary's.

If Rose's life story were to be retold with a simple shift of feminine to masculine pronouns, it might read very differently. No longer the familiar tale of unspoken, unrequited love, it might, in fact, sound remarkably like an equally familiar cliché: the Alger-American saga of the ambitious person who finds a patron, takes advantage of his opportunities, makes himself indispensable, and rises from humble beginnings to impressive heights of power and influence. His career is, indeed, linked with his patron's, but that is as ordinary a fact in politics as it is in other fields.

If Rose had been a man, the fact that she seemed to have no real life of her own aside from Nixon would have suggested not romance but obsessive ambition. The idea that a woman's life might center around the exercise of power is an unaccustomed thought. Yet power is surely what Rose Woods enjoyed when she alone controlled access to Nixon, when she doled out his time to those she considered deserving, in amounts precisely graduated on the scale of her opinion of their merits and influence. It is surely no accident that Rose and Haldeman eventually collided with such angry intensity: both of them wanted a power that was not felt by either to be divisible.

If what Rose wants is power, she must still depend on Nixon. Only a change in public opinion that would permit his return from exile could really restore her to a position of influence. A discredited fallen President in her background could be of little use to her future. Sharing his exile would do nothing to pave the way for his return. The more Nixon partisans who still maintain good connections with official Washington, the likelier a Nixon comeback seems. It is by helping Nixon that Rose can best help herself, and it need not be love that motivates her any more than it does any ambitious person, including her longtime boss.

The fact that the Gray-Woods alliance is still so close suggests that her assessment of her situation is a realistic one. For Bob Gray, inveterate partygoer that he is, is not frivolous, and most of Washington assumes that his relationship with Rose has always been based on something more than her Irish charm. Gray frankly admits that he makes no distinction between work and play; wherever he is, he is at work, and a major part of his business is influence. He heads up the Washington office of the largest public-relations firm in the world, Hill and Knowlton, a company with over five hundred employees in seventeen countries, offices in thirty-six cities within the United States, and an elaborate setup in Washington. What the company has to sell, at a minimum of $4,000 a month per client, is brought to bear at every level of government, and the clients who benefit are generally this country's largest corporations. Bob Gray has figured out that the corporations represented by his firm produce 14 per cent of the gross national product.

Close ties with a President's private secretary would obviously be a tremendous asset in Bob Gray's line of work. And Gray, a practical man, prefers to spend his time with people who have at least the possibility of influence. However much he may appreciate Rose Mary as a person and enjoy her diverting company, many in Washington cannot believe he would invest quite the amount of time and attention he does unless he felt she had a future. If that reading is correct, he must believe that Nixon does.

Before Richard Nixon can emerge from the shadows to take his place as elder statesman, party spokesman, or diplomat, he must satisfactorily explain his role in Watergate, exculpating himself and imposing his own vision of history on the American consciousness. He plans to do this—incidentally collecting some $2 million—by writing his memoirs. When he has set forth his account of what happened, when and why, and what he knew, Rose, with her well-known grasp of detail, her magnificent memory, will be an invaluable ally. Her visible, continuing loyalty will authenticate it all.

At the same time, Nixon cannot avoid the knowledge that Rose holds his reputation in her hands, because whatever she can corroborate she is also in a position to contradict. After all, she did transcribe those tapes, and she knows what is on them. As he said so long ago, Rose understands every detail of his job. He can trust her, because they are interdependent: her future depends on his, and she is ambitious. But it cannot be a comfortable interdependence. Contemplating Rose today, Nixon might not find it in his heart to call himself a lucky man.

Joanne Haldeman

Thank goodness Nixon won, because now Bob will
have something to devote his life to.

Jeanne Ehrlichman

John didn't know he swore like that.

"She is so attractive, with a natural, outdoors kind of good looks."
"Such warmth of spirit . . . "
"She has the loveliest expression."
"They're a wonderful family . . . outstanding kids."
"She believed so firmly in what he was doing."
"Their difficulties have brought them even closer together."
"She is the most remarkable woman I have ever known."

Accolades indeed, but for whom are they intended? Mrs. John Ehrlichman? Mrs. Bob Haldeman? Jeanne or Jo? Both? The words echo
through one interview after another as the listener gropes, almost
abandoning hope of ever distinguishing between the two. "They are
both," one Washington matron at last sums up the confusion, "absolutely wonderful human beings. I would be amazed if you found
anyone who had one critical thing to say of either Jeannie Ehrlichman or Jo Haldeman." And she is right.

"We have been lumped," admits Jeanne Ehrlichman with a
smile, adding, "Jo is darling, just a very real person." Jeanne is a small,
exceptionally pretty woman. Though she is approaching fifty and her
short, waving hair is gray, her rosy complexion, trim figure, and quick
smile combine to make her seem almost girlish. That impression is
supported by a vocabulary that lags a generation behind her age

197

(things tend to be "neat," or "super," or "fabulous"), but there is nothing forced or artificial about her. Rather, the impression she conveys is one of genuine sweetness.

"I don't think we'll ever know the real story behind Watergate," she says mildly. "I'm sorry, I just don't think we ever will." Yet even if the full truth never emerges—and to her that would be a disappointment, since she believes it would exonerate her husband —Jeanne Ehrlichman refuses to see Watergate as a catastrophe or even in any way unfortunate. Watergate, she says, "has just been a very fine experience for all of us."

First of all, it has brought the family closer than ever, and she feels that her children have had a chance to learn a great many lessons from it. They have had to test themselves, and they have found "that they really do have a rock on which to lean"—their love for their family and for their religion. She is sure her children are "better and more mature people because of this." Nor are they now unprepared to meet disaster, the "something tragic" she envisions that "might have happened to them later on in their lives."

That eventually, prepared or unprepared, they would have had to confront something of the sort she is quite certain: she believes that sooner or later into every life comes something very like a Watergate. It may be an illness, or a problem of human relationships, or something connected with a job, but she frequently reminds herself that her case, while it has been more publicized than most and thus is better known, is quite ordinary, simply an inevitable part of life. "If you think of it out of perspective," she suggests, "it becomes a big thing and you can hardly live with it. And that's why we've really worked to say, 'Look, it's no big deal.' "

But even beyond the effects of Watergate on her and her family, she sees benefits for others. "Good things are going to come out of this for everyone," she insists. "I've seen it already for ourselves, and it's true—when you have adversity, you really do come out better." Surprisingly, she reaches for the unlikeliest name she could invoke, her husband's accuser. "John Dean," she continues, "said something about that, and he really sounded like he was coming out better. He and his wife are closer. And everyone I've spoken to has felt that."

Jeanne does not say so, but if she sees Watergate as bringing such benefits to John Dean, she must believe it has brought them to Jo Haldeman as well. Jeanne's life and Jo's ran parallel during their years in Washington. Their worlds were overturned in almost the same moment. Surely the outcome cannot be vastly different for these two women. And when Jeanne thinks again about Jo Haldeman and the likeness people see between them, she acknowledges that. "We were wives," she says, accepting it, "who were working out their problems and family and children, and loving our homes. I don't know that we were all that different."

If Jeanne and Joanne seem at first glance interchangeable, their husbands are even more so. In their White House years their similarities were obvious: brusque, high on organization, low on frivolity, new to government and Washington, both were veterans of past Nixon campaigns. Both were Christian Scientists, a popular religious affiliation in the White House. Though both avoided the limelight, maintaining their personal privacy, their Teutonic names and zeal for efficiency were famous. They were known as the Berlin Wall, Hans and Fritz, and even, to dramatize their indistinguish-ability, Herdleman and Erdleman. By 1973 these two had helped design the Administration whose daily operations they regulated. They had staffed the White House with their protégés, surrounding themselves with the young and inexperienced, the unquestioningly loyal. They had easy access to the President, for it was they who not only transmitted Nixon's orders but helped shape them, and it was to them that others were forced to apply for admission to the Oval Office. After the President himself, they were the country's most powerful men.

When Nixon announced their resignations, he called them "two of the finest public servants it has been my privilege to know." Later, with Nixon on the verge of resignation, they tried together to wring from him a presidential pardon, which he, full of suspicion, refused. Now, in their fall, their unity was disintegrating. During the Water-gate cover-up trial, their separate lines of defense conflicted. And, as questioning elicited these divergent stories, the long relationship between the two families seemed, if not permanently inoperative, at least for the time in abeyance. Calmly, Jeanne Ehrlichman referred to the schism. "They are beginning to say different things," she admitted, "but we're all really very Christian kind of people, and we're not about to stand there and say 'You did this' and 'You did that.'"

The long interconnection of Haldemans and Ehrlichmans goes back to their college days at U.C.L.A. following World War II. John Ehrlichman, in fact, enrolled on the G.I. Bill, after flying twenty-six bombing missions over Germany as a lead navigator with the Eighth Air Force, and spent much of college talking politics with other young men who had shared the experience of war. He had been a lifelong Republican, although with a less visible passion than his classmate Harry Robbins (Bob) Haldeman. Bob's grandfather—another H. R. Haldeman—had been one of the founders of the Better American Foundation, an anti-Communist organization, and apparently Bob had listened early to his opinions. By the time he reached U.C.L.A., after a year at the University of Redlands and another in the Navy V-12 program at the University of Southern California, he was already an admirer of the young Richard Nixon and the effectiveness with which he had labeled Helen Gahagan Douglas a fellow traveler. At U.C.L.A. Haldeman flung himself into campus politics, the activity that brought him into contact with John· Ehrlichman, the real kingmaker in those days.

It was at U.C.L.A., too, that Bob met Joanne Horton, friend and sorority sister of his younger sister, Betsy. Looking back, the campus romance seems all but inevitable; the two just matched. Jo is the quintessential Californian—athletically attractive, outgoing, with a self-confident, casual grace. Like Bob, she was a Christian Scientist, had grown up in Los Angeles, attended private schools, and had felt no need to repudiate her family's values. Nor was she, any more than Bob, swayed by the liberal bent of the U.C.L.A. *Daily Bruin* and its then student editor Frank Mankiewicz.

Jeanne Fisher was a classmate of Joanne Horton's, both of them a year behind their future husbands, but they belonged to different sororities and barely knew each other. Jeanne did, however, get to know Bob Haldeman, because in her junior (his senior) year, they were co-chairmen of the U.C.L.A. Homecoming, an "enormous activity," on which they both worked hard and long. Bob, she says, looking back on it, was "fabulous and very organized and we worked very well together."

The closeness of the early relationship between the two couples has been much exaggerated in the publicity that has surrounded them in recent years. Contrary to almost every account, they never double-dated. (Ironically, the U.C.L.A. pair with whom the Haldemans frequently *did* double-date were Charlotte Mary Maguire and her future husband, Alexander Butterfield, who would eventually disclose the existence of the secret White House taping system, thereby inadvertently bringing down Haldeman, his old friend and the man to whom he owed his White House job.)

Another widely accepted—but untrue—story is that Bob Haldeman managed Jeannie Fisher's campaign for student body vice-president. It is true that Jeannie ran for that office, but he had nothing to do with her campaign. Even in those days, Bob had no time for lesser offices: he was working for a presidential candidate.

Another, even more colorful story, corollary to this, must also be disallowed. Some analysts of Haldeman's later political career have pounced delightedly on the rumor that in an attempt to influence the outcome of the vice-presidential race, Bob (still cast as Jeannie Fisher's campaign manager) released a poll showing her with a commanding lead, a stratagem revealed by her subsequent decisive loss. This has been put forward as Haldeman's first venture into the shady areas of vote manipulation. The true story is far less dramatic. Not only did Bob not manage the campaign, there was no poll. And though Jeannie had been expected to win, and indeed lost only by a narrow margin, she hardly knew Bob—or even John Ehrlichman—at that time. Looking back on the episode, though, she describes it as "a very interesting campaign" and one from which she "learned a great deal."

Though she and Jo Horton were still only acquaintances, Jeanne knew that Bob and Jo were dating, and later that they were engaged. When Jo left U.C.L.A. halfway through her senior year to marry Bob, John Ehrlichman and Jeannie Fisher were at the wedding. But the two couples did not see each other again until after both were married and happened to be living conveniently close. They then visited back and forth three or four times; thereafter, separated by greater distance, the two women corresponded by Christmas card until 1960, though their husbands were in closer touch. When Jeanne and Jo met again in the course of Nixon's first presidential campaign, they had not yet seen each other's children.

By the time of Jeanne's U.C.L.A. graduation in the spring of 1949, John had had a year at Stanford law school. Instead of prolonging their engagement until he finished, as they had originally planned, they married that summer and she went to work, teaching second and third grades. Soon after his law-school graduation, the Ehrlichmans visited Seattle. John Ehrlichman had spent his childhood there, and the pull of the Northwest remained strong. "I kept telling her about the water and the trees and the fishing," he once explained to an interviewer. "When we got there the sun was shining, the strawberries were big and fat. We came back to Los Angeles and the smog was terrible, the traffic was terrible, and we had a hard time finding a place to live. We decided to go back to Seattle."

There, life was pleasant. John made a quick name for himself as a real estate attorney, with a special interest in land use and conservation; Jeannie tended their rapidly expanding family. The Ehrlichmans loved the outdoor life—sailing, backpacking, climbing—and Jeannie especially enjoyed the fact that on these outings John, a former Eagle Scout, did all the cooking. Politics played little part in their lives; land use and zoning specialists have to deal with local and state officials of both parties, and John remained neutral so successfully that leading Republicans in the state hardly knew him. Inwardly, however, he was building an allegiance toward Richard Nixon, and this was largely due to the influence of his old college friend Bob Haldeman.

Bob had been moving up the corporate ladder at the J. Walter Thompson advertising agency, a career that would bring the Haldemans from Los Angeles to San Francisco, briefly to New York; and then back to Los Angeles, where by 1960 Bob headed JWT's Los Angeles office. He had never been what admen call the "creative type," but his organizational skills were formidable, and he won the loyalty of his staff, a group that included Ron Ziegler, Dwight Chapin, Larry Higby, and Bruce Kehrli, all of whom would eventually follow him to the White House. But though he inspired loyalty, he never allowed anyone to get very close. "Bob," confessed a JWT associate, "is not a warm and wonderful human being. People respect him more than they love him."

Jo Haldeman's life was a textbook example of the upper-middle-class American ideal. Her husband put in long hours at the office, but when the day ended, so did business. He rarely participated in social activities with clients, and dinner was a family meal. The four Haldeman children were all California-born, though once a very pregnant Joanne had to be flown from Connecticut for the event, because Bob was determined that all his children must be fourth-generation Californians. Theirs was a close and happy family, reinforced by tradition and religious conviction.

Outside the family, Bob Haldeman was not quite so virtuous. There was one controversy in his life that became so public that Jo could not have failed to hear of it. During Nixon's 1962 campaign for the governorship of California, registered Democrats received mailings from a group identified as the Committee for the Preservation of the Democratic Party. The supposed committee warned that left-wing extremists were influencing the Democratic candidate, a claim which, if heeded, could only benefit the Nixon cause. And indeed it was soon discovered that the committee had been invented by Haldeman himself, with Nixon's approval. Haldeman at the time was known to be unrepentant about this episode, considering it merely a normal, unexceptional political act. Jo Haldeman made no public statement.

Bob had been an advance man for Nixon in the 1956 vice-presidential campaign. In 1960 he persuaded his old friend Ehrlich-man to take a six-month leave and join him in working on Nixon's first presidential effort. Ehrlichman worked briefly again in the dis-astrous 1962 gubernatorial campaign, managed by Haldeman, and when Nixon decided to make one last all-out run for the presidency in 1968, Ehrlichman was tour director of that 50,000-mile campaign odyssey. Shortly after the election, Nixon offered him a job as White House counsel.

It was a difficult decision for the Ehrlichmans. John had promised to help through the transition, but he had not committed himself to move his family across the country and radically alter their way of life. They held a family council to discuss it. After all, they were very happy and comfortable in Seattle; John was successful; all of them were involved with friends and activities. But as they talked it over, they agreed that John had an obligation to accept, and that they all had an obligation to support his decision. Looking back on it now, Jeanne says, "John just really had a lot to contribute, and I really thought it was right, that maybe we'd be sorry if we didn't." Weigh-ing the question in retrospect, she adds, "We did it and we don't regret it."

They moved to Great Falls, Virginia, a subdivision in the midst of a rural area, where each house sits upon an acre. The houses there are roomy, and the grounds well kept, but it was not the Pacific Northwest or the warm, close-knit family life they had known. "They bought the house because they needed a place to live," one neighbor says, "and the house sort of showed it. They didn't have time to take a great interest in it, they were both so very busy." Indeed they were. John was in his car by 6:30 every morning, heading for a White House breakfast with top aides, to get the decks cleared before the chief awoke. At precisely 8:30 he met with the President before plunging into his long day's work.

Jeanne, with her husband so often away and her five children enrolled in school or college, was faced with a problem. She solved it by making a life for herself in volunteer work. As she says, practically, it was "the only thing to do." She organized and promoted concerts for children at Kennedy Center, and taught remedial reading in District schools, her hours of work adding up, friends say, to the equivalent of a full-time job. "She didn't have any more time than John did," one friend remembers. "They are *not* social people. They are hardworking people." But she did share her enthusiasm for public service with neighborhood women. "She got all of us involved in a teacher aide program," one says, "a pilot project she'd started in the

Great Falls schools, where she would enlist high school kids from the suburbs to tutor inner-city children."

The Ehrlichmans were not a staple on the Washington social scene. Part of the reason, of course, was disapproval. But in the main it was an effort to keep home and family central to their lives, despite the consuming nature of John's new commitment to government service. As Jeanne says, "I . . . not demanded . . . but I made it very important that if we didn't have quantity we had to have quality, so we worked very hard at this." The Ehrlichmans pared their social life to a minimum in order to spend as much time as possible with their children. As she explains, "you can go all week long to the various functions you have to go to, and then on the weekend if we had had our own normal social obligations or if we'd wanted to get to know some of the marvelous people in Washington, John wouldn't have had any time to see the children. So we decided to cut out of our lives any social life other than what was demanded, and that way we really did catch up on weekends."

The other thing they did was always to have dinner as a family, regardless of the time of John's arrival, which meant that they frequently did not eat until nine. When the Ehrlichmans first arrived in Washington, their two youngest children were eleven and nine, but "they stayed up and they sat down and we had dinner together every night, no matter how late he came home." Jeanne Ehrlichman notes that "it was a great sacrifice on the kids' part and they didn't always like it," but, she concludes, "it seemed like the right thing to do." And the system worked: family ties were not weakened. In fact, with a father so often absent, "having John home was so special the kids really didn't want to go off for anything, so they always made a big effort to be home on the weekend."

Jeanne still kept up her friendships, and the Ehrlichmans did occasionally entertain small groups. As Christian Scientists, they do not drink. Nor do they fill up others' glasses. "If you went there for dinner," says a neighborhood friend, "you'd have a choice of fruit juices before dinner, never even a glass of wine. You do not do that. You do not drink coffee, either. The body is a temple, and you don't abuse it."

There was tennis with the Haldemans at the McLean indoor tennis club; weekends at Camp David, where the children of the two families got to know each other. The two husbands saw each other frequently, of course, and continued to enjoy each other's company. The wives, though they liked each other, were not intimate. They never saw each other socially "except when we were together because the boys were together."

The Haldemans were even less visible on the social landscape than the Ehrlichmans. As Jo once told a reporter, "We are not as socially active as many people and just never have been. We haven't become involved in the cocktail party circuit." Bob, too, put in those long days at the White House, usually six days a week, and evenings were spent at home to allow him to unwind quietly. As Jo explained, "It's easier for him when he comes home just to be home and relax here rather than going out and doing something socially." Later in the evening Bob retreated to his study to work and read, and to listen to country-and-Western music on his stereo, but the early part was spent with the family. Sometimes he and Jo played chess, a slapdash version, since neither had taken time to study the game. "Our games are over in fifteen minutes," Jo confessed.

Even Jeanne Ehrlichman, hardly a social swinger, was surprised by the Haldemans' dedication to the hearth. "They really didn't go to any parties—or anything," she says. And a friend of Jo's tells of her constant efforts to encourage the Haldemans to enlarge their social circle, see more people, do more things, with almost no success. Perhaps it had something to do with the fact that Bob, as Joanne explained, was not interested in "small talk and ladies' chitchat." She once suggested, "I think he'd love it if tables at dinner parties were divided with the ladies at one end and the men at the other."

The Haldemans' sport was tennis. Jo had always played, while Bob's favorite outdoor activity over the years had been, in daughter Susan's words, "laying out in the sun." But in 1970, as a surprise for his wife, he started tennis lessons. The surprise was spoiled by a White House telephone operator who told Jo when she called one day that her husband was en route to his tennis lesson. Jo thought at first that the operator had them confused with Jeanne and John, who had taken up the game some months before, and insisted, "This is Mrs. Haldeman, not Mrs. Ehrlichman."

Bob, his secret discovered, was described by an amused Joanne as "crestfallen." She was pleased by this new interest of her husband's, but surprised since Bob "had never been interested in sports." In fact, she admitted, "he's really not very well coordinated." (Those who watched the Haldeman-Ehrlichman mixed doubles that followed tended to agree.) This recognition of a failing in her husband was rare for Jo, who generally views Bob as capable of anything he sets his mind to. "If he decided he was going to be a great piano player," she once told a friend, "I am totally convinced he would be a great piano player."

The home the Haldemans spent so much time in was a large $180,000 house in Kenwood, Maryland, a Washington suburb known for its broad, quiet streets and blooming cherry trees in spring. The place was red brick, vaguely antebellum in style, if of comparatively recent vintage, and spacious enough to be bought by the Australian Embassy when the Haldemans moved out. Though one visitor observed that the house looked as if it had been decorated dutifully by someone who did not much enjoy that kind of thing, the decor was greatly admired by others. "The whole house was a lovely gold," one neighbor says. "Lots of windows, flooded with light." Another woman, who looked the place over thoroughly later when it was up for sale, was awed by the quality of the housekeeping: she had never in her life, she said, seen a house so clean.

When the family dwindled from six to four in 1972, with only Peter, then sixteen, and Ann, fourteen, still at home, son Peter suggested that they move into the city, to Georgetown. His father, much to everyone's amazement, agreed. One White House aide, imbued with Nixonian scorn for the supposed liberalism and snobbery of the eighteenth-century quarter, jeered, "Bob has gone over to the enemy." Bob, characteristically, saw it as a time-saving move that allowed him an extra fifteen minutes of sleep each morning, and the Haldemans changed neither their politics nor their social habits. They lived near, but decidedly were no part of, Georgetown's social glitter. For them, life went on as before: family-oriented, outdoorsy, with occasional evenings of informal entertaining. Although as Christian Scientists the Haldemans rule out liquor for themselves, they do serve it to friends. As one occasional guest puts it, "Jo would very much want you to be at ease and enjoy yourself."

Joanne Haldeman struck much of Washington—or at least that rather small part of it that ever saw her—as understated, elegant, and aristocratic. In fact, aristocratic is a word frequently used in all discussions of the family: over and over, it is remarked that they were more than socially acceptable, with a wonderful background, and perfect taste, whether in Jo's elegant, understated clothes, or that debatable flair for decoration. Slim and tanned, and often dressed in slacks, Joanne has also been described as a California version of Julie Andrews.

She was not a daytime solitary. She did see neighbors. She gardened. She volunteered her services occasionally to the City Hall complaints center and to the Junior League. Her most personal contribution was the attempt she made to organize White House wives into a cohesive group similar to those formed by some other departments of government, and though she never quite managed this, she did help new wives orient themselves in Washington.

But her work did not fill up her life in the way Jeanne Ehrlichman's did. Her real interest continued to be her family. Jo, immensely proud of her husband's achievements, saw herself, first and always, as his helpmeet. When they first came to Washington, she began to collect clippings, photographs, and White House invitations for a scrapbook. Four years later she could point to eight huge books, some of them always prominently displayed on a coffee table in the Haldeman living room. She called them "the diary of our life in Washington" and her own "unique contribution" to "our" experience in public life.

When Joanne and Bob first came to Washington, she used to say, they had carefully considered their move. "We understood what it would mean," she said, looking back on it. "We went into it with our eyes wide open." And clearly she understood what the move really meant to her husband and their life together. Shortly after the 1968 victory she put it into words. "Thank goodness Nixon won," she said, "because now Bob will have something to devote his life to."

Stories of Haldeman's devotion to the President over the years abound. One reporter who accompanied Nixon and his entourage on a working vacation in the Virgin Islands returned with a particularly striking example. Haldeman had gone out for a sail one evening with some of his aides, but with one of those beepers so much a part of White House technology firmly strapped to his wrist in case the President might wish to communicate with him. With the boat half a mile out into the Caribbean sunset, the device began to signal Nixon's need of his right-hand man. Haldeman immediately scrambled to his feet and, impatient at the crew's inefficiency at turning the boat on command, hurled himself overboard to swim the distance back to shore. Apocryphal or otherwise, this story dramatizes the basic relationship of Haldeman and Nixon. Haldeman was always unquestioningly ready to subordinate his own wishes to Nixon's. He once told a friend that he did not mind wasting hour after hour dealing with "all the bitching and all the demands" of Tricia, Julie, and Pat Nixon, if by doing so he could make the President's life any easier.

Jo was well aware of her husband's attitude, for Nixon filled not only Bob's working days—and it was a rare evening when he was not repeatedly telephoned at home—but his leisure hours as well. It was

Haldeman's pleasure to record the life of Richard Nixon on film. Though official photographers were always at hand, Haldeman as self-appointed cinematic Boswell to the Nixon Administration, shot his own motion-picture film of presidential travels, at historic meetings, on the campaign trail. To get in proper position for the perfect shot, he was known to leap on car hoods, crawl behind speakers' podiums, dodge between pillars, crane from car windows. His plan was to make one highlight reel for each year of the Nixon presidency. As Haldeman used to say, his grandchildren might not be interested, but he would.

Bob had still photographs, too, and these were displayed in a study known to friends and family as the Nixon Room. "It was full of photographs that Bob had taken over the years," says a friend who was deeply impressed. "Excellent photographs. Bob had a tremendous flair for background, for interest. Nothing was run of the mill. It was history."

Never fully acclimatized to Washington's air-conditioned summers, Joanne continued to take the children to their California beach house for three months each year, with Bob joining them for a few days when and if he could. But that was rare; the longest vacation he ever managed after 1969 was five days. Yet Bob did not mind. Talking about the excitement of his job, he once explained: "The pace is pretty hectic, but I think that's what makes it fascinating. I used to take long vacations. I've found, and I think most of the people here have, that you get absorbed in this to the point that you don't want to be away, you don't want to miss anything. And you would rather be here than somewhere else." Then, making an approving if perfunctory gesture in the direction of balance, he added, "I look forward to when it's all over and I'll have a chance to unwind. But not with any deep yearning."

Jo Haldeman not only acquiesced in her husband's dedication to Nixon; she fostered it. When their twentieth wedding anniversary approached, she went to the President and asked him to copy out four sentences from his 1969 Inaugural Address. Framed and with presidential seal affixed, her anniversary gift read:

> Until he has been part of a cause larger than himself, no man is truly whole . . .
> The way to fulfillment is in the use of our talents. We achieve nobility in the spirit that inspires that use . . .
> As we measure what can be done, we shall promise only

what we know we can produce; but as we chart our goals, we shall be lifted by our dreams.

Jo Haldeman knew how very much those words would mean to her husband. They were his credo, the credo that justified his total devotion and unflinching service to Richard Nixon.

Jeanne Ehrlichman's husband, though deeply committed to his job, had never been quite so fully dedicated to the President. Yet even so, Jeanne found the shift in his priorities when they first moved to Washington extremely disconcerting. She had not realized what an impact his new career would have on their relationship. The fact that John was on twenty-four-hour call to the President and that therefore they had a White House telephone in their own room called for "a tremendous adjustment." As she explains it, "I had been No. 1 for a *long* time, and now I was No. 2. And that's probably the hardest thing that happens to a wife." To relinquish first claim on her husband was painful for Jeanne; Joanne had come to terms with the problem long before.

In the spring of 1973 both Jeanne and Jo, in their slightly different ways, had adjusted to their lives. They knew what to expect and could look to the future with confidence; they seemed enviably content. But the Watergate scandal was slowly undermining the foundations of this pleasant security, and in April Nixon accepted or exacted the resignations of both Haldeman and Ehrlichman.

The Ehrlichmans' six-bedroom Virginia house went on the market that June (for $139,000, a price the neighbors agreed was far too high). The following month John Ehrlichman appeared before the Ervin committee, ending his testimony with the stern warning: "Be prepared to defend your sense of values when you come here. You'll encounter a local culture which scoffs at patriotism and family and morality just as it adulates the opposite."

Finally, in August of that year, the Ehrlichmans moved back as renters to what had once been their own house in the prosperous Hunts Point section of Seattle. It is on a wooded peninsula that juts into Lake Washington, an enclave of $150,000 homes. Theirs (which they subsequently rebought) is a rambling yellow frame structure set on a wide lawn that slopes down to the water. Jeanne says the newspapers always describe it as "a fantastic house in a marvelous area." Actually, she says, it's a "funny old house," but they really love it. And of course there are friends nearby. "They're just a marvelous family," one neighbor said sympathetically at the time of the trial.

"It's just hard to believe he's in all this trouble. They always did everything right."

Yet despite the spreading scandal and their coast-to-coast legal troubles, the next year was good for the Ehrlichmans. The family could spend time together, and John, though suspended from the bar, could use his acknowledged expertise on a consultant basis. In the spring of 1974, Jeanne took a paid position as coordinator of family concerts for the Seattle Symphony, the kind of work she had done before on a volunteer basis. She says it is "a super job" that allows her a family-oriented nine-month schedule, with two summer months off and a month at Christmas.

Oddly, money seems not to have been a serious problem, though in 1972 Ehrlichman is known to have borrowed $20,000 from Herbert Kalmbach, then Nixon's personal attorney, to pay off a tuition loan. It is widely surmised that a prominent and wealthy uncle, Ben Ehrlichman, who had no children, left his money to John. To cover the Ehrlichmans' living expenses and allow them financial peace of mind in their present circumstances, that legacy would have had to be substantial. Legal fees continue to mount. In 1974 Jeanne Ehrlichman estimated that before they are through, the total expenses for all of John's defense will run in the "two hundred thousands"; others have guessed $300,000. Considering cross-country air fares, hotel bills, the cost of two trials and appeals—and there are other, less publicized suits pending—either estimate seems low. Durwood Alkire, treasurer of Ehrlichman's Seattle defense fund, will disclose no figures on money raised or spent; he says only that there has been "no very high-key or elaborate campaign to raise money, particularly lately."

The Ehrlichman children were with their parents in Washington in the summer of '74, demonstrating support by accompanying their father to the federal courthouse where the Ellsberg burglary case—in which he would be found guilty—was in progress. They survived the daily rush of cameramen, an onslaught that their mother admitted "made me feel like an animal" at first. When asked what sustained them through the trial, Jeanne and the children answered almost in unison, "Love for God . . . religion . . . love for family."

Jeanne knows that her husband's image in the press has not been likable, and she blames that on the job. "The kinds of things he was asked to do," she says, "were not the kind of things to win friends. He was the hard-nosed one who said no. The rest of them didn't. He did." But she does feel that he has had better publicity since the trouble started, and she appreciates that. She talks of the "hundreds and hundreds and hundreds" of encouraging letters they have received, and the number of people who have stopped John in the street to say, "Boy, stay in there, we're all for you, good luck." "Of course," she adds, "if people feel differently, they don't bother to say anything, but we've never had anybody say anything unkind."

If there has been a new image of John in the press, it is in large measure due to Jeanne herself. Since her husband's first trial began, she has repeatedly stopped to chat with reporters, invited them to the Ehrlichman hotel suite for private interviews, encouraged the children to speak out. And the message she has tried to get across is that John Ehrlichman is innocent, that the family is very much all right, and that the future is bright. During the Watergate trial, she said, "Today I couldn't feel better about where we are, at what point we are, and how grateful we are for the support and consecrated work that's gone on. The lawyers believe in John, I believe in John, and he believes in himself, so it can't help but have a good outcome."

As the Watergate conspiracy trial spun out its final days, Jeanne and John prepared to spend Christmas alone together in Washington. All six of the children (there is a new daughter-in-law) would be in Seattle with John's mother and an aunt. The Ehrlichmans had long since decided that even if the trial ended in time for them all to spend Christmas together in Seattle, this was the year to have "a *real* Christmas spirit, just a very spiritual Christmas," with no presents beyond "just candy, nuts, oranges, and all the little fun things." Jeanne Ehrlichman explained that none of them saw this as a hardship for the children ("It's marvelous that they'll all be together. We think that'll be kind of a unique experience for them"), adding, "They're thinking more of us." Any concern about their parents' possible loneliness, however, was clearly wasted.

After a three-month separation Jeanne at last had her husband to herself, and, radiating the pleasure she felt in their reunion, she explained, "That's why I can very happily say there are pluses to all this. I have a husband! It's *neat*. I mean it's just the most exciting thing!" Rejecting any sympathy for their isolation, she protested, "Oh, no, *no!* That really is the delight about this." Her faith in the future remained unshaken, too. Asked what they would do if all went well at the trial (she almost instantaneously answered "It will"), she explained that they would simply "go back to Seattle, our great old house there, and all the things we've been doing—a neat, fun life."

Joanne Haldeman, too, was in Washington to be with her husband throughout the trial. When the Haldemans had first left Washington, they had returned, as they had always talked of doing, to California. On arrival, they were lent a house—then on the market for $800,000—by an old family friend. Subsequently, they bought a place of their own, a "little four-bedroom house" they called it, in Los Angeles. From there Jo wrote optimistic notes back to all her friends in Washington, expressing her conviction that everything would turn out well, her faith in her husband and in the future.

Unlike Jeanne, she shrank from the press. Refusing all interviews, she left her husband to refashion his own image, which he did by smiling frequently and allowing the crew cut that had been his trademark to grow out. In previous years Joanne, who had never seen Bob with any other haircut, used to explain to friends that if he were ever to let it grow, he would never be able to manage it. He had very fine hair, she said, that would probably "end up in an Afro or something."

The week before the Watergate trial began, the Haldemans left California once again. Unlike Jeanne Ehrlichman, Jo did not have to be at home with younger children. Ann, who now goes to her mother's old school, and Peter, at his father's, were tended by two sets of grandparents in Los Angeles. "The families have been marvelously helpful," says a close friend. "The grandmothers are there, watching." For the duration of the trial, Jo, Bob, and daughter Susan—who had taken the term off from law school to help with her father's defense—took up residence in a small rented house in Alexandria. Every day they went to the courtroom at nine and stayed until five, five days a week, until the end. Jo had lost weight, her friends said, and looked tired. But there was no trace of bitterness.

For the Haldemans Watergate seems to have meant no loss of friends or respect. Certainly not in California, where family and friends have rallied round, raised money for the defense (though the Haldemans are rich), talked future jobs for Bob. And not in Washington either, or not so very much. In part this is due to Jo herself, to the genuine affection and loyalty she stirs in friends; but far more must be ascribed to the suspicion that haunts the nation's capital, that what has happened to the Haldemans could have happened to almost any one of them. One Washington woman tells of a nightmare her well-placed husband had recently, in which he found himself in the dock, a Watergate defendant. "If the President tells you what to do," she reports his reaction, "you certainly don't question it. You just do it."

As Jeanne Ehrlichman and Joanne Haldeman continued to stand beside their husbands, those husbands drifted into enmity. After so many years of personal and political friendship, "the boys" no longer presented a united front. Yet the similarities between the two women had never been more evident. Neither, apparently, was afflicted by a twinge of doubt about her husband's role, the ultimate outcome of Watergate, or the good life the future held.

The rock upon which all this certainty rests is surely religion, the foundation on which both these women have built their lives. "They feel it, they study it, they live it," says a friend. Christian Science is a faith that blocks out of the mind any negative thoughts or possibilities. There is no evil, no wrong, no injustice. "We are trained and disciplined," says Jeanne Ehrlichman, "to look for the good." Jo may be a little less careful in her religious observances than Jeanne. That occasional drink is, after all, served, and in recent months she has told friends with pleasure—despite Christian Science strictures on conventional medicine—of daughter Susan's romance with a medical student. But religion holds no less important a place in her life. "It has given her the ability to smile, to erase bitterness from her way of thinking," says a friend who saw her halfway through the trial. "She seems to feel only sadness at Mr. Nixon's condition."

Bitterness is the temptation, Jeanne Ehrlichman admits. ("When something has got out of control that's not your fault and you don't feel you've done anything wrong," she explains, "you're apt to look around to try to blame somebody.") But she does her best to resist that temptation. "We've really just stopped and not let ourselves point the finger," she says. "Some are bitter. We aren't. We've worked on that." Smiling, she adds, "That's the marvelous attitude John has had."

Of course, Jeanne Ehrlichman believes that her husband was totally ignorant of any wrongdoing throughout the Watergate period. When she asked him at the time what was happening, he used to tell her he had been assured "that everything was all right and you've got to run the country"—which, she adds proudly, "is just about what he was doing"—so he never took the time away from substantive things to find out exactly what was going on. If he had known, she contends, he would have considered many of those actions wrong. As for the President's own actions, the man on the tapes, she says, is not the man John knew. Her voice is tinged only by sympathy as she says, "John didn't know he swore like that."

Jeanne Ehrlichman admits that there were indeed wrongs to Watergate. Many of the revelations that emerged in court were, she says, very surprising, and she considers them "very objectionable." She refuses to describe such things as "politics as usual," pointing out that most of what was done was done by people who had never been involved in politics before. "Maybe," she muses, "the mis-guiding thing was to allow all those inexperienced young men . . ." Yet she does not want to blame them either, and draws back from the brink of criticism, suggesting that "a lot of it started back in the Eisenhower Administration, and it just got out of hand."

And in her view the good accomplished by the Nixon Adminis-tration far outweighs any of its possible ill effects. She has tried to keep that thought uppermost in her mind throughout her Watergate ordeal. When the Nixon pardon was announced, the Ehrlichmans' reaction was to "try to put things in our own perspective." They sat down and made a list of what Jeanne calls "all the good things that had happened in this Administration, which history will tell." By the time they finished, the list was four pages long. "It was very exciting," she recalls, "because we hadn't seen it anywhere, we hadn't heard anybody saying it for a while."

This resolute desire to emphasize the better aspects of everything extends to Jeanne Ehrlichman's view of Nixon, but as she hesitantly edges around her subject, unwilling to condemn, she nonetheless manages to communicate, if only by indirection, some considerable reservations. "As with every brilliant man," she begins, "I think there probably always are sides . . ." Without specifying what those less than admirable sides may be, she insists that "we knew, we weren't naïve about some of his . . . We didn't think of him as a god. We weren't idolizing him. We didn't put him up on a pedestal, *ever*." It was simply that Jeanne preferred not to see certain things. As she delicately explains, "There are probably some things about somebody that you think, 'Now, look, I want to work for the very *best*, and make use of the good'—because there was so much good —and I just think that the other little tiny things that we might have *suspected*—we just never gave much credence to, because they really weren't that important." Jeanne Ehrlichman does not recognize the man who spoke on the White House tapes, because "this isn't what we were associated with." She can only conclude that "he has a problem—with himself," one she has no wish to add to. "After all," she says, "he's got enough."

Yet evidently even this mild disapproval seems too much like condemnation. She is unwilling to abandon the fallen President without some last exculpatory gesture. After a pause, she offers one. "I think that any man who's President has a problem," she says thoughtfully, "in that he's under attack twenty-four hours a day, from people hoping he'll fall. It's shooting at the man on the moun-tain. The thinking that's gone on in this country has destroyed three

Presidents. Man's disdain for man ... look at the press. They're hoping he'll make a mistake." She looks up and, gently ironic, makes her point. "He really had a little bit against him to start with."

In the end, devout Christian Scientists find strength in refusing to grant importance to failure, doubt, discouragement, or pain, and Jo Haldeman and Jeanne Ehrlichman have found both strength and comfort in their religion. A favorite adage of Christian Science is that one must always try to turn stumbling blocks into stepping-stones. Up to the final day of the Watergate cover-up trial, Jo and Jeannie valiantly continued that effort.

There are few times when faces are truly naked to the camera, but in the tension and glare of that jam-packed courtroom, each revealed itself, suspended, shocked, absorbing the verdict of the jury. H. R. Haldeman, John Ehrlichman, John Mitchell, Robert Mardian: all guilty as charged. Kenneth Parkinson: the one free man. A Bronx cheer erupted in the silence, Dorothy Mardian's opinion of the jury. For Jeanne Ehrlichman and Joanne Haldeman, there was a moment of quiet before both turned to smile warmly at Pamela Parkinson, delighting in her relief, refusing to recognize any misfortune of their own. Then they rose to join their husbands.

Less than six months later, a Washington gossip column carried the news that the Ehrlichmans were separating. John, who had been living in Santa Fe since April, was out of touch with the family. Jeanne was said to have told a friend, "We had a wonderful marriage for twenty-five years, and I would have stuck by him forever if he had wanted me to."

Pat Nixon

*The tapes are like private love letters—
for one person only.*

For the First Lady of the land, there were no politics in the election year of 1972, few formal speeches, little controversy, yet Pat Nixon was out whistle-stopping her way across the country with an entourage of nine White House staffers, six Secret Service men, a hairdresser on loan from Elizabeth Arden, and a press delegation. In an unprecedented number of solo appearances she moved through crowds, hugging toddlers, shaking every last hand, lingering with the old. On platform after platform she sat at ease, always absorbed in the speaker's words, always smiling. She turned up where she was supposed to be, however rough the weather. As Pat Nixon says of herself, "I do or die. I never cancel out."

But no matter how carefully advance men scheduled her appearances, the 707 carrying the First Lady could not outfly Watergate. In Chicago Pat was confronted by the question, "When you and your husband discuss the election and the campaign, does the Watergate situation concern him?"

"We don't discuss it," came the terse reply, "because all I know is what I read in the papers. That's the only knowledge I have, so there's no reason to discuss it. I think it has been blown completely out of proportion." That was to be the standard answer for months to come. Sniping by the press was nothing new, after all, and the November election results soon demonstrated that hostile reporters did not reflect the feelings of the majority.

Clement Conger, the White House curator who helped the First Lady on restoration projects, says she carried on with their work to the very end. She never discussed Watergate, but if he raised the subject, obliquely, in sympathy, she would say simply, "They're out to get us, Clem. They want us out of here. But it's all politics and it

216

will go away." He explains that "she never seemed bitter and she always tried not to let it worry her."

There were signs of strain, of course. Once friendly, if always guarded, with reporters, she now recoiled from their questions. Irritated at being queried on Watergate at one official function, she retorted sharply, "I'll pray for the press." And to her closest friend, Helene Drown, she complained, "It's right out of *The Merchant of Venice*. They're after the last pound of flesh."

As the dark clouds of Watergate and impeachment gathered, Pat Nixon did what she had always done, as she always had. "Certainly she was upset," says the architect who advised her on the White House furniture collection, "but she's extremely strong. If her heart were broken you'd never know it. She'd say, 'We all have bad things to put up with in life.' " And to a reporter who asked how she had managed to maintain her calm throughout the bruising year of revelations, Pat Nixon replied: "The truth sustains me because I have great faith in my husband. He's an honorable, dedicated person. And when you know the truth, you have nothing to fear."

Then in July 1973 came the disclosure of the White House taping system. "She was appalled," says one old friend. "She couldn't believe the stupidity involved. She said the tapes should never have been used in the first place. It's something you just don't do."

According to her former press secretary, Helen McCain Smith, Pat Nixon said that the tapes were "wrong," and blamed Bob Haldeman for the installation of the system. Pat, she says, had never felt that her husband was getting the best advice from Haldeman and Ehrlichman; she suspected, too, that frequently he was not even informed of orders issued supposedly at his behest. "She'd say, 'I talked to him later and he didn't know anything about it,' " Helen Smith remembers.

As for the publication of the transcripts, Pat called it "foolish" and "silly," insisting that they were bound to be misinterpreted. Again holding Nixon aides responsible for what she considered a mistaken decision, she could never understand why the tapes had not simply been destroyed.

Months later, disclosing that she had read every published transcript, Pat told a friend she felt the tapes should have been considered "like personal, sensitive diaries ... never to be released to anyone." On another occasion she said, "The tapes are like private love letters—for one person only." Her own faith in Richard Nixon, however, was unshaken, and she reiterated her confidence. "He simply would not lie to me," she told her press secretary up to the very end. "I know it, I just know it."

About a week before the resignation Pat Nixon called Clement Conger about the project the two of them had been working on, the new White House china. Her voice, he says, was quivering, but all she told him was, "I won't explain, Clem, but don't go ahead with the porcelain. Call it off."

On the morning of August 9, the White House maids wept as they said goodbye to the First Lady, but she herself shed no tears. She hugged Julie and David Eisenhower, then quickly crossed the lawn to the helicopter that would take her away for the last time from the presidential mansion. "Pat was drained, but there was no letting down," says an old friend who was there. "She's too proud for that. It was a matter of dignity."

Pat Nixon has always endured. In her world, will power and self-discipline are the prerequisites for self-respect. "You can do anything you put your mind to," she once said. "You can adjust to anything if you want to." It is a credo that has shaped her life.

Thelma Catherine Ryan was born in Ely, Nevada, on March 16, 1912. Her father ("100 per cent Irish," according to Pat) was a miner who had trekked West in search of gold, her mother a German-born widow with a son and a daughter of her own. Katharina and Will Ryan had two sons, Tom and Bill, and then came Pat—born on the eve of St. Patrick's Day and dubbed by a delighted father with the good saint's name. When Pat was still an infant, the family moved to what they called a ranch, a ten-and-a-half-acre truck farm on the southern fringe of Los Angeles. As a child, Pat helped harvest fruits and vegetables in the fields; as a twelve-year-old she stayed up nights nursing her mother through the final months of cancer. Five years later, the dashing father she adored was dead, too, a victim of the miner's disease, silicosis. Pat had been running the household for her father and two older brothers, but now the family broke up and, in the Depression year of 1930, the seventeen-year-old girl was on her own, determined to "make something out of myself."

The first year of independence was spent at nearby Fullerton Junior College, where she paid her way by sweeping out a local bank each morning, returning as its teller in the afternoon. Then, offered the opportunity to drive an elderly couple across the country to New York City in their "huge and ancient" Packard, Pat Ryan set off to seek her fortune in the great world. "It took days," she recalled later. "In the desert we broke down because we were overheated, and in the mountains the brakes gave out every now and then, and we had flats. I was eighteen—driver, nurse, mechanic—and scared." But she managed.

Pat remained in New York for two years, working as a secretary and as an X-ray technician. Someone who knew her during that time—and surely someone must have—should come forward with a memoir about those years. Failing that, one can only assume that she concentrated on amassing the money to fulfill her ambition, which was to go through college and become a department-store buyer. Having saved enough, she returned to the West Coast and enrolled as a merchandising major at the University of Southern California. Despite the fact that she continued to work at a variety of part-time jobs, including one as a movie extra, she graduated with honors in 1937.

She never did become a department-store buyer. Instead, an offer to teach commercial subjects in the high school in Whittier, California—at a "fabulous" $190 a month—proved irresistible. In Whittier she met Richard Nixon, a young lawyer just setting up practice. The local amateur theater group attracted both. Many years later, Pat called it destiny and claimed that at the very first glance "I thought he was absolutely smashing." More recently, she explained to a friend that from the beginning she was "completely captivated by his resonant voice." At the time, however, the attraction must have seemed less compelling, for Pat Ryan, pretty and popular, did not encourage her new admirer. Though he proposed the first night they met (a most uncharacteristic gesture, she decided when she got to know him better), she dismissed him then as "some kind of nut." Later, a friend recalls, "she had Dick dating her roommate, and all he did when he took the roommate out was talk about Pat."

Dick Nixon was no dashing suitor. At law school he had been known as Gloomy Gus, and was described by one classmate as "too intelligent to be much fun." During a six-year romance with the daughter of the local police chief (a girl who in later years would explain that she was attracted to Richard Nixon mainly for his mind), he had been inveigled into learning to dance, but by all accounts he was bookish, withdrawn, lacking in wit, charm, or athletic ability, hardly the man to attract the spirited, fun-loving young teacher. But he was persistent.

The most striking feature of their early relationship is the fact that sometimes Dick Nixon drove Pat Ryan into Los Angeles when she had dates with other men there, and even waited around to drive her back. This story is no floating rumor (it appears in Richard

Nixon's authorized biography), and it surely suggests some unusual things about the two of them and their courtship.

One thing it suggests, of course, is that when Richard Nixon decides he wants something, he will do anything, truly anything, to get it, however implausible the prospect of success. But of course one might have guessed that the man who made what is conceded to be the most unlikely comeback in American political history must have been willing to grit his teeth, bear any amount of humiliation, and persevere.

The mystery is why, two years after that first meeting, Pat Ryan finally said yes and chipped in to buy her own engagement ring. What went wrong? What failure of nerve or imagination could have betrayed that spirited, ambitious, and apparently self-sufficient girl into a relationship that bears all the earmarks of a second choice?

A romantic imagination cannot resist the speculation that perhaps Pat Ryan had been wounded—or at least disillusioned—by one of those Los Angeles men, and that perhaps Richard Nixon had predicted it. It is difficult to believe that he would have presided over those dates in Los Angeles if a clear threat to his interests had been involved. It seems far likelier that he was convinced that whatever relationship this was could have no favorable ending, and that he had made up his mind to stand by until Pat was ready to share his realistic assessment of her situation. At that point Dick Nixon's two-year record of constancy, presaging a future of near-total security, would make him the logical choice.

Pat was twenty-eight when she married Richard Nixon (ten months her junior) on June 21, 1940. Their wedding was so modest that no picture or record of a reception has ever been unearthed, and the young couple set up their frugal ménage in an apartment over a garage. During the years her husband served in the Navy, Pat continued to work, hoarding her earnings toward the eventual purchase of a house. But on his return those savings were spent instead on Dick's first congressional campaign in 1946. That was the year their first daughter, Patricia, was born, but Pat was at her husband's side, his office manager, his entire staff, his indispensable support.

From that time on, she seems to have abandoned all wish for personal independence, completely submerging herself in her husband's life. Eventually she would be one of America's most admired women, but Pat Nixon never believed that people who were critical of Dick could possibly like her, or even see her as in any way separate from him. She thought of herself only as Mrs. Nixon, and she would often say, later on, that she asked nothing more from history than to be remembered as the "wife of the President."

From the start, Pat was one of her husband's major political assets, but his career was not of her choosing. There had been no talk of such a thing when they first met. The question did not, in fact, arise until Nixon was offered the chance to run for Congress after his return from the Navy. According to Pat, she "didn't feel strongly about it either way." As she has explained that original decision, "I felt that a man had to make up his mind what he wants to do. Then after he made it up, the only thing I could do was to help him." Yet submerge herself and her own wishes as she might, she underlined the point that the decision had been something of a sacrifice on her part, adding, "It would not have been a life that I would have chosen."

She once told a reporter that in 1955 she had persuaded Nixon to agree to retire rather than run again in 1956, and had him note the date and the decision on a slip of paper tucked in his wallet. And when, after five nonpolitical years in New York, Nixon decided to make another try for the presidential nomination—a decision he revealed during a restaurant dinner with friends—Pat is said to have left the table alone and in tears.

Yet whatever her own wishes, there is no question that Pat Nixon not only acquiesced in but vigorously supported her husband's political career. Nixon himself has told the story of his last-minute despair over the Checkers Speech. Three minutes before he was to go on the air, he turned to his wife to announce, "I just don't think I can go through with this one." This time, apparently, Pat did not feel that "a man had to make up his mind what he wants to do." She did not hesitate. "Of course you can," she told him, and according to Nixon she spoke "with the firmness and confidence in her voice that I so desperately needed."

And in November 1960, when John Kennedy defeated Richard Nixon for the presidency, she stood beside her husband as he delivered the concession speech. With cruel clarity, the cameras showed Pat Nixon—always previously so poised and gracious—struggling for control. Her smile was tight, frozen with tension, and then came sudden, painful tears. If she could not share his exhilaration in politics, she could at least partake of his bitter disappointments.

She shared her husband's dedication to hard work as well. As she once said, "Work is our enjoyment." Other people might seek pleasure, ease, self-expression: she chose instead to follow the path of duty, a narrow and difficult one that she had laid out for herself. She loved children and sympathized with the disadvantaged, but there was always a trace of resentment in her attitude toward the affluent and the indolent. Of the rebellious students of the sixties she explained, "They think the world owes them a living." And once she told a reporter, "I'm not like all you . . . all those people who had it easy."

Asked whom she admired, she said, "I never had time to think about things like that—who I wanted to be, or who I admired, or to have ideas. I never had time to dream about being anyone else. I had to work." Then she invoked the images of her toilsome life. She had been the girl who chauffeured that ancient Packard across the country, worked her way through college, drudged away the years of her husband's absence in the Navy. She was still the hardworking woman who put duty first. "I haven't just sat back and thought of myself or my ideas or what I wanted to do," she continued. "Oh, no, I've stayed interested in people. I've kept working. Right here in the plane I keep this case with me, and the minute I sit down, I write my thank-you notes."

Indeed Pat Nixon was always hard at work. For years—though she certainly could have afforded help—she proudly did the housework, sewed drapes and slipcovers. She insisted on doing her own hair. In the course of a 1954 interview she told a reporter that she had recently had a rare evening of leisure all to herself. What evening's entertainment had been the choice of the wife of the Vice-President of the United States? "I took down all Dick's suits," she revealed, "and pressed every one. Of course, I didn't have to. But when I don't have work to do, I just think up some new project."

As First Lady, Pat Nixon was even busier. Her best-known innovation was the installation of floodlighting around the White House, but a major part of her time was spent conferring over the continuing process of redecoration, and in this area her achievements and expertise were impressive. Pat's friends suggest that Jacqueline Kennedy's accomplishments, so much better known and more highly praised, pale by comparison.

Convinced that it was her duty to share the White House with the American people, Pat was proud of the fact that by 1972 more of them had passed through it during the Nixons' tenancy than ever before. In her very first year, 45,313 were entertained. In addition to this constant hospitality, Pat Nixon soon became the most traveled First Lady in history, racking up a total of 123,245 miles in the course of visiting twenty-nine countries, either with her husband or alone.

Her mail is said to have averaged over three thousand letters a week, and Pat, who might well have chosen to acknowledge this postal eruption with printed cards, insisted on reading each one. She even read and signed—and sometimes amended—the replies written by her staff. Often she stayed up late, after official entertainments, to work for hours on her mail.

She set high standards, and not everyone could measure up. Even Richard Nixon long ago admitted that if Pat has a fault it stems from this. "She's a stern disciplinarian in her own life and in her home," he said. "She runs a shipshape house, but tends to do too much her-self—and she is sometimes impatient with inefficiency." Daughter Julie and Pat's old friend Helene Drown agreed that Pat's only fault was that, possibly because of her own perfectionism, she "expects too much of other people."

This constant striving for self-improvement brought Pat such honors as Outstanding Homemaker, Mother of the Year, and Na-tion's Ideal Housewife, but it also gave rise to the persistent feeling that Pat Nixon was unreal, too good to be true—in short, Plastic Pat. Her descriptions of her life have always been so rosy, so determinedly optimistic, that it is hard for ordinary mortal dwellers in an imperfect world to accept her as a fellow human being.

If she cannot achieve perfection by effort, she sometimes seems to do so by proclamation. Pat Nixon is a woman who by her own account is never tired, never afraid, and never sick. She is never bored. She has complete control over all her emotions and physical sensations. If it is cold, she tells herself it is not—and does not feel a chill. If it is hot, she tells herself it is not—and keeps her cool. And she is always perfectly happy.

One must wonder how much this almost superhuman control has to do with the relationship between Pat Nixon and her husband. That she loves or wills herself to love him seems clear. During the 1972 campaign, asked if she were happy, Pat hastened to assure the questioner that indeed she was, because "I've got the greatest guy in the world." Clearly, too, she shares his background, his view of the world, and his passion for hard work; she can identify with him. And she has always provided a strength and courage that he in some measure lacked.

But to the outside eye the Nixons' relationship never seemed to offer much emotional sustenance for Pat. Much of Richard Nixon's leisure was spent in recreation with his male friends. Hour after hour he is said to have used them, not his wife, as silent sounding boards for his ideas. The Nixons seemed, in fact, to spend little time together, and did not even share a bedroom. (Nobody could sleep with Dick, Pat explained, because of his habit of rising periodically to read or dictate.)

Suggestions of charade permeated their public appearances. When they flew together, Nixon sequestered himself with his aides, leaving Pat to herself, remembering her only on arrival. Then she was summoned as the plane taxied to a stop so that the Nixons could emerge together arm in arm. It has been reported, too, that when the Nixons left a White House entertainment to head for their private elevator, they were the picture of a devoted couple as they moved off down the hall, heads close in murmured conversation, his hand cupping her elbow. Once out of public view, however, like actors leaving a stage, they separated. Neither touching nor speaking, wrapped in their own concerns, each walked on alone.

One Nixon staffer who saw the former President almost daily for more than a decade insists that in all that time, "Pat's name never once came up in a conversation." Even in his emotional farewell speech on his last day as President, Nixon mentioned his dead mother but not his wife.

Some of those closest to the Nixons wished at times that he could have been a little more open in expressing the affection they are sure he inwardly felt. "They just weren't a gift-giving family," one explains apologetically. But these loyal friends insist that the marriage is nonetheless warm and close. "They have perfect rapport," says a Washington matron who has spent much time with the Nixons. "Not one special occasion goes by without some thoughtful, tender gesture—if only a big bunch of red roses." She herself, she continues, often advised the busy President on what his wife had fancied on one of their shopping expeditions together and was sometimes commissioned by him to have it sent to the White House as a gift for Pat. As for more intimate expressions of affection, by word or touch, she explains, "He's shy. Besides, the White House is not the place for demonstrative gestures."

Helen McCain Smith is sure that Nixon expressed his feeling for Pat in private, if not in public. "He wrote perfectly darling notes," she says, "affectionate notes, tucked in beside her pillow." Most of these messages seem, as she reviews them, to have been acknowledgments of services rendered. "He might say she'd done a wonderful job," Helen Smith explains. "I do think he knows what a tremendous asset she's been."

And recently Richard Nixon himself has issued an uncharacteristically florid public tribute to his wife. As he explained to an interviewer at San Clemente, throughout his postresignation brush with death Pat was always at his side, and "if it hadn't been for her, I might not have survived. I think it's her immense capacity to comfort and encourage that pulled me through. Pat's devotion kept me alive—I doubt if I would have made it without her. Her love, her strength, her constant reassurance, her faith in me as a human being and as her husband led me out of the depths."

Yet even this, of course, is tribute to Pat's devotion, not his own. Whatever his own emotions may be, we are left to guess. "You can imagine my feelings," Nixon told the interviewer, "just knowing she was with me." A remark once made by son-in-law David Eisenhower seems remarkably apropos. "Mrs. Nixon is always there with a shoulder to lean on," David said. "But whose shoulder does she have to lean on?"

Today Pat Nixon shares her husband's San Clemente exile. The white stucco house of Spanish architecture that sits high on a bluff overlooking the Pacific Ocean is cloaked in silence. The five acres surrounding it, once splashed with garden colors, lie untended, the rosebushes uprooted at Pat's request. And surely there must be something profoundly dispiriting about those empty rooms, the sudden absence of official ceremony, the steadily dwindling entourage. Today Pat has only Fina, her maid, and Manolo, Nixon's valet; vast piles of unopened mail; and the care of her ailing husband.

Friends dwell on the enjoyment she finds in walking the beach, digging and weeding in her garden, the new freedom away from the demands of White House life. Julie and Tricia remain in daily contact with their parents, and—as Pat's friends hope—perhaps there will be a grandchild. Helene Drown rejects the notion of her friend as "a pathetic figure—and she's not a little shrinking violet either. She's a very heroic woman, and I don't mean from the standpoint of wearing a black veil when there's a tragedy in the family. I've never seen her do that. She's a very, very unique human being."

Pat herself is reportedly optimistic. "I hate complainers," she said long ago. "And I made up my mind not to be one." As she prepares to help her husband in the writing of his memoirs, her only worry is said to be whether or not she will live to see the day when people will remember the wonderful things her husband has done. "Like everyone else," she told an interviewer, "he has probably made mistakes—no one is infallible. But he has done many good things for our country and the world." Above all, she hopes that Richard Nixon's achievements will not be forgotten, and that eventually people will "concentrate on a fair assessment of him and his presidency."

Pat Nixon once explained that when she was young, "life was sort of sad, so I tried to cheer everybody up. I learned to be that kind of person." She learned that lesson well. The independent girl who set out across the country to seek her fortune never did find adventure, excitement, or wealth of spirit. Her high expectations, her playfulness, her love for dancing and skating, her gaiety, all were extinguished along the way, and in the end her journey led her to San Clemente. Yet all along she had been forging an awesome strength of will, and when disaster came she was ready for it. Ironically, no life could have been better preparation for this last sad chapter of it.

Epilogue

When Watergate was at its height there was no shortage of moral indignation and outrage on both sides. Because polarization always oversimplifies, the voices of conviction drowned out a variety of arguments and doubts and reservations representing all shades of moral judgment.

With the fall of the mighty, Watergate seemed to have defined itself, measured itself by its effects. What brought the disintegration of an Administration, the first presidential resignation in American history, could have been nothing less than an enormous cause. Though polls revealed that 25 per cent of the people remained unreconciled, they were silent. The accusers were no longer required to berate, exhort, or condemn. In fact, as the sorry drama approached its end, there was talk of being "bored with Watergate," as if it were simply some popular entertainment that, spun out too long, had lost its hold upon our interest. When Ford decided to pardon the former President, there were many to protest what they saw as unequal justice, but many more who were relieved at what they, like Ford, welcomed as the closing of a tragic chapter in American history.

Watergate, then, is past, and Americans look to the future. But as time passes, Watergate is being transformed. It, like any other historic event from the siege of Troy to the battle of the Little Big Horn, will eventually become whatever people believe it is. It will have whatever significance we assign it. The sum of our individual judgments will be known as history's verdict.

"What was this?" Richard Nixon once asked rhetorically. "What was Watergate?" Answering his own question, he sloughed it off as "a little bugging." Then he went on to pay lip service to its moral implications. "I mean a terrible thing," he said; "it shouldn't have been done, shouldn't have been covered up. And people shouldn't have and the rest, but"—for him this was a time for action, not reflection—"we've got to beat it. Right?"

The question still hangs in the air. What was this? What was Watergate? If we waive our hard-won right to do our own thinking, there are always others ready to do it for us. And as everyone knows, those who refuse to learn from history are condemned to repeat it. One by one, the women of Watergate have found their answers. We must find our own.

BARBARA JORDAN

ELIZABETH HOLTZMAN

PATRICIA COLSON

JILL WINE VOLNER